Do You See What I Mean?

TOP: *James Earthboy, 1988, at Snake Butte, Fort Belknap Reservation, Montana. Photograph by Phil Deloria.*

BOTTOM: *Rose Weasel, 1988, outside her home at Fort Belknap Agency, Montana. Photograph by Phil Deloria.*

DO YOU SEE WHAT I MEAN?

Plains Indian Sign Talk and the Embodiment of Action

BRENDA FARNELL

UNIVERSITY OF TEXAS PRESS
Austin

Substantial portions of Chapter 3 appeared in "Nak'ota Mąk'oc'e: An American Indian Storytelling Performance," *Yearbook for Traditional Music,* vol. 23 (New York: International Council for Traditional Music, Center for Ethnomusicology, Columbia University, 1991). Used by permission.

"Night Hawk" and "Harlem, Montana: Just Off the Reservation" are reprinted from *Riding the Earthboy 40,* by James Welch. Copyright © 1990 by James Welch. Reprinted by permission of Confluence Press at Lewis-Clark State College, Lewiston, Idaho.

Portions of the Introduction and Appendix B appeared in "Ethno-graphics and the Moving Body," *MAN* 24(2), December 1994.

Library of Congress Cataloging-in-Publication Data

Farnell, Brenda M. (Brenda Margaret)
   Do you see what I mean? : Plains Indian sign talk and the embodiment of action / by Brenda Farnell.—1st ed.
      p.   cm.
   Includes bibliographical references and index.
   ISBN 0-292-72480-2 (alk. paper)
   1. Indian sign language—Great Plains.   2. Assiniboine Indians—Folklore.   3. Folklore—Great Plains—Performance.   4. Storytelling—Great Plains.   5. Culture—Semiotic models.
   I. Title.
   E98.S5F37   1995
   302.2'22'08997077—dc20
                                                                94-21820

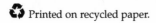 Printed on recycled paper.

For James Earthboy, Rose Weasel, and their families

*. . . tell me, do you see these stories when I tell them
or do you just write them down?*

ZUNI STORYTELLER TO DENNIS TEDLOCK (1983)

CONTENTS

PREFACE

In the pages that follow, I approach the Cartesian bifurcation of the person into mind and body as a dancer-turned-anthropologist who finds herself caught in the late-twentieth-century academic borderland between science and art. In this thought world that is dominated by words and the new hegemony of "text," I try to locate a theoretical space for a semiotics of the moving person, that is, for the embodiment of language and social action. This ethnography about Assiniboine language practices has been written in the interests of articulating such a post-Cartesian discourse that may better serve interpretations of indigenous theories of meaning. I try to show how bodily action can be viewed as integral to discursive practices and so central to social action generally. Such a view demands a radical restructuring of conventional notions of person, movement, and language away from the Cartesian legacy. If mind is socially constructed, I argue, then it is so in conjunction with physical being. Such physical being is not static; social actors consistently and systematically use bodily movement as a cultural resource in discursive practices and not simply in addition to them.

As a dancer and dance educator in England during the 1970s, I initially turned to social and cultural anthropology in order to understand dances and dancing in cultures where such forms of meaning making were held in greater prestige than in my own. I eagerly approached work on social action with the naïve expectation that it would, at least in part, encompass my own assumption that "action" meant physical movements of the body. Ironically, I found myself in an alien culture composed of two opposing camps equally committed to the exclusion of the moving body from what counted as social action. On the "macro" level, action referred to social determinisms such as roles, rules, institutions, and all forms of social collectives. On the "micro" level, action involved all kinds of disembodied individualist notions such as intentions, motivations, subjective experiences, and interpersonal relationships through talk. In both camps the person as active embodied agent was nowhere in view. Apart from a tiny island called the anthropology of dance, body movement entered the picture only peripherally as "nonverbal communication," forever cut off from mind and language.

More recently, despite the postmodern discovery of "the body," the embodied person *as actor* remains absent from social theory. Giddens (1984), for example, has reminded us that despite the linguistic turn, accounts of social action have yet to find ways to connect saying with doing. In philosophy and the social sciences this linguistic turn has not yet rotated far enough to transcend the discursive practices that stem from Cartesian mind/body predicates, and so the actions of embodied actors as agents in signifying acts other than speech acts remain obscure. Even Brian Turner (1984), who has examined this issue so well, does not manage to reach the moving body.

One of the fundamental reasons for this continued absence is Cartesian dualism, the epistemological tradition in Western thought that separates the mind—as rational, thinking, immaterial, private, mental substance, and the only essential part of human being—from the body—as irrational, mechanical, material, or physical substance that merely provides public, physical extension in the material world. This bifurcation of the person into mind and body has in turn led to a host of other dualisms: subjective versus objective, knowledge versus experience, reason versus feeling, theory versus practice, and verbal versus nonverbal, among others. Such familiar terms continue to play an important role in the discursive practices of anthropology, but the Cartesian epistemological presuppositions that inform them go largely unexamined.

On the one hand, Cartesianism has led to the exclusion of the body from social theory, but on the other hand, and equally unhelpful, there has emerged a view of the body and its movement as the last refuge from language and the intellect. Equally Cartesian but with the center of privilege reversed, a "somatic" or "lived" body is romantically positioned as the last bastion of the "natural," the "unspoiled," the "preconceptual," and the "primitive," a retreat from the moral responsibility and complexity of the "verbal" condition. Conversely, as Ardener has suggested, for others, language has long been a refuge from materiality (1989:173).

This Cartesian bifurcation of the person is tenacious in most Western academic circles, and this means that most anthropologists (although they are certainly not alone in this) literally do not *see* movement empirically. Where they do, it is viewed as behavior, not action; thus, many find it hard to imagine how movement might "mean" at all, far less contribute anything to our understanding of persons, language, and social action. Exactly how such an omission must surely undermine anthropological practices has yet to be made clear. The visualism identified by Fabian (1983) as characteristic of our representative endeavors turns out to be a static visualism that not only separates subject from object but is one in which the kind of knowledge that can be framed in charts, diagrams, and maps is deemed most real. I here invite the reader to take a daring leap across the epistemological chasm facing us at this juncture in order to reach an understanding that human movement is not a series of still positions like a Muybridge motion study or a movie seen frame by frame, but rather a dynamic medium and a human resource essential to the ongoing construction of self and Other.

It is also my conviction that the search for a truly reflexive anthropology will be severely compromised if allowed to rest content with having injected new political sensitivities into its practices. The portrayal of multiple voices, situating the author in the text, and criticism of our modernist colonial ancestry are indeed necessary and important, but we are mistaken if lulled into complacency by thinking the task ends there. A reflexive anthropology, in my opinion, also requires an explicit authoring of the metaphysical assumptions that stem from our own Western cultural traditions, and this requires nothing less than the forging of a different kind of relationship between philosophy and anthropology than has existed in the past. It demands that we inquire as deeply into the epistemological and ontological presuppositions that inform our own personal, disciplinary, and cultural beliefs and practices as we do into the metaphysics of our various Others. Pocock (1973) captured this notion succinctly twenty years ago with the idea of a "personal anthropology" building upon the insights of Polanyi (1958). I hope the ideas discussed in this book provide a further example of how fertile such a perspective may prove to be for a reflexive anthropology.

ACKNOWLEDGMENTS

Nothing I could say here would be adequate to express the affection and gratitude I feel toward the people of Fort Belknap Reservation, Montana. Their hospitality, generosity, and patience in sharing their knowledge with me and helping me to understand what little I have so far knew no bounds. In particular, James Earthboy spent many, many hours helping me to record and understand his stories and the sign talk; *minekśi, nina óta ųspemąkiya, pinamaya*. Likewise, Rose Weasel and her daughters, Josephine Mechance and Ruth La Mere, also allowed me into their lives and generously shared their knowledge of Nakota storytelling with signs. I spent many delightful hours in the homes of friends Leo and Isabel Wing, Emma Lamebull, and Juanita Tucker, learning Nakota and much besides; *ak'e pinamaya*.

In addition, Fort Belknap Community College and the education department generously provided working spaces for me over an extended period of time, and I wish to thank most sincerely former college president John Spence, current president Margie Perez, tribal archivist Preston Stiffarm, education director Lauren (Bum) Stiffarm, and John Strike for their help and cooperation. The Lily and Quentin Fox family became my Montana family and are so very special for their ongoing love and generosity to me at all times. Conversations and time spent with George Shields, Sr., Joe and Alphradine Iron Man, Max and Francine White, Selina Ditmar, Minerva Allen, Wanda Allen, Mike Talks Different, Tommy Christian, Kenny Ryan, Harvey King, Poncho Bigby, and Jenny Gray have all been important. At Fort Peck, David and Susan Miller provided extended periods of delightful hospitality. In addition, I would like to thank Connie Fox, Josephine Red Elk, and Lois Red Elk, also of Fort Peck, for their interest in my work and for sharing their knowledge of Plains Sign Talk with me.

I am indebted to several institutions for their support. The anthropology department at Indiana University made my graduate study possible with Skomp Fellowships and graduate assistantships, in addition to two summer field school grants. A Wenner-Gren Award, together with a fellowship from Indiana University Graduate School of Arts and Sciences and a grant from the Philips Fund of the American Philosophical Society, made my long-term field research possible. A short-term Smithsonian Fellowship, followed by a postdoctoral year, also provided the opportunity for historical research which has informed the work throughout. Financial and technical support from the Center for Innovative Computer Applications (CICA) at Indiana University facilitated the initial printing of the movement texts. Ilene Fox, director of the Dance Notation Bureau, provided important advice on writing Plains Sign Talk with Labanotation. Extraordinary creative and technical support for the production of the CD-ROM came from Jen Rogers, David Guttenfelder, Robert McBurney, Joan Huntley, Greg Easley, and Fran Burns at Second Look Computing, University of Iowa. To all these agencies and their faculties and staffs I am deeply grateful.

In addition, I am indebted intellectually to several extraordinary teachers and colleagues, including Drid Williams, Bonnie Urciuoli, Raymond J. DeMallie, Richard Bauman, Michael Herzfeld, Anya Royce, and Karen Hanson, each of whom provided exactly the kind of expertise from his or her own specialty that I had hoped for, and in the best possible way. Special thanks must go to Drid Williams, who supervised my master's degree in the anthropology of human movement at New York University, and to my doctoral advisor, Raymond J. DeMallie, whose steadfast encouragement never wavered. Charles Varela has also provided unwavering moral support, intellectual guidance, encouragement, and good humor in times of doubt, for which I shall be eternally grateful.

In this era of the late twentieth century labeled post-industrial, an age of information is heralded that eagerly embraces the technological means to transmit information anywhere, anytime, to anybody. The Euro-

American perspective, umbilically connected to the metaphor of progress, tends to take it for granted that this is a common good. But information is not knowledge, and knowledge removed from the cultural context that gave it meaning requires a recontextualization that meets conditions of appropriateness and respect for the people to whom this knowledge belongs. The Assiniboine elders and storytellers whose knowledge is shared in this book were eager to embrace a recording technology that would preserve their knowledge for future generations, but they were also concerned that it be treated with respect when made available to non–Native Americans. In giving me their permission and assistance to create this book and the CD-ROM that accompanies it, they also entrusted me with the responsibility to inform the reader and the viewer of that which is appropriate and respectful. Some traditional Assiniboine stories and events, for example, cannot be recorded at all— and they have not been; others should be told only in the winter season and at night. Of the 2¹/₃ stories transcribed and translated in this book, "Inktomi and the Frog" and "The Star Children" are *ohųkaka*—nighttime stories best told in the winter season. We wish readers to take this into consideration in their use of this book.

Closely related to this type of appropriateness and respect, in my view, is the idea that anthropological reflexivity means something other than a narcissistic use of the Other as mirror of self, and something more than multiple voices and an explicit political agenda. Reflexivity in this case has meant placing my exploration of Assiniboine theories of language and person on an equal footing with a critical examination of certain basic tenets in Western philosophy. The fact that our struggle to articulate a post-Cartesian position takes us ever closer to the non-Cartesian worldview of Native America does not mean, however, that we should try to become the Other. On the contrary, it provides a means of sharpening our own post-Cartesian move without losing the distinctiveness of either view, the problems being worked out from our respective contexts, to our mutual benefit.

The knowledge I have learned among Assiniboine people has altered my thinking and theorizing and the way I live, when I am with them and away from them. It has not, however, led me to abandon the critical and systematic rigor involved in a post-positivist notion of science as providing the best possible way of using our minds for critical thinking. As Krupat (1992:54) has noted, ethnography's postmodern move beyond science frequently sets up a science that is a straw man, one whose positivistic paradigm has long since been abandoned in theory, if not always in practice. The modernist illusion that the Cartesian quest for certainty is somehow intrinsic to the nature of science or philosophy has already been destroyed (Toulmin 1990). In my view, rejecting the *grands recits*—the overarching explanatory narratives of historicism, philosophy, and science—does not mean abandoning theory in the name of a naive humanism. Rather it means recognizing that theory is another form of discursive practice—one that must be made suspect the moment it looks like a metaphor of the social ideology. In any case, we now recognize that anthropology cannot, in any absolute sense, engage innocently with another culture. It turns people into cultural subjects of inquiry that become objects of its knowledge. The question is whether it is worth pursuing certain projects of inquiry in the interests of mutual understanding and respect for differences. Obviously, the existence of this book and the CD-ROM means that I do consider such artificial academic boundaries permeable and the pursuit of mutual understanding worthwhile.

Do You See What I Mean?

. . . in those sequences of interpersonal behavior which form the greater part of our daily lives, speech and action supplement each other and do each other's work in a web of unbroken pattern.

EDWARD SAPIR (1933)

INTRODUCTION

It is probably the case that storytellers in all cultures use manual gestures to add meaning and dynamics to their tales, but the extent to which this is the case and the extent to which the semantic load is borne by such actions await investigation (but see Havilland 1986; Kendon 1989; McNeill 1985, 1992; McNeill and Levy 1982). Among the Assiniboine or Nakota people of northern Montana, whose storytelling traditions provide the focus for this study, there are storytellers whose hand gestures draw upon a unique action sign system that can also be used independently of speech.[1] This system has been known generally as Indian Sign Language but is more accurately called Plains Sign Talk (PST).

PST was well documented during the late nineteenth and early twentieth centuries by Colonel G. Mallery of the Bureau of American Ethnology and a number of other army officers, missionaries, and interested amateurs whose curiosity led them to make extended dictionary-like collections of signs.[2] These outside observers saw the sign language in use as an extensive intertribal lingua franca among Plains people who spoke very different languages. During the past hundred years, however, since the establishment of reservations, increased isolation from neighboring groups and the forced accommodation to the English language has led to the gradual replacement of the sign language as a lingua franca. Its gradual decline mirrors that of many spoken languages on the Plains. Today, fluent sign talkers are not common but can be found in various locations on Plains reservations, among elders who learned it as young people and where deafness in a family or among old people has preserved its usefulness (e.g., on the northern Plains, at Fort Belknap,

Crow, Northern Cheyenne, and Blackfeet reservations in Montana, and at the Blood Reserve in Canada).[3]

In addition, there has arisen a contemporary performance genre in which young people, usually young women, perform signed translations of the Lord's Prayer and hymns and songs (some with an educational message) at many kinds of public events, such as powwows, church services, and school graduations. This genre seems to have originated during the 1940s when churches were eager to display the results of their missionary efforts. Such performances were ideal for this purpose in that they combined the innocence of young women performing "their" culture (i.e., they dressed in traditional costume and made signs) with a display of Christian beliefs. This has since been reappropriated by Native Americans as an acceptable display of ethnic identity, and today such performances serve as exhibitions of "Indian" traditions to Native Americans and Euro-Americans alike. At a mass celebrated during the pope's visit to Arizona in 1988, for example, at least twenty people from as many different Indian nations performed sign-language versions of the Lord's Prayer.

When I began research at Fort Belknap Reservation, one of the first things I noticed was that many older Nakota speakers, who denied any explicit knowledge of the sign language, appeared to accompany their speech with manual gestures that I recognized from the nineteenth-century documentation as belonging to that system.[4] Upon mentioning this observation I was told, "Of course, it's part of the language," and my remark was considered to be rather obvious (if not altogether stupid). This alerted me to the consideration that the understanding obtained from the historical record—of Indian Sign Language as a distinct and primarily intertribal language—is grossly misleading. It may be a product of what Roy Harris (1987) called "the language myth": the artifactualization of languages as "fixed codes."

Instead, in Assiniboine communities at least, a continuum exists from the informal use of manual gestures that accompany or replace speech in everyday interactions to more formalized contexts such as storytelling performances (and signed songs, although frequently performers only know as much sign talk as is contained in the performance pieces). In former times, the continuum extended to the use of a widely conventionalized intertribal system that could exclude speech altogether.

In the context of storytelling performances, both speech and manual

Photo 1.1. A moment from a contemporary performance of Plains Sign Talk at Fort Belknap Reservation in 1988. Hays/Lodgepole high school students Quannah Steele, Clarissa Bell, and Kelly Chandler rehearse a sign language translation of the hymn "How Great Thou Art" for their Christmas pageant. Photo by Pat Bear.

Photo 1.2. The Hays/Lodgepole students were taught by Wanda Allen (right), seen here coaching the author. Photo by author.

gestures provide an integral part of the narrative sense, and the latter are not simply dramatic enhancement nor a repetition of the spoken narrative. In view of this, it seemed appropriate to explore storytelling performances not as multimedia events in which two languages go on at the same time but as crossmedia events, where action signs and speech integrate. This better represents the way Assiniboine people conceive of language and, as I soon discovered, this practice of using speech and signs extends beyond the storytelling context to everyday interaction.

For the Assiniboine, speech acts are at once vocal and manual. Both vocal gestures and manual gestures create utterances that are considered to be "talking," hence the use in English of the term "sign talk." My consultants prefer the designation "sign talk" over "sign language" because the latter is felt to denote a system altogether separate from speech, which is not the case here. Happily, the appellation "Plains Sign Talk" also helps to focus our analytic attention away from language as system and toward linguistic practices.

Evidence for an Assiniboine conception of language as constituted by both vocal and manual gestures emerged gradually during the course of my research. On one occasion, for example, when I asked one of my teachers for the spoken equivalent of a signed utterance by saying, "How would you say that in Nakota?" the reply was, "Like I just showed you." Further evidence for a combined conception comes from the use by Assiniboine sign talkers of the English lexeme "word" to refer to either a vocal or a signed utterance.

"Nakota" is the self-designation of these people in their language and also refers to any Indian person. "Assiniboine" is now used as an "English" name, but in fact is derived from French traders' attempts to pronounce the Ojibway name for their western neighbors: *Asinipoels* 'they cook with stones'. This distinctive method of cooking is probably also the origin of the term "Stoney" for cultural and linguistic relatives of the Assiniboine in Canada. "Nakota" has been a convenient designation for linguists because it serves to illustrate links with other Siouan languages such as Dakota and Lakota. In keeping with this, I use the term "Nakota" when referring to the spoken language and "Assiniboine" when referring to the group of people, but the reverse would have been equally valid.[5]

The close association between spoken and signed utterances expressed by Assiniboine people themselves leads me to say that for Nakota speakers PST is indeed "part of *the* language." Perhaps it is the case, however, that such embodied action is most fruitfully conceived as "part of language" in a more general sense. The Assiniboine case offers an interesting challenge to the definition of language as traditionally constituted in Western thought, whereby only those components of language practices that can be represented with the Roman alphabet (and its extension into phonetic alphabets) have counted as truly linguistic.

TOWARD AN ACTION-CENTERED THEORY OF DEIXIS

The parity of spoken and signed utterances in Assiniboine conceptions of language sets up the first problem of the study. The traditional approach to language and communication has been to separate analyses according to the medium. Investigations have therefore been linguistic and verbal (dealing with sound) or they have been nonverbal (dealing with gesture, facial expression, and other bodily movements). These in turn have been divided into linguistics "proper" and paralinguistics, separate from kinesics (microanalysis of body) and proxemics (space) in ways that may have distorted indigenous models of events.[6] The problem is how to overcome this, both conceptually and methodologically, so that analyses of events better present indigenous models.

In order to examine the way in which spoken and signed utterances may integrate, I have focused on an area in which both media are dealing with the organization of persons in space and time. In linguistics this area of concern has been called "deixis" and is one aspect of indexicality in language use that refers to the way in which speech acts are bound to a particular place and time by expressions such as "here," "now," "then," and "there," all of which work by virtue of relations to the current act of speaking in which they occur. These are indexical expressions that, along with pronouns and tense, create spatio-temporal grids that locate persons, not only in physical space-time but, most importantly, in psychosocial space-time (Harré 1984:60–61; Hanks 1990).

Assiniboine narratives contain a multitude of indexical manual gestures performed in conjunction with many spoken language deictic terms. The second problem, then, is how to reorient traditional treatments of deixis toward an action-centered theory, one in which embodied actions—whether spoken (vocal gestures) or signed (manual gestures)—are viewed as signifying acts performed by persons using culturally grounded resources and strategies to create and communicate meaning. Central to this endeavor was recording body movement with the Laban script. Only by including movement texts could both modalities be given equal analytical weight. The inclusion of movement writing alongside the words of the stories means that the reader can actually read all of the actions that the storytellers made rather than read *about* them.

The third problem is a historical one. Sign languages generally and PST in particular were widely known about and of great interest to late-nineteenth-century anthropologists in both England and the United States. The problem is why inquiry into possible relationships between PST and spoken languages of the Plains still awaited investigation one hundred years later. Was this neglect due to inadequate theory and method or are deeper philosophical reasons involved?

SYNOPSIS OF CHAPTERS

As discussion of the last problem helps to elucidate the first two, I examine the historical and theoretical context inherited from nineteenth-century interests before turning to the ethnographic context. Chapter 1 centers around the work of E. B. Tylor on "the gesture language" and is an examination of the nature of relations between power, language, and the body in nineteenth-century anthropological and linguistic thought. I identify a general bias against the iconic in Chapter 2 and discuss relations between icon, index, and symbol in order to situate the use of indexicality and deixis in subsequent chapters.

Chapters 3 and 4 present different aspects of the idea that lived space is a personally achieved structuring and that grammar maps this through indexing devices and names. While the grammatical structure of movement-based systems has category features uniquely based in bodily action, much is shared at the semantic level. The narrative that provides the focus for Chapter 3 introduces the context of my study at Fort Belknap Reservation. It is a narrative about Assiniboine territory as it was conceived prior to the setting up of the reservation system, and it provides the reader with an entry into the lived reality of Assiniboine conceptions of space-time. The story tells how geographical space has been molded by political and historical events. Deixis here provides opportunity for the creative use of past and future, here and there, I/we and they, in achieving socially constituted ends. The narrative was performed in both speech and signs, and the spoken and movement texts on which the subsequent analysis was based are presented together, thus taking one step further Tedlock's notion of a "performable script" (1983:62).

Williams has suggested that lived spaces are simultaneously physical, conceptual, moral, and ethical (1986:6). While Chapter 3 focuses on geographical and historical spaces, Chapter 4 continues the theme by noting how spoken and signed languages integrate naming practices and language about landscape to locate the actor in various moral and ethical spaces.

Chapter 5 illustrates how the system of spatial orientation and use of deixis identified in the "territory" narrative is shared by the community. The system is effective because of shared localized relationships and personal histories that are consistently brought to bear in the use of language. Through a recognition of the embodied nature of this use of narrative, where signed and spoken languages integrate, we begin to gain entry into the daily lived experience of such powerful cultural symbols as the four directions and the circle. The four directions emerge here as an important organizing principle. The idea of the circle is added in Chapter 6, and the central role it plays in both the form and the content of storytelling performances as well as in everyday contemporary life and interaction is examined.

Many investigators of native North American peoples have noted the importance of these two spatial ideas, and my initial inclination was to downplay the importance of what seemed to be well-worn clichés. However, when their role as fundamental organizing principles kept appearing again and again, I reconsidered my initial reluctance. I also realized that while the circle and four directions have been mentioned often in the context of religious symbolism (e.g., Neihardt [1932] 1972; Brown 1953; Walker 1980), exactly how such symbols are encoded in action signs that play a central role in the ongoing activity of everyday life, as well as in the grammatical structure of PST, had not been articulated. Clichés are so, perhaps, precisely because only the obvious has been understood.

The uses of PST and speech examined in Chapters 3 through 6 suggest that a very different notion of language exists among Assiniboine people than that defined by the European and Euro-American philosophical and linguistic traditions. Chapter 7 therefore sets out to examine how an Assiniboine philosophy of being-in-the-world might be structured so that body movement as a way of knowing is central to meaningful social life. Evidence is drawn from pictographs, mythology, and concepts of persons, as well as indigenous classifications of sign morphology, to see how this might be achieved. Spoken and signed language use regarding "thinking" and "feeling" are also examined, as is the use of the complex vocabulary surrounding verbs of coming and going insofar as it contributes to this theme.

The final chapter concludes that deictic concepts apply not only to the organization of space, time, and persons via speech but also via physical being in the use of manual gesture, spatial orientation, and actual locomotion between "here" and "there." The implications of the Assiniboine case for articulating an adequate conception of relations between language and social action are discussed.

Before embarking upon the ethnographic journey through the text, readers interested in theoretical and metatheoretical assumptions and issues may wish to read the remainder of this introduction so as to be clear what is meant when terms such as "agency," "action," "action signs," "movement," "gesture," and "embodiment" are used. Readers not so inclined may prefer to skip it. An alternative strategy would be to return to it after reading the ethnography.

THEORETICAL AND METATHEORETICAL ASSUMPTIONS

Dell Hymes warned us that in studying Native American oral literature, "if we do not deal with the means, we cannot possess the meanings" (1981:5). To date, however, despite some interest by those studying Native American storytelling (e.g., Sherzer 1983; Tedlock 1983; Wiget 1987), we still know little about how the manual gestures used in oral performances become a part of those means. This study begins from Hymes's premise and seeks to widen the notions of "discourse," "verbal art," and "performance"[7] to include a consideration and interpretation of not only "the surprising facts of device, design and performance inherent in the words" but also those in the "action signs"—the manual gestures and bodily/spatial orientation. The aim is thus to embody the study of language-in-use, and to dissolve the unfruitful Cartesian division between verbal and nonverbal communication.[8]

There has been a series of developments in the study of language in culture that make such a project timely, because they emphasize a discourse-centered approach to speech activity and promote the inclusion of context in linguistic analyses. The focus has shifted from language as primarily grammar and system to language as indexical, including speech acts within speech events as ordering the meaning and value of social action.[9] These developments provide a theoretical space within which to add the embodiment of social actors to the notion of language-in-use, thereby connecting embodied actors as movers *and* speakers to the conversational spaces in which they are located so that they are viewed not merely as acting in terms of one modality (speech) but as being involved in semiotic practices that include signifying acts achieved with vocal gestures (speech acts) and manual gestures (action signs) in socially constructed spaces. My theoretical project is to introduce embodied actors into the general field of social action through the particular operation of indexicality in language use.

The study brings together insights from anthropological linguistics, semiotics, and philosophy. In particular, sociolinguistics, poetics, discourse analysis, and the ethnography of speaking complement insights from semiotics and from a semiological approach to the anthropology of human movement called semasiology.[10] Of major importance in overcoming the limitations of Cartesian dualistic talk about bodies and minds have been the philosophy of Wittgenstein ([1953] 1958) and the social constructivist perspective on "mind" (and therefore "person") espoused by Harré (1984, 1986a, 1987), Coulter (1979, 1989), and Warner (1990). Such social constructivism is grounded in the new realist philosophy of science articulated by Harré (1986c) and Bhashkar (1978).

The works of Lakoff (1987) and Johnson (1987) have also been of interest in that they expand considerably on their earlier pioneering efforts (Lakoff and Johnson 1980) to expose the inadequacies of the objectivist philosophical tradition in its rigid separation of mind from body, cognition from emotion, and reason from imagination. Their work articulates theories of meaning and cognition in which physical experiences and body movement are seen as the means by which language, imagination, and our entire conceptual systems are possible. However, these stimulating contributions compromise their post-Cartesian thrust somewhat by retaining body/mind predicate talk in the assumption that there are entities called conceptual systems that have to find concrete embodiment in linguistic practices (Lakoff) or physical experiences that work their way up into mind as mental operations (Johnson). The elusive notion of "concept" and its associated terminology (such as "schema") would seem to promote the ontologizing of symbolic practices in unfortunate ways. Following Harré's lead, I have attempted instead to base my interpretation of Lakoff's and Johnson's work on the formula that "to have a concept is to be able to use the relevant words [and actions]" (Mühlhäusler and Harré 1990:6). The same struggle to avoid mentalism applies to my reading of "psychological structures" as proposed in McNeill's contributions (1985, 1992).

One of the aims of this ethnography is to illustrate exactly how a semasiological perspective, grounded as it is in a conception of persons and agency arising from the new realist philosophy of science, offers a cogent alternative to the pendulum that has been swinging between Cartesian intellectualism and phenomenological, existentialist subjectivism for several decades. Descartes' position was that the whole nature of the body consists of its being an "extended thing" and that there is absolutely nothing in common between thought and extension ([1641] 1986:93).[11] Stemming from this radical separation of mind (as rational, nonmaterial [i.e., occult]) from body (as irrational, mechanical, sensate matter) are objectivist views of human movement as "behaviors," or as "raw" physical data of some kind, the result of biologically triggered impulses, survivals from an animal past perhaps. The Cartesian perspective therefore privileges mind as agency to the exclusion of the body, but the agent is in fact powered from nowhere because mind is an occult nonmateriality; as Ryle (1949) put it, we are left with a ghost in a machine.[12]

In opposition to Descartes but equally reductionist, Merleau-Ponty (1962) swung the pendulum as far as possible in the other direction and attempted to reclaim the body within a phenomenological existentialism grounded in the subjective experience of the "lived body." Unfortunately, instead of successfully transcending Descartes' mind/body dualism he posited a "bodily intentionality" that appears to relocate an equally ambiguous notion of agency *in* the body. Although this was an important and sensitizing corrective at the time, it must now be seen as transitional. As Varela (1992) has shown (and see also Grene 1985), such a conception cannot offer a definitive solution to the problem of the disembodied actor in the behavioral sciences. The proper location of causation and agency and a genuine conception of the person are required. As Varela puts it:

> The reversal of the center of privilege in Cartesian dualism is ultimately rooted in the tacit acceptance of the conceptual incompatibility of causation and agency prescribed by the Humean tradition. After all, if mind *is* a ghost in the machinery of the body, moving or not, the body is the only "reality" for the location of causation *and* agency. But if the body as machine, the objective body, is rejected as such because of its deterministic status, then the body as "lived," the subjective body, must, it is thought, be accepted as the only alternative. Somehow then, as a Jamesian act of faith, it is viewed as nondeterministic as long as it is "lived." And so the subjective body is mistakenly viewed as the only proper location for agency. (1992:7)

Varela's analysis articulates several conceptual errors found in recent attempts to return to the work of Merleau-Ponty in order to find ways to transcend the exclusion of "the body" from social theory.[13] To emphasize Merleau-Ponty's existential phenomenology and ignore his later emphasis on a new ontology, in which he was reaching toward language (1962:197–199) and saw the need to connect manual gesture with vocal gesture, is, in fact, to bring his approach to a dead end. Indeed, Varela argues that in order to accept Merleau-Ponty's invitation to discover that connection between language and manual gesture one must go to theoretical and philosophical resources beyond Merleau-Ponty's work itself. Such resources exist in the new realist philosophy of science articulated by Harré, and the ethogenic standpoint that he has developed from it for the purposes of sociocultural investigations. It is these resources that provide the ground for Williams' semasiological approach to human movement and that inform my use of her work. In my view, these developments together successfully transcend Cartesian dualism without renouncing the significance of Merleau-Ponty's suggestions.

As mentioned above, resort to "the body" as lived, experienced, or intentional does not transcend Cartesianism because agency remains a ghost, and we are left with what Hamlyn has been tempted to call a "solipsism with a body" (1987:328). The new realist philosophy of science argues instead for a definition of agency that properly connects it to a conception of substance that is compatible with causation (as causal power, not the Humean variety). Without causation there can be no agency, and for causation to be possible there must be substance for its grounding (Harré and Maddon 1977). A new conception of substance has been articulated that is neither the materialist nor the phenomenalist version but a dynamic one: an immaterialist model of substance as a structure of powers and capacities in which, in our case, the natural powers for agency grounded in the structure of the biological human organism make possible the realization of personal powers that are grounded in, and thus afforded by, social life. Causal powers thus belong to the person, not a pre- or acultural biological organism, and the Cartesian material/immaterial dichotomy underlying the body/mind duality becomes obsolete. The key is the primacy of the person, gesture (including vocal gestures), and social action, not the primacy of the body (as precultural organism) experience, and individual perception.[14] Since powers are grounded in social life, the biological organism, in becoming a person empowered for agency, is thus transformed into the body viewed as a *biocultural* entity. Embodiment, the cultural fact of the body, is therefore the result of the social construction and empowerment of the person.

The new realist position thus neither loses nor obscures substance and cause and thus recovers person and genuine authorship. The person is a substantial being who is causally empowered to author dialogues with other authors. Such a conception of substance and cause is important to an anthropology of physical being and of human movement. This transcendence of the Cartesian material/nonmaterial dichotomy forges a view of embodied persons as personal agents in the utilization of action signs and words.

Table 1. The Objectivist versus Subjectivist Pendulum

Descartes	Merleau-Ponty
"I think"	"I can [experience]"
Intellectualist Fallacy	Phenomenalist Fallacy
Talk *about* the body	Talk *of* the body
Third-person objectivist	First-person subjectivist
Body as "it" (not me)	"I" feel, experience
"*I can* see it"	"*I can* feel my . . ."
A reduction of body to	A conflation of body
biological organism	with organism
or social object	
Model of Causality	*Model of Causality*
= a substance and its qualities	= substanceless qualities
Ghost *and* the machine	Ghost *in* the machine
Talk about actions using	Talk of actions using
word glosses	word glosses

In order to avoid the current theoretical stalemate summarized in Table 1, it is useful to reinterpret Merleau-Ponty in terms of the new realist perspective.[15] Merleau-Ponty's major shift was to take the Cartesian "I think" and convert it into "I can." If left there, however, we would have only the opposition between the intellectualist and the phenomenological perspectives (our current terminology would label these as objectivist and subjectivist positions, respectively). Merleau-Ponty's "I can" is itself ambiguous but need not be interpreted in such a way that we are left with an opposition. "I think versus I can" (according to Merleau-Ponty) is actually "I think versus I feel." If, however, "I can" is interpreted according to the new realist perspective as indicating our natural capacities and powers for all kinds of action (thinking, feeling,

Table 2. New Realist/Semasiological Perspective

Talk *about* the body	Talk *from* the body	Talk *of* the body

First-person agentic
"I" act
"I can act as a person"
Agentic entitlement through causal powers
and capacities: the body as cultural entity
enacted by the person socially entitled to be
a certain kind of actor

Model of causality = dynamical immaterial

Records of actions via
movement scores

talking, and enacting the body), it remains useful. Clearly, Merleau-Ponty reduced this general power of "I can" to one specific power of feeling as experience.

Table 2 summarizes several ideas around this theme. We now have three perspectives rather than an opposition between a fallacy and its corrective. A person can think objectively and talk *about* her own or anyone else's body; a person can feel and talk *of* her bodily experiences; and a person can act (i.e., move) and thus "talk" *from* her body. The point is that none of these positions removes the moving body from the person as agent: *bodies do not move and minds do not think—people do.* This book takes as its point of departure an interpretation of the Merleau-Pontian "I can" as "I can act." In this way, instead of a standoff between two opposing perspectives—in which one is labeled a fallacy and the other the only alternative—we now have three genuine agentive alternatives, different kinds of linguistic practices with their appropriate rhetoric and purposes. The "I can" is not in opposition to "I think" but is an indicator of our natural capacity to be socially and personally empowered through membership in a culture to engage in all kinds of semiotic practices.

ACTION

Stemming from this new realist conception of person and agency is a specific concept of "action" that differs from other uses of the term in the social sciences and philosophy. From a semasiological standpoint, action is body movement that is intended by meaning-making agents who are language users with a hierarchy of powers and capacities that are specifically human (Williams 1975, 1982; see also Best 1978; Harré 1984).[16] An "action sign" is a unit of movement recognizable as such by its users, and "action sign systems" are conventional systems of movement that are best understood in a sociolinguistic sphere of human life, that is, in conjunction with (but not subordinate to or the same as) the kinds of conceptions possible through spoken discourse. They cannot be separated from the capacity of humans to create and use multiple and complex levels of meaning in other kinds of semiotic systems. This is not so much a theory of movement as "a theory of culturally and semantically laden actions couched in indigenous conceptual models of organization as they apply to various idioms of dancing, signing, liturgy, greeting systems, martial arts and such" (Williams 1982:164).

In 1975, Williams had to argue for this position against positivistic and reductionist views of the body and human movement that stemmed largely from Cartesian conceptions of the body as merely sensate matter. There is no doubt, however, that the Western Christian tradition of the body as flesh (the locus of sinful desire) has also played a considerable role in the exclusion of the body from social theory (see Turner 1984; Varela 1992).

The term "action" in the context of semasiological theory implies certain assumptions about the nature of human beings that differ in important ways from concepts of social action used elsewhere in social theory. Parsons (1978), for example, considered himself an "action theorist" and called his version of social science the "action frame of reference." But, as Giddens has sought to show, a satisfactory conception of action cannot be found in Parsons' work because it lacks any real conception of agency, having "no room for the knowledgeability of social actors as constitutive in part of social practices" (Giddens 1984:xxxvii). Parsons is trapped between Durkheim and Freud in the sense that actions are viewed as the result of adherence to social norms at the one end, and determined by personality at the other. In addition to the absence of any conception of persons as agents in the Parsonian scheme, there is also no room for embodied persons.

Elsewhere in sociology, Goffman's work on social interaction has been of importance because it includes recognition of gesture, posture, and the locations of participants. He did not, however, make any systematic attempt to discover exactly how actions fitted with speech to contribute to the ongoing creation and interpretation of meaning.[17] His classic development of the "dramaturgical model" (Harré and Secord 1972, Chap. 10) focused on "role" as the determining basis of action, which made external structures and expectations determinative and left no room for individual choices and the negotiation of meaning according to personal histories.[18] In his later work (1974, 1981), the idea of "frames," while certainly useful, does not escape the constraints of role theory, since they too are taken to be preexisting devices employed by people to create conversations. "Alignments" between participants are presumed to exist prior to speaking and shape interaction, rather than actual relations being jointly produced in the very act of conversing (Davies and Harré 1990:55). Dynamic aspects of encounters are thus missing.

Such dynamics have been referred to as the fundamentally "dialogic" nature of language by followers of Bakhtin (see Holquist 1990, Todorov 1985). Although Bakhtin never took his work in the direction of semiotic systems other than spoken and written language, the idea of "dialogue" certainly applies in a Bakhtinian universe conceived as endless semiosis. However, this endless semiosis of dialogue—that is, the emphasis on dynamic relations and differences—loses sight of the "natural kinds of things," in this case people as embodied persons, who are causally empowered to produce that dynamic dialogue and those differences. In Bakhtin's dialogism, as in the work of his contemporaries Cassirer and Dewey (who also argued for relations, and fields of relations, in constant dynamics), substance and cause and therefore person and authorship are at least obscured, if not lost.

Dialogism certainly focuses on language as discourse and locates it socially and interactionally but, like Derrida's "grammatology," limits itself to a narrow focus on visible signs as graphic, rather than being inclusive of a socially located person that produces visible signs in interactive space.

Derrida's "logocentrism" has acted as a corrective for the prioritizing of vocal signs, but he doesn't quite escape the metaphysics he is combating because he substitutes writing or "arche-writing." He thus ends up with a visual rather than an auditory metaphysics, but the person remains disembodied. Derrida even indulges in the fantasy of a more evolved human being that would need a body only to press buttons—a keyboard, presumably! Nor does Derrida consider the possibility of visible signs that are like auditory ones in being transitory. While I am in sympathy with the criticisms implied by the Derridean term "logocentric," I obviously do not hold to his vision of such a diminished role for any future "body," but neither do I hold to the view that the answer lies in a championing of "the body" in opposition to spoken language meaning.

ACTIONS AND MOVEMENTS

In philosophy also there has been a great deal of discussion of the concept of action, the most fruitful for social theory being the work of Hampshire (1965), MacIntyre (1986), Taylor (1985), and Harré (1984), all of whom have been working toward a view of persons and personhood in which action and agency are central. To date, however, only Harré (1992) and Hampshire (1965) have included physical being in that conception. Concordant with these philosophers' views, and especially that of Harré, Williams' semasiological conception of action takes things one step further because it has as its basic premise a conception of physical being in motion that is inseparably linked to the new realist notion of human agency.

Within this framework it is necessary to make a clear distinction between gross physical movement and action: "Actions are, by contrast, taken to be movements or comprehensive sets of movements that *have* agency, that is, intentions, language use, meanings, rules . . . human actions are couched in a system consisting of reflexivity" (Williams 1982:177).[19] The post-Cartesian theoretical thrust of semasiology is therefore to link human physical action to the capacity of humans to create multiple levels of meaning and to overcome the physiological reduction of personal being to the identity of a material organism.

This task has been further complicated by one particular aspect of the Cartesian legacy. Descartes' insistence upon the material nature of the body in contrast to the nonmaterial nature of mind not only made it impossible to link thinking with moving but also severely limited conceptions of physical being. This in turn has created difficulties in communicating the idea that investigating and understanding movement of the body is the study of people using semiotic systems of some complexity and not a matter of physiology or kinesiology. It involves understanding exactly how people create and provide ongoing meaningful cultural resources through manipulating various and multiple body parts to produce dynamic spatial pathways as they move through (at least) four dimensions of space-time. These meaningful patterns are then, like speech, produced by a substantial person but are not usefully described in physiological terms. They are meaningful precisely because they are connected to mind, culture, and language.

However, even though explanatory control at the highest metalevels of explanation in semasiological theory is not given over to biology and natural history, biological or somatic processes are not ignored; they simply do not have a privileged position.[20] Jackson (1983) has concluded somewhat misguidedly that such approaches "play up the intellectual and linguistic characteristics of human social existence to the exclusion of somatic and biological processes." Equally unhelpful then, Cartesianism has also meant that the realm of human movement has long been, for some, the last refuge from language and it is romantically viewed as a last bastion of the "natural," the "unspoiled," the "preconceptual," and the "primitive," a retreat from the moral responsibility and complexity of the "verbal" condition.[21] Conversely, as Ardener has suggested, for others language has long been a refuge from materiality (1989:173).

Earlier objectivist views of human movement, typical of approaches from nonverbal communication that entered the anthropological arena, have proved barren, and ever more detailed microanalyses of visible movement (e.g., Birdwhistell 1970) led nowhere because, from an anthropological perspective, it is the nonobservable features involved in social organization, cultural values, and the beliefs and intentions of persons that give meaning to the visible. Max Weber (1947) recognized this in his definition of action.[22] It is social taxonomies of the body and the semantics attached to time and space as they emerge in specific cultural contexts and historic moments that create the signifying person.

ACTIONS AND PRACTICES

Related to the developments that shifted language and then speech acts to center stage in anthropological theory and practice, these changes in the concept of action have deeply affected the kinds of relationships that could be said to exist between movements of the body and spoken languages. Giddens, for example, while admitting the central significance of the "linguistic turn" in social theory, considers the term to be a misleading one, for "the most important developments as regards social theory concern not so much a turn towards language as an altered view of the intersection between saying (or signifying) and doing" (1984:xxii). Giddens' concern, however, like Bourdieu's "habitus," is restricted to what he calls "practical consciousness," unreflective commonsense knowing and habit that agents make use of in the routine of daily lives. This conception I find problematic on three counts. First, the emphasis on "practical" perpetuates a division between movement as "instrumental" (the everyday "routine" tasks and interaction) and movement as "symbolic" (as found in ritual events, dance idioms, etc.) that is unhelpful.[23] We do not divide spoken languages in this way, separating the everyday usage from poetry, for example, because the latter would not make sense without an understanding of the former, and it is an appreciation of the whole system and the full range and diversity of language-in-use that informs our understanding. The same is true of the medium of movement, but part of the problem here is the lack of any notion of shared cultural practices or "systems" in relation to human movement.[24] There is no room in the schemes of Giddens and Bourdieu for all the uses of human movement that are neither "practical" nor tacit (e.g., rituals, theater, ceremonies, choreography, sign languages).

In addition, Giddens' tripartite division into "discursive consciousness," "practical consciousness," and "the unconscious" sets up a *divi-*

sion between speaking and doing, not an intersection. There is an implicit assumption that "knowing how" (Ryle 1949)—knowledge that is not normally put into words (which is not the same as "cannot be")—lies somewhere between discursive consciousness and the unconscious, rather than simply being part of a different semiotic and out-of-focal-awareness through habit. Like "everyday" actions, much of everyday speech tends also to be out-of-focal-awareness through habit, but this much-overlooked fact does not remove either mode from the realm of intended action. One is hard put to know exactly what could be different about the *kind* of consciousness involved. The hegemony of the discursive continues, for there is no room at all in this scheme for nondiscursive semiotic systems that are not "practical," such as the visual arts, music, or architecture, nor for those that involve our senses of smell and touch, for example.

Third, Giddens' use of the word "consciousness" in the phrase "practical consciousness" ties him in unfortunate ways to theories of mind that posit an "unconscious" of the Freudian variety, despite his attempts to create a "Freud-free zone" (Varela, in press). I have used Ryle's (1949) term "knowing how" (distinguished from propositional knowledge or "knowing that") to refer to those aspects of human life that are out-of-focal-awareness through habit, and to refer to skills that are not normally put into words (Polanyi called this "tacit knowledge"; see Polanyi 1958:55–65, 1967; Sperber 1975).

Bourdieu's (1977) notions of "habitus" and "practice" share some of these problems with Giddens, especially in the repeated references to the unconscious character of practical logic. The notion of habitus is helpful because, despite ambiguity surrounding "dispositions" and exactly how the habitus connects with practices because the problem of agency has not been dealt with adequately, it has focused attention away from "rules" and toward strategies and shared habitual ways of acting and evaluating actions. Hanks, in his recent work on Mayan deixis, considers Bourdieu's "practice" a solution to the dichotomy between "abstract objectivism" and "individualistic subjectivism" as it relates to language (Hanks 1990:9). In view of this commitment, it is puzzling to find that Hanks deems it necessary to return to the former subjectivist position, as expressed in Merleau-Ponty's phenomenology, in order to attempt to incorporate embodiment into his work on deixis. I suggest that this is because Bourdieu's habitus, while it certainly champions embodiment, in fact offers no theoretical or methodological strategies for its systematic inclusion.

It is not surprising to find that in spite of Hanks's stated recognition of the way in which deictics can make a special contribution to the anthropology of the body (because "speakers make reference to the body with deictics but, more interestingly, they make reference to the world relative to the body"), he can only talk *of* the body and not *from* the body: he fails to get to the person *moving* in deictic spaces. Thus we find in this important contribution to deictic studies that gesture is treated as a side issue. Only a brief inventory of four conventional gestures, a few references to "pointing," and two descriptions in word glosses (relegated to footnotes) are included. Word glosses take the place of movement scores because Hanks's theoretical commitment to Merleau-Ponty prevents him from relocating agency so that the person, not the body, can be viewed as the locus, not only of spoken language but of all kinds of semiotic systems, including action sign systems. We learn later on that in fact Hanks considers gesture to be extrinsic: "Linguistically extrinsic factors in the organization of deictic practices [include] . . . the pervasive reinforcement of verbal acts by bodily gestures" (Hanks 1990:512). Gestures are merely duplication, a reinforcement, peripheral and not a part of the means.

Like Kendon (1983:13) I use the term "gesture" rather loosely to delimit a field of interest, applying it to any action by which meaning is given to bodily expression. I expand the conventional referent, however, to include speech viewed as vocal gestures. This reintroduces an expression used by G. H. Mead (1933) and suggested by Merleau-Ponty (1962) in their anti-Cartesian explorations. Juxtaposition of the terms "vocal gestures" and "manual gestures" places these two types of semiotic practice on more equal theoretical ground and will perhaps provide a means to further Stokoe's earlier challenge to the conventional boundaries around our definition of language (Stokoe 1960). I hope it will open up theoretical space in linguistic anthropology for the combined study of vocal and manual gestures in discursive practices.

Gesture involves bodily action that is intentional and voluntary, excluding movements and sounds that are symptomatic, such as tics, scratching, sneezing, or coughing. Unlike Kendon, however, I do not rule out "practical actions" per se, because of the aforementioned problems associated with separating the "practical" from the "symbolic" in many situations. In the context of telling stories with a sign language, it is possible, however, to make a clear distinction between gestural utterances in PST that may be interrupted by the actions necessary to take a sip of coffee, for example. Such actions I would consider external to Plains Sign Talk, but not external to the body language(s) of Assiniboine culture generally.[25]

Kendon and I agree that the modality of manual gestures is as fundamental as the vocal modality as an instrument for the representation of meaning (Kendon 1983:38).[26] The manual gestures that create PST are movement utterances produced by the arms, hands, head, and torso in a limited area of physical space that I have called the PST signing space. In Assiniboine linguistic practices, these utterances are performed at the same time as vocal gestures that create spoken utterances produced by air moving through the mouth and throat. Like that of Kaeppler and Williams, however, my interest is not confined to sign languages and manual gestures per se, but sees these systems as part of an all-embracing anthropology of human movement that is inclusive of dances, theater, martial arts, sports, ritual practices, and ceremony.

THE ANTHROPOLOGY OF THE BODY

The postmodern fascination with "the body" appears to have triggered a groundswell of interest in the physical body as cultural construct in current anthropological discourse. Much interest has been stimulated by Foucault's important contributions on the body and social control, but current interest also connects to several important antecedents in anthropology.[27] As is the way with anthropological categories, however, one wonders whether the very notion of "body" may retreat from us as a valid category almost as soon as we have arrived at the serious consideration of it, and our interests may be better served by the terms "physical being" and "person." Aihwa Ong's study of Kmer refugees, for example, tells us that they see acquiring a biological body as a specifically American experience; to act as an American one must become an inhabiter of this thing called "a body."[28]

Foucault (1973, 1978, 1979), Armstrong (1983), Brain (1979), Freund

(1982), Hudson (1982), Martin (1987), Turner (1984), and others have focused attention upon such important topics as the social construction of the sexual body, the medical body, the civilized body, the decorated body, and so forth. These developments are extremely fruitful because they draw attention to the ethnocentricity that has made systems of meaning other than spoken language peripheral to anthropological concerns. However, in these developments, in addition to the agent-centered philosophical contributions of Harré and Hampshire mentioned above, there remains one major lacuna—the human "body" as a *moving* agent in a spatially organized world of meanings.

Despite Mauss's seminal paper "Les Techniques du corps," first published in 1935, until Bourdieu reintroduced the notion of habitus in 1977 (and see also 1984, Chap. 3), there has been only peripheral interest in the moving person. Yet, if social theory is to embrace fully the notion of "person," it would seem necessary not only to treat the actor as embodied agent but also to recognize that this embodied person moves. In other words, theories of social action without the action can no longer be deemed adequate.

Unfortunately, and as a result of the same Cartesian legacy, when attention has been paid to a moving body, it often appears to have lost its mind. In addition to the phenomenological approach discussed above, many earlier approaches to human movement that acquired the appellation "nonverbal communication" were for the most part behavioristic and scientistic (cf. Argyle 1975; Hewes 1955; Hinde 1972; Lomax 1971). The label "nonverbal" is itself problematic because, apart from being a logocentric maneuver, as a negative appellation—the designation of something in terms of what it is not—it tends to direct attention away from the many ways in which complex semiotic systems and practices as diverse as sign languages, dance idioms, martial arts, religious ritual, ceremonial events, and fighting are deeply integrated with spoken language concepts and practices and depend equally upon the human powers and capacities for meaning making. These attributes are essential to an agent-centered notion of what Harré (1971) has usefully called "an anthropomorphic model of man." In addition, to reduce such complex systems to "communication" is to ignore their many other functions and so commit a pars pro toto fallacy.

MOVEMENT LITERACY: THE LABAN SCRIPT

We know as much as we do about the speech component of discursive practices because we remove them temporarily from the flow of "real time" by writing them down for the purposes of analysis. We are able to do this because of the invention of the alphabet and because we are literate in relation to speech. The production of written movement texts using the Laban script supplies the same conditions for the analysis of the bodily, spatial, and dynamic components of actions. The storytelling performances that provide the data for this study have been transcribed with both scripts so that equal attention can be paid to both spoken and gestural action.

Frequently, in ethnographic accounts, while great attention is paid to translations of spoken language meaning, manual gestures and other action sign systems are not granted the same status, and gestures are interpreted according to an entirely "English" set of rules of interpretation (Chapman 1982:134). Translation is not thought to be necessary, and even where actions are noted as conveying meaning, word glosses or static photographs are assumed to provide an adequate transcription and translation. The lack of an adequate transcription system has been a major factor here, but can no longer stand as a reason for such neglect. The kinds of meaning and structure encoded in Plain Sign Talk that are discussed in this study would not have been possible without the creation of the movement texts. I have only subsequently attempted to translate relevant movement passages into words, where it was necessary to assist an understanding of the analyses. I have also used admittedly inadequate word glosses (in upper case letters) to represent signs, for those unable to read the movement texts themselves.

The Laban script is not simply a recording technology, however. Ardener has reminded us that events which are registered are inseparably tied to the mode of registration used and our definition of events depends upon the modes of registration available to us (1978:104). The Laban script becomes a mode of registration in and of itself, a means to apperceive and conceive of movement without the necessity of translating into spoken language terms but in ways that offer the same kinds of awareness of the medium that spoken language literacy provides. As Williams has put it:

[M]ovement texts undermine the ways we normally think about human acts and actions because they force us, cognitively, to put images of human bodies into events and into our thinking about events. When you are confronted with a movement text, you can no longer live solely in a notionally abstracted world of words alone. (Williams 1990:122)

While the limitations of any script, as well as the history of relations between literacy and power, deserve serious attention (see Goody 1977a, 1977b; Harris 1980; Herzfeld 1987:39), in my view the value of literacy en route to gaining an understanding of the medium remains indispensable.[29] For those who would cry "scriptism," let me simply say that advocating movement literacy is not a legitimizing strategy but rather a proposal for new creative language and a ferocious critique of the dominant culture. The hegemony imposed by traditional linguistics in determining that only those things which can be written down are to count as "linguistic" is not a motivating factor here. It is my view that the atomistic nature of analysis is a temporary but necessary component, and indeed creates a discourse of its own, but it is not an end in and of itself. It is employed in the service of piecing together again so that a deeper appreciation of the whole is thereafter possible.

In stressing the "alphabetic" nature of the Laban script I wish to point out that the level of representation parallels a phonetic rather than a phonemic or phonological level. I think the difference offers some important possibilities. There is a residual Cartesianism at work in the traditional separation of phonology from phonetics. The phoneme, Tedlock argues, is a product of alphabetic literacy and on that ground has excluded from analyses all those features in an acoustic signal such as amplitude, pitch, duration, and silences that also add meaning to language performances (Tedlock 1983:204). The investigation of sound as "phonic matter"—the physical voice—has been excluded from phonology. It is a realm from which all materiality has been exiled and whose constituent phonemes, Jakobson insists, exist outside of measurable time (Jakobson 1978:69). Even where phonology allows for intonational features such as "pause juncture," "stress," and "vowel quantity" they are denied duration. These features, then, are condemned as paralinguistic to lie at the borders of proper phonology, often treated as suprasegmentals rather than segmental, prosodic rather than phonemic. This is another way of saying that each one poses problems for alphabetic writing (Tedlock 1983:204). In a semiotics subservient to linguistics (which is the inverse of Saussure's vision), such features will always be relegated to the boundary or conceived of as subcodes. Bringing acoustic features into the semiotic field as Tedlock has done has demanded a transcendence of the Cartesian material/nonmaterial dualism. The same is true of the incorporation of physical action. Tedlock suggests that "the exploration of the problems requires not that we refrain from making transcriptions, but that our transcriptions begin to give visible expression to the durations of the sounds of the voice and the silences between them" (Tedlock 1983:215). To this one would only want to add, "and to the actions of the remainder of the body and the stillnesses between them." Happily, the fact that the Laban script necessarily incorporates duration and timing along with several other features of the dynamics of action in performance means that it offers several advantages over the traditional notion of "alphabet."

In our eagerness to be aware of the limitations of scripts, it is important to remember that literacy also provides tremendous possibilities *for* the imagination. Poets and novelists as well as anthropologists cannot do their work without writing. Musicologists and (most) Western composers require their musical notation systems—indeed, the revolt against the rationalism of traditional Western tonal music was facilitated through the invention of new notation systems, not without or in spite of them. Movement literacy too provides that kind of possibility for the imagination, the creation of alternative cartographics.

It is not altogether surprising that the notion of movement literacy, rather than being recognized as an exciting methodological breakthrough, appears to arouse a negative response on the part of many social scientists. Not all of this has to do with an anticipated tedium of having to spend time and energy learning to become literate. There are deeper cultural reasons. For example, perhaps the overall advocacy of a publicly visible acting self so deeply challenges Western individualism that writing actions appears to threaten the solipsistic Cartesian conviction that one's "real" self is essentially private and unavailable to inspection by others (see Wittgenstein [1953] 1958). Varela has commented:

Social scientists are body-dead because they are conceptually brain-dead to signifying acts within the semiotics of body movement. As a consequence, there is a systematic neglect of the fact and importance of literacy in the performance and study of human movement. [It is] . . . not surprising that some may argue, even in principle, against any such position. . . . there is the professionally alarming consequence that renouncing movement literacy closes off future developments of research, knowledge and understanding concerning movement systems. The deeper point is an underlying issue concerning the suitable expansion of our conception of rationality beyond the restrictive version provided by the positivist tradition. This will itself be foreclosed by any dogma against literacy. Intellectualism (deductivism, efficient rationality, formal rationality) may well entail literacy, but the reverse is not necessarily true. It is high time that the fight against the bogeyman of intellectualism in the name of freeing new forms of imagination, being and feeling, be abandoned. Literacy itself provides the occasion for the freeing of such forms. (Varela 1992)

The ethnography that follows illustrates my conviction that ultimately understanding "talk *from* the body" means embracing the idea that actions (movements) themselves can be transcribed and read.

Chapter 1

The real foundations of his enquiry do not strike a man at all.
Unless that *fact has at some time struck him.*

LUDWIG WITTGENSTEIN (1958:50)

THE NINETEENTH-CENTURY LEGACY

The study of sign languages in anthropology has never provided a satisfactory way of actually connecting sign talking to speech talking. To understand and account for this disjuncture, it is necessary to examine some nineteenth-century ideas about the nature of language and about relations between speech and manual gesture. While some of these ideas have been modified in the light of ethnographic evidence, the metatheoretical assumptions remain intact and systematically inform current attitudes. A study of the anthropological legacy in this regard reveals some ongoing fundamental concepts about power, language, and the body in the Western intellectual tradition. E. B. Tylor, for example, said:

> Gesticulation goes along with speech, to explain and emphasize it, among all mankind. Savage and half civilised races accompany their talk with expressive pantomime much more than nations of higher culture. The continental gesticulation of Hindoos, Arabs and Greeks as contrasted with the more northern nations of Europe, strikes every traveller who sees them; and the colloquial pantomime of Naples is the subject of a special treatise. But we cannot lay down a rule that gesticulation decreases as civilisation advances, and say, for instance, that a Southern Frenchman, because his talk is illustrated with gestures, as a book with pictures, is less civilised than a German or an Englishman. ([1865] 1964:37)

The statement contains the seeds of an entire worldview, for despite Tylor's polite disclaimer, the prevailing message is that the more gesticulation used, the lower the position on the evolutionary ladder. Tylor's suggestion is that the French, while certainly colleagues in civilization because European, are slightly less equal because they are less literate, being dependent on the "pictures" provided by gesture. Europeans are civilized because literate, but some are obviously more literate than others in Tylor's view (Herzfeld 1987:137).

Spoken language and particularly literacy are assumed to represent the pinnacle of all things civilized:

> We English are perhaps poorer in the gesture language than any other people in the world. We use a form of words to denote what a gesture or a tone would express. Perhaps it is because we read and write so much and have come to think and talk as we should write, and so let fall those aids to speech which cannot be carried into the written language. (Tylor [1865] 1964:37)

The courteous modesty that concedes the English to be "perhaps poorer" in gesture should not mislead us here. Tylor subtly argues that the English have voluntarily "let fall" the crudities of gesture. Such practices are primitive "survivals" in other civilized nations. The "expressive incontinence of gesture" is appropriate only for those who remain in an infantile stage of cultural development (Herzfeld 1987:137).

> The upper-class Victorian English regarded gesticulation as a "natural" act, and therefore as "rude" (cf. Latin rudis, "raw, unformed"). As a feature of the savage stage in human evolution, and indeed as the only expressive recourse of true savages, it could be treated as both universal and fundamentally invarient; and in this regard it contrasted diametrically with the precise language of educated people—especially of the Europeans, whose linguistic diversity was but one mark of their transcendant unity. (Herzfeld 1987:136)

The power of literacy is also involved here. Ong has suggested that to dissociate words from writing is psychologically threatening to most literates, because a sense of control over language is closely tied to its visual transformation (1982:14). It is no surprise then to learn that the

Victorian ideal was to talk as one should write—a legacy that remains with us, of course, in the accepted norms for the performance of academic scholarship. Unfortunately, we also find a Victorian evolutionary attitude surviving in much of Ong's work. "Primitive" cultures have been replaced by "oral" cultures in which people are deemed to be more "agonistic" (read physical and combative) than in literate cultures.

An important impetus to the development of this kind of social evolutionism in social anthropology was the shift to a secularized and naturalized time scale that followed Lyell's *Principles of Geology* (1830), despite important points of departure from Darwinian principles (see Fabian 1983, Chap. 1). Unable to relinquish prior convictions about "progress" and the notion that time accomplished things, relationships between parts of the natural and sociocultural worlds were to be understood as temporal relations; dispersal in geographical space reflected evolutionary sequence in time. Those peoples farthest from the geographical ethnocenter of Victorian England, such as Australian Aborigines and American Indians, were taken to be the most primitive. Not unsurprisingly, both peoples used sign languages extensively. Those on the margins of Europe, as implied by Tylor's mention of "Hindoos, Arabs and Greeks," who, along with the Italians, gestured frequently while speaking, fell uncomfortably somewhere in between. Fabian has argued that since this spatialization of time, "anthropology's efforts to construct relations with its Other by means of temporal devices implies affirmation of difference as *distance*." Given this view of time-space, control over the body and its movement is already an important criterion for placing on the evolutionary "tree."

To understand why gesture should occupy this position, it is necessary to examine the often implicit yet predominant philosophy of mind/body relations in Victorian England that allowed human movement to be viewed as a marker of primitiveness. It was constituted, at least in part, by the Christian tradition in which the body as flesh was viewed as the location of corrupting appetite, sinful desire, and private irrationality. Bryan Turner (1984) has built upon Weber's work on the Protestant ethic and capitalism to suggest that alongside the emergence of a modern form of consciousness set within a rational tradition, new forms of discipline emerged that regulated and organized the energies of the human body. The moral stability of the individual was bound inextricably to the equilibrium and control of the body (cf. Foucault 1973, 1978, 1979; Hudson 1985).

Through European eyes, the fact that the "savages" gestured profusely when speaking and spent a great deal of time dancing appeared as markers of irrationality, indicative of a potentially dangerous lack of control over the "passions" of the body, in defiance of a rational mind. Linnaeus' seventeenth-century taxonomy of human groups highlights these associations between control of the body and the social control deemed appropriate to civilization. Europeans have "close clothes" and are governed by laws; Asiatics have "loose clothes" and are governed by opinion, while those without clothes at all but "body grease" (African) and "body paint" (American) are ruled by "caprice" and "custom" (see Hodgen [1964] 1971:425; Herzfeld 1987:97).

Douglas has articulated how margins, both bodily and social, are frequently considered dangerous as potential sources of social pollution (1966, Chap. 7). It is not surprising, therefore, to find that for Euro-Americans, bringing "civilization" to the "savages" in the North American context involved radical alterations to the margins of their bodies through hairstyle, clothing, and daily bodily practices. It involved gaining control not only of their bodies but also of the spaces in which they moved. The control of geographical spaces, for example, that came with the setting up of the reservation system in the late nineteenth century also brought control over personal, linguistic, social, and moral spaces.

Elderly consultants today at the Fort Belknap and Fort Peck reservations vividly recall their own painful and humiliating experiences in this regard. Other adults remember stories told by their parents, who, as young children, were torn away from extensive kinship networks in order to comply with the requirement of forced attendance at boarding schools. Along with the complete ban on Native American spoken languages in such schools, long and flowing hair was cut and loose-fitting, fringed clothing was discarded for European styles that outlined and confined the body. In addition to confinement in the classroom, the ethic that preached salvation through discipline and hard work imposed strict regimes of household tasks. Farming, eating, and sleeping practices, as well as religious ones, were enforced by the threat of severe physical punishment (see Fey and McNickle [1959] 1970:125–141). Bodily comportment and norms of interaction were brought under control by teachers, missionaries, and Indian agents alike. Under aggressive government policies of assimilation, Indian agents in charge of reservation administration were instructed to ban dancing of all kinds as detrimental to the Indians' "advancement" and "stirring the passions of the blood." [1]

From a European perspective, land squared off into fields, placed under individual ownership, and occupied by permanent rectangular dwellings represented space and nature under control because it was marked by clearly defined boundaries. The Protestant work ethic of most Euro-American immigrants centered on staying in one place; they were *settlers*. People who traveled frequently across land that had no visible, artificial boundaries were therefore viewed as having undisciplined lives dangerously full of movement and outside of any rational and therefore moral control.

GESTURE AND THE ORIGINS OF LANGUAGE

Given this kind of perspective on movement and the body, gestures and sign languages became of interest to nineteenth-century anthropologists because it was assumed that these systems could provide evidence of the origins of language. Those "races" that used a great deal of gesture were "savages" and so, ipso facto, gesture was most probably a primitive precursor to speech. This idea had a corollary: the languages that such people spoke must also be simple and underdeveloped. The underlying assumption was that languages were linked to the mental capacities of the races that used them and that language itself was physically determined. Sayce (1880) claimed that "the gesture language" represented a distinct separate stage of human utterance through which humans passed before they came to speak. Tylor never supported this claim, but felt it quite plausible to maintain that

> in the early stages of the development of language while as yet the vocabulary was very rude and scanty, gesture had an importance as an element of expression, which in conditions of highly organized language it has lost. ([1865] 1964:10)

He wrote of Plains Indian Sign Talk:

As a means of communication, there is no doubt that the Indian pantomime is not merely capable of expressing a few simple and ordinary notions, but that to the uncultured savage, with his few and material ideas, it is a very fair substitute for his scanty vocabulary. ([1865] 1964:32)

"Pantomime," although originally a genre of Greek theater, had become in Tylor's England a humorous form of popular theater, aimed primarily at children. The connection between children, frivolity, and the gestural communication of "primitives" was certainly not lost to Tylor, especially given the widespread acceptance of Haekle's evolutionary dictum that ontogeny recapitulates phylogeny (see Gould 1977). Neither is the Platonic disdain for *mimesis* as imitation absent here. Viewed as mime, as mere iconic representation of objects and action, gestures and sign languages could make no claim to grammar.

By the mid-nineteenth century in England, tales of entirely "dumb" races were no longer in vogue, at least, Tylor tells us, among "authors worthy of credit." Nevertheless, there were a number of accounts of peoples halfway between "the mythic dumb nations and ourselves and having a speech so imperfect that even if talking of ordinary matters they have to eke it out by gestures" (Tylor [1865] 1964:62). Tylor investigated several reports that primitive spoken languages were more dependent upon gesture than his own, but found these nonconvincing and concluded, quite accurately from a contemporary standpoint, that in any spoken language context in which two persons do not speak the same language, gesticulation accompanied by unusually loud and simple talking usually occurs.[2] It may seem obvious to us today that this does not indicate any deficiency in the spoken languages of the peoples concerned, yet travelers' reports of such situations led to a myth that became well established in anthropology, that savages were dependent upon gesture for communication (Henson 1974:18).

In line with what Whorf identified as early as 1936 as a dualistic mode of thinking in the Western mind, a major problem encountered here is what might be called either/or thinking: either a word or, in the absence of adequate vocabulary, a gesture (1956:59). That this combined use of speech and gesture might instead indicate choices between two equally available and expressive media according to convention and context was entirely overlooked in this theoretical framework.

Much can be learned about nineteenth-century attitudes toward so-called primitive languages and gesture by examining some of these reports in more detail. In one case, a Dr. Milligan, speaking of the language of Tasmania and the variations in its dialects, actually blamed the use of gestures for a lack of clarity in the spoken language:

> The habit of gesticulation, and the use of signs to eke out the meaning of monosyllabic expressions, and to give force, precision and character to vocal sounds, exerted a further modifying effect, producing, as it did, carelessness and laxity of articulation, in the application and pronunciation of words. (Milligan 1859, quoted in Tylor [1865] 1964:63)

Another example is provided by Spix and Martius (1823, cited in Tylor [1865] 1964:63) about the Puri and Coroado peoples of Brazil. Noting that these different tribes conversed in signs, the authors complained of the difficulty, nevertheless, in making them understand by signs the objects or ideas for which they wanted the native names. That such evidence contradicted the assumed universality of signs went unnoticed. Signs with the hand or mouth were necessary to these people to make themselves understood, reported Spix and Martius, and they cited as an example the sentence "I will go into the woods." "The Indian uses the words 'wood-go' and *points his mouth like a snout in the direction he means*" (emphasis added). Confronted with an unfamiliar use of the face, these writers effectively reduce the Coroado and Puri people to the status of animal.

The tendency to blur the boundaries between animal and human already had a long history in European conceptions of the Other. Ever since the days of discovery, tales of fantastic creatures and half-human monsters had been brought back from far-off shores (see Hodgen [1964] 1971). Even today, however, slippery thinking and unfortunate uses of language in behaviorist or observationist studies of human movement continue to frame simplistic comparisons between human and animal movement in ways that studies of sound do not.[3] At work usually is the fallacious assumption that what looks the same means the same. This problematic status for human movement is one of several problems that stem from the Cartesian view of mind/body relations that, along with religious attitudes, contributed to the Victorian disdain: while the mind and spoken language are deemed to be *cultural*, the body and its movement are seen as essentially *natural*.

In the North American context, the idea that "savages" were dependent upon gesture gained ground from reports such as that of an unknown observer on the Plains who declared the Arapaho language to be "a cross between a whistle and a grunt that needed gestures to eke out its meaning" (Scott ca. 1928). The Arapaho language also came under fire from Captain R. F. Burton:

> Those natives who, like the Arapahoes possess a very scanty
> vocabulary, pronounced in a quasi-intelligible way, can hardly
> converse with one another in the dark; to make a stranger under-
> stand them they must always repair to the camp-fire for "pow-
> wow." (1861:123)

Burton's ethnocentric contempt for the native languages of America, typical of his time, is again illustrated in the following derogatory description:

> A story is told of a man, who being sent among the Cheyennes to
> qualify himself as an interpreter, returned in a week and proved
> his competence; all that he did however, was to go through the
> usual pantomime with a running accompaniment of grunts.
> (1861:123)

The "usual pantomime" obviously refers to the use of PST, which was in fact a most appropriate language for an interpreter to learn at the time, given that it was in use as a lingua franca throughout the Plains region. In Burton's view, learning such a skill obviously did not demand anything as complex as "real" language learning. Reference to the Cheyenne spoken language as "a running accompaniment of grunts" once again reduces its users to a subhuman level.

Ethnocentrism aside, it was the inadequacy of sources of information in the 1860s that permitted such speculations about "primitive" spoken languages. Nineteenth-century fieldwork methods for transcribing oral languages were limited by a phonetic notation adapted from that used to record European languages. Philologists did not describe a language in its own terms but used the semantic and grammatical categories of the main European languages for comparisons. The lack of overlap was then explained by a failure on the part of the "primitive" languages (Henson 1974:12). While methods of transcription for non-European oral languages later improved, there was no conception of any need for a transcription system for gesture or signed languages. The gestural component, upon which many of these languages were reportedly dependent, dropped out of consideration altogether because "real" language was conceived of strictly as a system of sounds. Boas, for example, although certainly interested in gestures and dances, and familiar with Mallery's extensive collection of the Plains sign lexicon, chose to exclude "the gesture language" from the *Handbook of American Indian Languages*. He justified this omission by aligning gesture with "musical means of communication" (Boas 1911:10).

Although couched in deeply ethnocentric terms, ironically what was probably a fairly accurate observation about the importance of gesture in many non-European (and some European) linguistic practices was prevented from being viewed as a challenge to definitions of language precisely because of epistemological and ontological aspects of that ethnocentrism. Cultures that fully utilized movement of the body in discursive as well as nondiscursive systems of meaning were kept at a safe distance, outside the boundaries of the "civilized world," by the evolutionary notion of stages of development and the close association between "real" language and literacy.[4] Any challenge to the foundations of European definitions of language and ways of knowing that might transcend Cartesianism by including bodily actions other than those performed by the throat and mouth was thus avoided.

Four ingredients have emerged from this discussion that, when blended together, offer some explanation as to why, despite widespread interest in gesture and sign languages in the nineteenth century, possible connections between sign talking and speech were not explored.

The ongoing Platonic/Cartesian separation of rational mind from irrational, sensate body was accompanied by a particularly Victorian reading of the Christian disdain for an uncontrolled body. These factors were complemented by the social evolutionary fervor of the time which placed gesture in a more "primitive" or, in Tylor's term, more "natural" category than speech. All this was topped by an equation of civilized language practices with literacy. The theoretical leap from the available, albeit scanty, evidence to a consideration that perhaps the notion of "language" needed to be expanded to *include* gestures, was never made. This potent brew contributed not only to the theoretical neglect of any connection between sign talking and speech talking but to the absence of "the body"—that is, the embodied and moving person—in social theory generally, a legacy which has remained salient.

The ongoing exclusion of sign languages from linguistics was tenacious. Not until 1960 did William Stokoe manage to persuade some members of the profession that American Sign Language (ASL) was a real language, and only subsequently did linguistic research into the grammatical structure of ASL gain credibility. At about the same time, West (1960), supported by Kroeber (1958) and Voegelin (1958), attempted to devise a transcription system for PST and apply it to a descriptive linguistic analysis. The theoretical implication of these intrusions into the conventional definition of language as systems of speech sounds has yet to be realized, however. Sign languages are frequently viewed by linguists as substitutes for speech by special people in special circumstances, and so it has been possible to retain the implicit assumption that sign languages are marginal cases. Accompanying this is the further assumption that sign languages and the manual gestures that accompany speech are somehow different in kind. The continuum between the informal use of manual gestures with speech and the use of signs without speech in the Assiniboine case is important in this regard, because it opens up the tight boundary that has surrounded linguistic phenomena as conventionally constituted.

Chapter 2

Perhaps you are in danger of falling into some error on consequence of limiting your studies so much to Language.

CHARLES S. PEIRCE TO LADY WELSBY[1]

Linguists will have to distinguish the semiological characteristics of language in order to place it properly among the systems of signs; the task of the new science will be to bring out the differences between these diverse systems as well as their common characteristics.

FERDINAND DE SAUSSURE (PARAPHRASED BY ROMAN JAKOBSON)[2]

BIAS AGAINST THE ICONIC

Iconicity was—and still is—devalued and distrusted in Euramerican sign systems. This has long-standing philosophical roots in interpretations of the Platonic disdain for the arts as *mimesis*—imitation.[3] The problem for sign language analysis is that the arbitrary relationship used to define linguistic signs in contrast to other types of sign-referent relations has been accorded a kind of prominence in traditional linguistics due to the valorization of the Saussurian principle, the Swiss master's call to semiology notwithstanding. Aspects of sign relations that are iconic have on these grounds been viewed as nonlinguistic and less complex than other sign relations, despite the fact that spoken language systems too are shot through with iconicity. The trio of sign-referent relations articulated in the semiotics of C. S. Peirce—icon, index, and symbol—is particularly useful here as a means both to identify the problem as inherited and to transcend it. In this chapter I shall again draw upon the nineteenth-century legacy to trace this bias against the iconic as it has persisted into current strategies for linguistic analysis. It was the predominance of iconicity at the level of "signs"[4] in sign languages—in contrast to the predominantly arbitrary nature of spoken lexemes, for example—that laid the ground for nineteenth-century claims that "the gesture language" was universal, primitive, and natural.

UNIVERSALITY AND "THE GESTURE LANGUAGE"

As I noted earlier, gestures, as the expressive recourse of "savages," could be treated as both universal and fundamentally invariant, hence the name *"the* gesture language." Tylor's *Researches into the Early History of Mankind*, first published in 1865, investigates the gesture language in some detail, over half the volume being devoted to the nature and origins of language. This was unusual, for apart from Tylor, the most influential early British anthropologists largely ignored the problem of language (Henson 1974:39); the subject was the realm of philologists.

Tylor paid detailed attention to "the gesture language" as a complete and independent language as "it" was used by "the deaf and dumb," Cistercian monks, Greek and Roman actors, and the "Indian Pantomime." The point of departure for Tylor's ideas was the work of two French priests, Abbé de l'Epée (1776) and Abbé Sicard (1808), who pioneered the use of signing in the education of the deaf. Sicard considered the sign language used by his pupils to lack grammar and therefore to be closer to thought and more natural than speech. Its elements were expected to be universally recognizable, one of the reasons Tylor chose to investigate it so thoroughly. He studied firsthand the sign language used in the Berlin Deaf and Dumb Institute and compared it to a similar system in England.[5]

Tylor believed that whereas "there are many hundreds of mutually unintelligible tongues . . . the gesture language is essentially one and the same in all times and countries." The universality of signs was proved by the "ease and certainty with which any savage from any country can be understood in a deaf and dumb school" ([1865] 1964:46).

Mallery (1881), at the Bureau of Ethnology in Washington, D.C., whose voluminous work on "Sign Language among the North American Indians" was a direct application of many of Tylor's ideas, conducted an experiment on this topic in 1881. He took seven visiting members of the Ute tribe to the National College for the Deaf in Washington, where Thomas Gallaudet, who was then president, oversaw a "thorough test" in which the Indians and seven deaf pupils each told narratives in signs, which were then interpreted by college officers and a Ute interpreter.

The situation was complex, to say the least. Misunderstandings occurred because of numerous vocabulary differences, and what mutual understanding was achieved was probably the result of explicit miming combined with trial and error, rather than the use of either sign language. Both groups were already very skilled in using the medium and no doubt rose to the occasion with creativity. Also, as became known later, Indian sign talkers, probably out of politeness, were adept at adapting their own signs to accommodate a stranger's attempts.[6]

However, seeing only what he wanted to see because of his theoretical position, Mallery concluded from this experiment that signing represented the direct expression of thought, which seldom failed to communicate because it was without the "mental confusion of conventional sounds" (1881:323). Following Tylor, he felt his own studies indicated that there was but one "gesture speech of mankind—of which each system is a dialect." In the Plains context, it was General Hugh Scott (ca. 1930) who later strongly disputed this universalist position, asserting quite accurately from a contemporary standpoint that to claim universality for sign languages was the same as saying that Japanese and English were the same language because they shared the medium of sound!

It is difficult to ascertain exactly what Tylor meant by "same" when he stated that the gesture language is essentially one and the same in all times and countries. He quite clearly wrote of one language with several dialects:

> The Indian Pantomime and the gesture language of the deaf and dumb are but different dialects of the same language of nature . . . I have now noticed what I venture to call the principal dialects of the gesture language. ([1865] 1964:28, 36)

But in a footnote he adds:

> There is much in each [dialect] that differs from the others in detail though not in principle, that they may I think, be held as practically independent, except as regards grammatical signs. ([1865] 1964:14 n. 8)[7]

From later discussion in the same chapter, it becomes clear that when Tylor uses the term "the same," he is not referring to lexical content in itself but to the principle and process by which *iconic* features are utilized to create signs. This is no different, of course, than saying that all spoken languages are the same because for the most part lexemes share an arbitrary relationship between sign vehicle and entity signified. It may be true, but it is not an acceptable criterion for the claim that all languages are therefore dialects of each other.

ARBITRARINESS AND ICONICITY

Tylor divided languages into two types because he felt that "the gesture language" worked on a different principle from that of spoken language. It was this principle, he posited, that allowed the gesture language to be universally understood, and its lack in spoken languages that created hundreds of mutually unintelligible tongues. This principle was "to seize the most striking outline of an object or the principal movement of an action" ([1865] 1964:16) and, by imitating it, create the signs of the language.

Tylor's concern was to prove that there was a past when the selection of signs was "natural," that is, based upon reason and not at all arbitrary. He believed that in a sign language the reasons for the choice were always obvious and that "the relation between sign and idea not only exists but is scarcely lost sight of for a moment" ([1865] 1964:16). A study of both the gesture language and picture writing would, he felt, reveal in some measure a condition of the human mind that underlies even the lowest dialect of spoken language.

Following the terminology of Peirce, what Tylor seized upon here are the iconic aspects of many lexical units in a sign language. Tylor did not wish to venture far into a comparison of the gesture language with spoken languages, but he did make some cautious statements about two different processes involved which had parallels in spoken language terms:

> The gesture language uses two different processes. It brings objects and actions bodily into the conversation, by pointing to them or looking at them, and it also suggests by imitation of actions, or by "pictures in the air," and these two processes may be used separately or combined. This division may be clumsy and in some cases inaccurate, but it is the best I have succeeded in making. ([1865] 1964:51–52)

Citing the work of Max Müller and the division of Sanskrit root forms into two classes, Tylor suggested that the sign language of the "deaf and dumb" could be divided roughly into "predicative" and "demonstrative" signs, thus anticipating a current distinction in linguistic terminology between "semantico-referential" signs and "indexical" ones.[8] Before investigating further the implications of Tylor's classification, brief exposition of the terms "icon," "index," and "symbol" will clarify the argument.

ICON, INDEX, SYMBOL

A sign, in the general sense in which this term is used by the philosopher C. S. Peirce, is defined as something that represents or signifies an object to some interpretant (the person who understands the sign or device that interprets it). Peirce devised a complex taxonomy of signs, a part of which concerns the nature of the relationship between the entity signaled and the signaling entity.[9] Peirce divided this category into iconic, indexical, and symbolic sign types. Burks (1949) and Friedrich (1979) stress that Peirce's trichotomy of signs into icon, index, and symbol has to be understood as a functional differentiation, not an ontological differentiation: it designates aspects of symbolism (in the wider sense), not kinds of symbols. As Friedrich suggests, "[Signs] are not objects or entities that can be sorted into their respective pigeonholes, but, rather, are aspects of the relation between idea and form" (1979:18). This relationship becomes established through use that both creates convention and is based on convention. All signs are at least partly conventional, and all conventional symbols have iconic or indexical aspects. Eco's (1976) shift of focus from signs to sign functions also emphasizes this point.

Iconic Signs

Iconic signs or icons in the Peircian schema are those signs in which the perceivable properties of the signifying form itself are seen to resemble the signified concept. For example, many road signs are iconic in that they show pictures of "falling rocks ahead," "road junction on the right," and so on. In a sign language like PST, the sign glossed in English as TIPI is an iconic sign because the index fingers on each hand are held up and crossed at the fingertip end so that they re-create the shape of a tipi with the poles crossed at the top.

In spoken languages sound, sight, and movement all provide iconic representations in ideophonic words. They are iconic because they are understood as attempts either to duplicate the sound (e.g., onomato-

Photo 2.1. Rose Weasel has made the sign glossed as TIPI, in which the index fingers of both hands iconically represent the shape of this distinctive Plains dwelling.

poeic words such as "buzz," "meow," and "swish") or to denote some quality of the object such as the visual appearance or texture (e.g., the sound cluster /sl/ in words such as "slimy," "slippery," and "slick") or movement (e.g., zigzag, wigwag, flip-flop) of the thing represented. In all these examples of what has come to be known as "sound symbolism," the sound of the word forms is felt to be appropriate to the meaning and so is in an iconic relationship.[10]

Sapir carried out an interesting experiment on "expressive symbolism" (iconicity) in contrast to "referential symbolism" (arbitrariness) in 1929. Nonsense words with the vowel /a/ seemed consistently to English speakers to symbolize a larger size than did words containing the vowel /i/. Sapir suggested, and his subjects agreed, that there was an acoustic and/or kinesthetic reason for this symbolism in that the "volume" of the vowels in the mouth is different due to the position of the tongue and available space for the vibrating column of air. When pronouncing /i/, the tongue is higher and the air more compressed through a narrower resonance chamber than is the case with /a/ where the tongue is lower and also retracted: "the spatially extended gesture is symbolic of a larger reference than a spatially restricted gesture" (Sapir [1949] 1985:70).

But visual, kinetic, kinesthetic, and acoustic ideophones are also tropes, because they are conventional renditions of iconicity. Onomatopoeic words, for example, have a greater homology to the natural sound but differ from one language to another. So, for example, the sound of a sneeze is "achooo" in English and *pśa* (psha) in Nakota. The sound is assimilated into the phonemic pattern of the language. This kind of assimilation is frequently found, thus giving a remarkable variety of representations in different languages of the "same" sound, the "same" texture, the "same" movement.

A similar process of assimilation also occurs with iconic aspects of signs in a sign language. What counts as the most salient feature of an iconically based "lexical" item in a sign language relates to the kinemic pattern of that language. In other words, even so-called iconic signs, instead of being natural and universal, are highly conventionalized and system-specific.

The term "kineme" refers to a level of representation equivalent to a phoneme in a spoken language. That is, it is a unit of movement, or shape of the hand, for example, that provides a constituent part of a sign recognized by native speakers as making a difference in meaning. Figure 2.1 shows the representation of TREE in Danish, Chinese, American (ASL), and Plains sign languages. All do indeed display iconic features, but obviously the concept of "treeness" is not the same in these different cultures. In PST, for example, the sign combines three kinemes. A particular handshape, palm facing, and movement create the sign, which can be written as shown in Figure 2.2.

For PST the iconic aspect of the sign uses notions of branching and growing; in Danish Sign Language the perceived shape of the finished product from top to bottom is portrayed; in Chinese Sign Language it is the solidity of the trunk that is most salient; and in ASL it is the branched shape that moves in the wind.

Likewise, the sign glossed as DANCE in PST is an iconic representation of an alternate stepping action, a basic step pattern found in many otherwise radically different dance styles on the Plains. That this action does refer to "dancing" might seem transparent once given a word gloss in translation. The unobservable cultural value and meanings attached

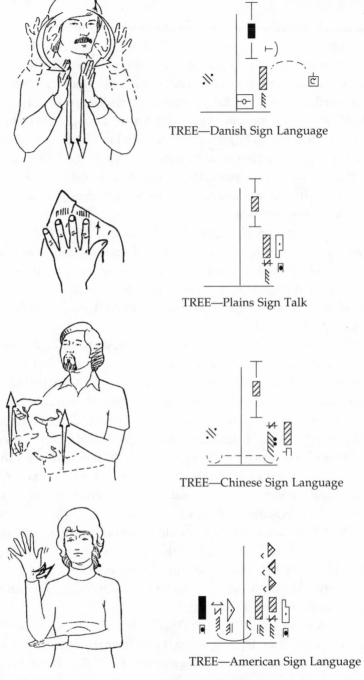

TREE—Danish Sign Language

TREE—Plains Sign Talk

TREE—Chinese Sign Language

TREE—American Sign Language

Figure 2.1. The iconic representation of TREE in four sign languages. From Klima and Bellugi 1979:21 and Tomkins [1926] 1969:56. Used with permission.

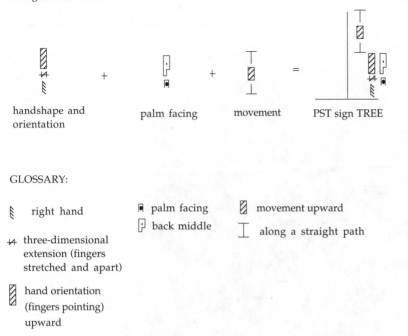

handshape and   palm facing   movement   PST sign TREE
orientation

GLOSSARY:

  right hand   palm facing   movement upward

                         back middle   along a straight path

three-dimensional
extension (fingers
stretched and apart)

hand orientation
(fingers pointing)
upward

Figure 2.2. Components of the PST sign TREE.

to the notion of "dancing" for Plains Indians are entirely misrepresented in the English gloss, however. The sign in ASL for DANCE, for example, also means PARTY, a conception which would be quite foreign to the concept of dancing to any Plains Indian, given the religious significance of traditional dance forms. Although such translation problems in spoken language situations are usually given serious attention, they are frequently overlooked when it comes to gestural representation precisely because of naïve expectations of iconic universality.

Iconicity such as that found in sign languages can probably be more easily understood than spoken language only among people who share conceptual bases that deal with the body, space, and time in similar ways. The degree of conventionalization in such iconicity has been blurred not only by a lack of knowledge about different sign languages and gestural systems but also by the tendency of investigators to draw upon examples from their own culture, where familiarity of context and shared conceptual bases play an important role in understanding the iconicity.

Closer attention to the selected examples Tylor used to demonstrate the general principle by which signs are made clearly illustrates the con-

Photo 2.2. The PST sign BUFFALO involves an iconic
representation of the horns of the animal.

ventionality of so-called universal signs. The tacit cultural knowledge
involved in understanding "imitative" signs for such apparently transparent things as a flower garden, house, man taking off a hat, and roast-
ing a goose are far from trivial. They demand, at the very least, experience with the notion of garden, the shape of European domestic architecture, a style of clothing fashion, a method of cooking, and a bird that
comes under the category of food.

Likewise, the PST sign BUFFALO (representing horns) is perfectly
transparent in the context of a discourse about hunting or trading on the
Plains, but out of context and without any word gloss in explanation
such a sign could, for a European, equally refer to the devil, any sort of
horned animal, or even some kind of hat or hairstyle.

Experiments in ASL research have shown that most ASL signs are not iconic enough to be understood without being told their meanings (Klima and Bellugi 1979, cited in Baker and Cokely 1980:39). Once someone learns the meaning of a sign, however, then an iconic relationship between the form of the sign and its meaning can often be perceived. According to Frishburg (1975), signs in ASL have become less iconic over time, but perhaps the reasons are most productively viewed as changes that have occurred in the interests of brevity and speed of production and to accommodate a smaller and more focused visual field, rather than as evolution from a more primitive form into a more arbitrary and therefore "real" language. Such has been the hegemony of spoken linguistics, however, that it has led researchers to attempt such justifications for sign languages.[11]

Tylor himself, in a discussion of various systems of greeting, noted confusions that arose from the unexpected conventionality in gestures of beckoning in India. The Indians' arm motion was likely to be taken for a gesture of motioning away by a European.[12] As Boas observed, the Baffin Islanders raised their eyebrows instead of saying yes; wrinkled their noses to indicate no; frequently shook their heads in saying "I don't know"; and for saying "it may be" raised their shoulders.[13]

Sign language and other gestural systems have been systematically devalued precisely because iconic aspects of signs have remained in focus to the exclusion of both arbitrary and indexical aspects that also exist at all levels of their linguistic structure. The lack of a writing system for movement has no doubt contributed considerably to this lopsided focus. Meanwhile, the iconic in spoken languages has been minimized, for it is certainly the case that spoken languages too are shot through with iconicity. In addition to the sound symbolism mentioned earlier, as Jakobson pointed out in 1965, the temporal order of speech events tends to mirror the order of narrated events in time or in ranked importance; in declarative sentences the predominant basic order for nominal subject and object is one in which the former precedes the latter; the combination of words into syntactic groups and morphemes into words agrees with the Peircian definition of diagrams and their iconic nature. Likewise, in morphology, an increased length of form can mirror the gradation of the signified (as in high, higher, highest and the addition of plural morphemes). In rhyme, there is often a phonemic allusion to semantic proximity (e.g., father, mother, brother). In poetic language particularly, Jakobson reminds us (and see also Ullmann 1962), the iconic value of phonemic opposition comes to the fore. He summarizes, "While predominantly symbolic in character, the iconic and indexical constituents of verbal symbols have too often remained underestimated or even disregarded" (Jakobson 1965:426). The operation of iconicity as an external motivation for grammatical structure remains a study in its infancy, according to Croft (1990:202).

Symbolic Signs

Symbols, in the Peircian scheme, are those signs deemed most languagelike in the traditional sense. Sign vehicle and entity signaled (Saussure's signifier and signified) are related only through convention.[14] Thus a red traffic light by conventional agreement alone means "stop." Likewise it is the conventions of a particular language that determine which sounds can be used to represent what. So, for example, the sounds /tri/ in English identify a tree. In German the sounds /baum/ do this, and in Nakota the sounds /c'a/. Symbols form the "arbitrary" signs spoken of as the fundamental kind of linguistic entity. All words in any language are arbitrary symbols in this sense, even when they are also iconic (as in onomatopoeia) or indexical (e.g., "this," "that").

Indexical Signs

An example of an indexical sign would be the act of pointing to a book. The sign (pointing) creates an existential connection to the book and so is in an indexical relation. If the pointing were replaced by the words "this book," then "this" becomes an index because the object being referred to is in existential relation to the word. In both spoken and signed languages, examples are found in demonstratives—such as THIS and THAT, HERE and THERE—as well as pronouns (I and YOU), all of which depend upon the actual speech situation for their meaning. Peirce (1956:108–109) said that the function of an index is to refer or call attention to some feature or object in the immediate environment, and this is precisely why such signs become important in the analysis of many speech events: they situate the actors in a particular context. Deictical features in language are devices that locate actions in time and space relative to the speaker. Personal pronouns, verb tenses, demonstratives, and time and space adverbs all point outward from the actor's location, from the speaker who is "I" in the "here and now"—a location that is sometimes referred to as the "zero point" of deictic space (Lyons 1977) or the deictic "origo" of the speaker (Bühler [1934] 1982).

Traditional treatments of deictic reference have tended to assume a "natural" stance toward this I-here-now of deictic reference, as if the speaker's body is merely a concrete organism located in physical space. It is, however, not a body (reduced to organism) that deals with deictic reference, but a person, whose bodily and spatial experiences are socially constructed in interactions with other persons. Subjectivist assumptions have also tended to mask the sociocentric nature of acts of deictic reference, grounded as they are in social relationships and interactions between persons (see Hanks 1990:5–9).

INDEXICALITY AND LANGUAGE-IN-USE

Although indexicality is not new to inquiries in philosophy, linguists have taken this category as a basis for forging new relations between language and culture. Indexes can be explored as they relate to the persons, time, space, and social setting of the speech event itself in creative ongoing acts of defining self and others; "Indexes create the social person" (Urciuoli 1988). Friedrich (1979), for example, notes that linguists have shown growing awareness of indexicality, specifically in relation to a large class of grammatical units usually called "shifters" (after Jesperson 1923).

Roman Jakobson ([1957] 1971) used the term "shifter" to describe the kind of referential index that depends on factors of the speech situation; in other words, the reference "shifts" according to the speech situation. For example, temporal categories—such as the past tense—compare the time referred to with the time of utterance. The time of the speech event (now) is the fixed point of comparison in referring to another time (then). Jakobson referred to these referential indexes or shifters as "duplex structures" operating at the level of code and message simultaneously: the general meaning of a shifter cannot be defined without reference to its function. All languages incorporate these duplex signs, which anchor the "semantico-referential signs" in the actual speech event by making the propositional reference dependent on suitable indexing (see Silverstein 1976).

For example, personal pronouns, one type of shifter, are symbols in that they have an invariant relationship through convention. "I," for example, is only related by the conventions of English to the person uttering it (*"ich," "je,"* etc., performing the same function in other languages). But the linguistic utterance "I" cannot represent its object without being in existential relation to the speaker: "I" means the addresser and "you" the addressee of the message to which it belongs, and, as this reference shifts according to who is speaking, pronouns also function as indexes. Other shifters include the categories of person, demonstratives, mood, and tense.

Silverstein (1976) suggests distinguishing between two distinct types of linguistic signs that merge in the apparent structure of utterances: semantico-referential symbols (names) and shifters (indexes). Indexing can be presupposed—that is, taken for granted, because "you" and "I," "now" and "then," "this" and "that" achieve understood reference—or it can be creative. Creative indexes are features of speech that do not contribute to achieving reference (in the restricted linguistic sense); rather, their meaning is pragmatic. Indexing is performative, for example, when I choose to address you as *"du"* instead of *"sie"* in German, or as "uncle" instead of "Jim," according to the social relations I want to emphasize between us.

A common example of creative indexing found among Assiniboine people is the way in which an illocutionary speech act (Austin 1962:98– 108) such as a request is made in the presence of relatives. Often such a request will be made only obliquely, perhaps by mentioning a particular event and the work needed to be done. In this way social etiquette, which requires that relatives never refuse to help one another, is not violated. Indexing the request means that no one is actually compelled to voice a refusal, but a person does not have to offer either. Individual autonomy is not curtailed and individual moral choice remains reasonably intact, dependent upon other commitments and feelings of obligation.

Creative or performative indexicality and many areas of language labeled in the past as paralinguistic are coming to be seen as part of a functional grammar of language-in-use. Indexes previously labeled paralinguistic, for example, include accent (Urciuoli 1984) and sound symbolism (Nuckolls 1990). Indexes previously labeled nonverbal but emerging as integral to linguistic analysis include gesture and spatial orientation, as seen in the recent work of Havilland (1986), Kendon (1989), McNeill and Levy (1982), and McNeill (1985), in addition to the present study.

Silverstein notes that in order to distinguish analytic subparts of culture, such as language, we have traditionally distinguished among types of communicative events on the basis of the signaling media. In the case of language, the signaling medium has been considered to be articulate speech, and events have been isolated on this basis. This segmentation of speech from other signaling media has been justified in the past because of its symbolic sign function. According to such analysis, a speech event consists only of a sequence of "speech behavior in which some speaker or speakers signal to some hearer or hearers by means of a system of phonetic sign vehicles called speech messages or utterances" with an overt goal in view in a socially shared system of such purposive functions (Silverstein 1976:13). Emphasis upon this single function and type of reference has led to what Wittgenstein calls "a particular picture of the essence of human language" (1958:1). This is an Augustinian view, which he rejects, for "in this picture of language we find the roots of the following idea: Every word has a meaning. This meaning is correlated with the word. It is the object for which the word stands" (1958:1). Wittgenstein suggests that the question be rephrased to ask not "what is the meaning of . . . but how is it [a word or sign] used" (1958:1). This is a major shift away from a view of language as primarily a naming device.

Silverstein draws attention to the limitations of traditional analyses of spoken language due to an overemphasis on analytic techniques and formal descriptive machinery designed to categorize referential signs. The social functions of speech have not been built into analyses (1976:14; 1977). It might also be the case that the predominant physical metaphor in linguists' talk about language has contributed to the exclusion of gesture from conventional linguistics. Talk about the temporal and organizational dimensions of actual and idealized segmentable speech has "used up" the spatial and temporal dimensions of the metaphor, as it were. Ironically, then, there isn't any space left for aspects of communication that take place in "real" physical space, so they are largely ignored (Lawler 1979).

Urciuoli (1988, 1992) adds a political aspect to this by noting that indexicality is a property that spoken language shares with all sign systems, maintaining and creating social connections anchored in experience and the sense of the real. Her research on code-switching and accent among Puerto Rican immigrants in New York illustrates how indexes in discourse extend beyond pronouns, adverbs, and verbal categories to the sounds and shapes of speech that identify the actor with a particular group and profoundly affect a person's social status and lack of political power (1984). She notes that not all sign systems are equally valid in all societies; certain sign types will not be recognized as legitimate systems of meaning, or, if recognized, will have less status than others:

> Euro-American societies, for example, privilege speech over text
> (and text over speech), the systems most displaced from the body,
> so that the public self that counts most is the self that can be
> spoken or written (preferably written). Politically this becomes
> dangerous when a society is in a position to dictate what is or is
> not a valid system. Thus Euro-American epistemologies have long
> been reproduced by institutions that can privilege speech and text
> as universally valid and *natural*. Especially privileged are the most
> text-like aspects of speech—the referential—where context (which
> is embodiment) counts least in the creation of meaning. The flip
> side of this, of course, is that any sign system that cannot be
> reduced to reference, falls outside the charmed circle, and entire
> populations are robbed of valid ways of being in the eyes of the
> elite. (1988:4)

The connection between this and the view of gesture and sign languages discussed above is that these movement systems have been labeled primitive and robbed of validity in relation to spoken language systems because of the predominance of iconic signs. In the privileged semantico-referential category of traditional linguistics, signs are supposed to be arbitrary and symbolic, not iconic.

The stress placed upon the difference between signed and spoken languages due to iconicity and arbitrariness has been confusing because of a failure to realize that each medium utilizes both kinds of sign relations but in different ways and at different levels of linguistic structure. At the level of the lexicon, it may indeed be the case that spoken language units predominate at the arbitrary end of a continuum and signs of a sign language predominate at the iconic end. In relation to sign languages, however, it may be the case that insufficient attention has been paid to the medium of expression itself. It would seem perfectly logical to expect a language using a visual medium to maximize both the shape and the movement of objects in the naming of them. As Saussure himself stressed, however, whether or not a sign is arbitrary, it gains meaning from its place *within a system of signs*. In other words, once in a linguistic context, the degree of iconicity or arbitrariness becomes a feature that is interesting but irrelevant for what counts as a "real" language.

Chapter 3

*Then Inktomi called the Raven and told Raven,
"My brother, fly in one direction and see how far this land is.
See if it is big enough for us to survive. . . ."*

FLOOD STORY BY JAMES EARTHBOY

It is not down in any map; true places never are.

HERMAN MELVILLE (1963:68)

GEOGRAPHICAL AND HISTORICAL SPACES: ASSINIBOINE TERRITORY AND THE EMBODIMENT OF DEIXIS

It was Whorf (1941) who drew attention to the fact that grammatical structures of specific languages allow speakers to presuppose certain classifications of experience. In like manner, the grammatical structures of gesture-based systems have category features that allow actors to presuppose classifications of experience. Persons move (their bodies) in spaces that are simultaneously physical, conceptual, moral, and ethical (Williams 1988:6). Lived space is therefore not a given physical "reality" but an intentionally achieved structuring, and grammar maps this through indexing devices and names. In this chapter, indexing will provide the main focus.

Indexing is both presupposed—that is, taken for granted—and creative (Silverstein 1976). Deixis is a centrally important element here because it keeps pointing away from and back toward the speaker/mover in time and space, providing opportunity for the creative use of past and future, here and there, I/we and they, in achieving socially constituted ends.

What is achieved by a speaker/mover necessarily relates to the body itself ("I," as a person, including my body, "am here" or "was there") for the speaker no less than for the sign talker, and many aspects of deixis are shared by both media. For the sign talker, however, the realization takes place in visible space, and because the medium of movement structures grammars differently, many aspects of both presupposed indexicality and creative or performative indexicality are achieved differently.

The narrative that provides the focus for this chapter introduces the context of my study at Fort Belknap Reservation, northern Montana. It is a narrative about Assiniboine "territory" and its history, and provides an entry into the lived reality of Assiniboine conceptions of space-time, realized as geographical space that has been molded by political and historical events. Throughout the discussion a tension is maintained between two different speaker loci, the Native American and the Euro-American, the latter of which has always been taken as more "real." I suggest that the imposition of non-Indian constructed forms, boundaries, and routes contrasts strongly with indigenous "maps," both cognitive and geographical.

As a starting point, consider the words of Luther Standing Bear, a Lakota Sioux author, who eloquently contrasts the view of the landscape held by the indigenous people of the Plains with that of the "white man":

> We did not think of the great open plains, the beautiful rolling
> hills, and winding streams with tangled growth, as "wild." Only to
> the white man was nature a "wilderness" and only to him was the
> land "infested" with "wild" animals and "savage" people. To us it
> was tame. Earth was bountiful and we were surrounded with the
> blessings of the Great Mystery. Not until the hairy man from the
> east came and with brutal frenzy heaped injustices upon us and
> the families we loved was it "wild" for us. When the very animals
> of the forest began fleeing from his approach, then it was that for
> us the "Wild West" began. (1933:38)

Contrast this with the words of Lieutenant Colonel Richard Irving Dodge, a seasoned army officer:

> When I was a schoolboy my map of the United States showed
> between the Missouri River and the Rocky Mountains a long and
> broad white blotch, upon which was printed in small capitals "The
> Great American Desert." (1877:2)

Finally, consider the description of British author Sir Arthur Conan Doyle:

> In the central portion of the great American continent there lies an

arid and repulsive desert which, for many a long year, served as a barrier against the advance of civilization. From the Cordillera to Nebraska, and from the Yellowstone River in the north to the Colorado in the south, is a region of desolation and silence . . . enormous plains which, in winter, are white with snow and, in summer, are gray with alkaline dust. They all preserve the common characteristics of barrenness, inhospitality, and misery. (Quoted in Allen 1985:207)

To early-nineteenth-century Euro-Americans, the vast expanse of land west of the Mississippi was a wild and dangerous place: a region of vast deserts and impenetrable mountain ranges, inhabited by unpredictable savages. While it might provide an ample playground for the foolhardy adventurer, it was deemed quite unsuitable for civilized habitation. By 1877, when Colonel Dodge wrote the memoirs from which I have quoted, the Great American Desert had become for many the Great Plains, a romantic frontier land not only of adventure but also of possibility. When compared to an ocean in its vast extent and monotony of vista, the metaphor also evoked the romance of the ocean as a place full of opportunities for masculine heroism, where "the nerves stiffen, the senses expand and a man begins to realize the magnificence of his being . . . the true grandeur of his manhood" (Dodge 1877:3).

This shift in perspective was neither simple nor universal, nor was it free of political considerations. As Allen points out, at any given time during the 1800s a number of images were in vogue, arranged on a continuum of opinion, with the Great American Desert and the Garden of the World occupying polar positions (1985:209). Acceptance of any particular view depended upon social position and the motivations and goals of the perceivers. The desert concept was most prevalent among urban northeasterners who were opposed to western expansion. The idea of the lands within the new Louisiana Purchase being a rich garden, with fertile soils and benign climates, found more favor among the rural populations to the south and west who favored aggressive westward expansion. By the 1870s the livestock industry had moved north out of Texas, and this successful economic activity gave rise to a new conception of the Plains as "the all year grazing country" and "the great western pastoral region" (Allen 1985:217). To midwestern farmers, the railroad companies, and land speculators, however, this was too exclusive, and they promoted phrases such as "the continental wheat belt" and "the northern tropical belt" to describe the Plains. Propaganda about the farmer's paradise on the Plains came mainly from railroad companies eager to sell the land along their routes given to them by the government. Their promotion prompted thousands of farmers to move onto the Plains in the 1870s, unprepared for the harsh realities of uncertain rainfall, grasshopper invasions, drastic heat, and winter blizzard conditions. Nearly half the population that moved onto the Plains in the 1880s moved out in the 1890s and talk of the great agricultural bonanza declined (Allen 1985:217). Allen suggests that this Garden-Desert continuum remained a feature of American thought but only among the occupiers of the land itself, depending upon conditions at the time. It no longer represented differences in attitude between an eastern elite and a rural folk population.

The romantic image of the Plains found among non-Indian people in the eastern United States and Europe was furthered by the paintings of traveling artists such as George Catlin, Karl Bodmer, and Samuel Seymour.[1] These men joined explorers of the region who followed Lewis and Clark's pioneering journey up the Missouri River and across the northern Plains and Rocky Mountains to the Pacific Coast in 1804 and 1805. The idealized images of the region and its inhabitants that these artists produced reflected European artistic and literary trends. They concentrated their efforts on preserving what they perceived as "the truth and correct delineation" of what they saw.[2] Not unsurprisingly, this turned out to be highly colored by their romantic expectations, and they depicted an expansive Garden of Eden inhabited by an idyllic unspoiled natural man, the virtual embodiment of Rousseau's noble savage, who was, nevertheless, at the same time a wild and unpredictable heathen. Belief in the superior qualities of untamed nature over society's demoralizing artifices was ascribed to many artists and writers of the time, as clearly expressed in this comment by artist Alfred Jacob Miller, who made an excursion to the Wind River region with Scottish nobleman Sir William Drummond Stewart in the summer of 1837. Such untamed virtue is an embodied one, that is, expressed through an ideal physical appearance.

Among this tribe we found some as fine specimens of Indians as any that we met. They reminded us strongly of antique figures in Bronze, and presented a wide and ample field for the sculptor; nothing in Greek art can surpass the reality here. . . . Sculptors travel thousands of miles to study Greek statues at the Vatican; but here at the foot of the Rocky Mountains are as fine forms stalking about with a natural grace (never taught by a dancing master) as ever Greeks dreamed of in their happiest conceptions. ("Rough Drafts for Notes to Indian Sketches, Sketch 37," quoted in Hunt 1982:17)

Convinced, albeit sadly, of the inevitable demise of the magnificent Indian people they met, these artists set out to document as fully as possible the ways of life set out before them.[3]

Their predictions of demise were not unfounded, for a mutually advantageous fur trade that had existed for two hundred years was about to collapse.[4] A combination of smallpox and other diseases, increasing intertribal wars due to displacement, the ever more numerous encroaching settlements of non-Indians, broken treaties, and the virtual extermination of the great buffalo herds by avaricious and opportunistic non-Indian frontiersmen were soon to ravage Indian cultures all over the Plains. Employing a rhetoric of "civilizing the savages," missionary activity and government agencies alike proceeded to undermine the religious, political, economic, and social structures of indigenous Plains communities. Peoples whose subsistence and culture were based on freedom of movement across large tracts of land without boundaries other than those posed by enemy groups quite suddenly found themselves confined to smaller and smaller areas of country and increasingly dependent upon U.S. government rations because the land was now devoid of game. Not only had buffalo provided food, clothing, housing, and myriad utensils, but they also had been a vibrant source of religious inspiration and empowering symbolic capital. The Assiniboine people shared and survived this tragic series of events with other Plains tribes.

This complex history has been well documented by both historians and anthropologists.[5] This chapter focuses instead on the notion of "territory" on a less grand, but equally complex, scale by looking at one particular Assiniboine conception of the tribal territory during the period of intertribal wars prior to the establishment of the reservation system. This differs somewhat not only from non-Indian histories but also with those of other Indian tribes; that of the Gros Ventres, coresidents of the Assiniboines on Fort Belknap Reservation, for example. No one version of this history can be privileged as "truth," nor should the truth value of an indigenous account be "bracketed" by interpreting it as "symbolic" (Rabinow 1983; cf. Luntley 1989). Instead, each particular history, like all histories, is best understood as a highly selective and complex weaving together of a number of collective representations. Each particular history is itself situated historically in an intellectual and moral universe of meaning, as well as being a creative response to contested truths that have very real consequences in terms of identity and political power.[6]

My analysis adds another dimension to Fowler's discussions of the shared occupation of Fort Belknap Reservation by Assiniboine and Gros Ventre people,[7] in which documented evidence and former, as well as contemporary, rhetoric are used to show how political power and ethnic identity are negotiated through interpretations of oral history regarding "who was here first" (Fowler 1987, Chap. 3).[8]

The narrative was told to me, and to the camera, by James Earthboy one day in 1988 in a basement room of the Fort Belknap tribal building. He has been my teacher for several months now, teaching me Plains Sign Talk and spoken Nakota simultaneously. We are a strange pair: Earthboy, age 73, has lived at Fort Belknap all his life as son, father, and grandfather. As a young man, a warrior of the United States Army, he visited my country, England, but I am the nomad here. Earthboy is fluent in Cree, Nakota, English, and Plains Sign Talk; pleased to have his knowledge preserved for future generations; sad that his sons and most of his daughters speak only English. "My niece," he says to me, "what story shall I tell today." "*Minekśi* [my uncle]," I reply, "tell me again that story about Assiniboine territory, we should record that one." "*Hą* [yes]," he says, "let's do it, are you ready?"

Nak'ota Mąkoc'e

Mąkoc'e Hokśin(a) woknaka

Assiniboine Territory

Told by James Earthboy

1. Waną—kaś

    nen
    Nak'ota úpi
    ec'ake nen
    úpiśį.

2. Tók'iya nówa t'éhąhą i úpi.

3. Mąk'oc'e ne

    tukten ihąke że

    snokyapi.

4. Sáp'a że

    t'oka żéc'a úpi c'en
    żec'iyaś yápiśį.

5a. Nąka
    c'ąku wak'ą eyapi ne akasam

5b. mąk'oc'e wążi.

6. "Wazihe," eciyapi.

7a. Tá—ku k'ápi k'o snokwayeśį

    įś wanuh "wa" żec'a
7b. "zi" żec'a eśta
    wahąksica żéc'a
    ġi żec'ac' k'ápi k'o

7c. snokwayeśį eyaś
    "Wazihe," eyapi s'a.

1. Lo—ng ago

    the Indians that live here
    now
    did not always
    live here.

2. They lived at many far-off places.

3. They knew

    the boundaries

    of this country.

4. Beyond that

    lived those who were enemies
    so they did not go there.

5a. Nowadays
    beyond what they call the
        "mysterious line" [Canadian
        border]

5b. there is a place.

6. They call it "*Wazihe*."

7a. Wha—t the meaning is I do not
        know
    but "*wa*" means "snow"
7b. "*zi*" means yellow/brown
    and "*wahąksica*" a grizzly bear
    it's brown perhaps that is what
        they mean
7c.   I do not know
    they usually just say "*Wazihe*."

8. Żéc'etahą
    hąwi įsaye iyaye netam.

8. From there
    one goes over this way where
    the sun goes down.

9. Íyą żec'
    t'ąkt'ąkac' maktapi néc'en
        kak'en tahą
    en.

9. There are large rocks that form a
    cliff
    over there.

10. "Íyą Waokma," eciyapi.

10. "Writing-on-Stone," they call it.

11a. Że ec'en
     żetahą sam néc'akiya
     hąwi įsiya iyaye néc'akiya
         żen
11b. íyahe
     tóna
     mośneśnen.

11a. Then from there
     farther this way
     where the sun goes down but
     more this way
11b. there are mountains
     that come to a point.

12. "Aíkpoġa Oyuze," eciyapi.

12. "Cedar Gathering Place," they
    call it.

13. Ak'e żetahą ka akasam
    wiyotahą ne táp'akiya

    yápi hą́ta.

13. From there again
    when they go over there

    going across toward the south.

14a. Wakpa wą́żi t'ą́kac'
14b. "Miniśośe," eciyapi żen.

14a. Over there is a large river
14b. "Muddy Water," they call it.

15. Ak'e sam

    T'uki yápi Wakpa eya.

15. Farther that way

    is Clam River they say.

16a. Ak'e sam
     Heħaka Wakpa eyapi
16b. eyapi żen.

16a. Farther on
     Elk River is over there
16b. they say.

17. Żetahą hąwihinąp'e netahą
        yápi.

17. From there they go toward
        where
    the sun rises.

18. Ká—k'i
    t'é—hą

    T'ac'eži Wakpa
    eyapi.

18. Fa—r over there
    a lo—ng way

    is what they call Tongue River.

19. Ak'e žen ípi hą́ta
    sáp'akiya yápi.

19. When you reach there
    you go farther still.

20. Mąk'aha Skána yápi.

20. To White Earth [River] they go.

21. Žen ípi hą́ta
    ak'e žetahą
    c'ąku wak'ą eyapi ne.

21. After you get there
    again you go from there
    to what is called the "mysteri-
    ous line."

22. Sáp'a.

    Nak'ota úpi žen ípi hą́ta.

22. Farther on

    when you get there it is where
    the Assiniboines live.

23. Žetahą ak'e nec'

    "Waziĥe," eyapi žen ípi hą́ta.

23. From there, going this way
    again
    you arrive at the place called
    "Waziĥe."

24a. Že— įskoya že nen
     Nak'ota úpi e

24a. So— that much of it is here
     that land where the
     Assiniboines live

24b. že mąk'oc'e že
     t'áwapi.

24b. it belongs to them.

25. Že t'i mahen
    táku úpi ne nówa.

25. Inside there
    all kinds of things lived.

26. Wįc'ak'ute wįc'ayuta úpi.

26. They lived by shooting them
    and eating them.

27. Že mąk'oc'e že
    ųkiųkit'awapi.

27. That land was ours.

The short text of Earthboy's story provides a deceptively simple descriptive account that turns out to be laden with meaning if we know where to look. Following Tedlock I have attempted to create an open text in which the reading eye meets a "practical poetics" in the peculiarities of good speaking rather than bad writing (1983:7). The volume of speaking is quiet and steady throughout. A line after vowels indicates lengthening of the sound, and the length of lines, and spaces between lines, represent the rhythm of speaking and silence.

After an examination of the Nakota spoken component, I will take Tedlock's idea of producing a "performable text" one step further by adding a transcription of the gestural component. The goal here is to create a level of notation that in many ways parallels that of a musician's score. To recreate a song from notation, for example, a musician reads the musical staff and the text of the words of the song simultaneously in a process we call sight-reading. The same kind of sight-reading can be done with the Laban texts. Having opened up our ears to the sounds of performance with the help of Tedlock's work, we now have a clear path for opening our eyes to the sights of performed action.

The texts, both spoken and movement, only approximate the performance, of course, and here serve only the purpose of analysis. Both texts are certainly poor substitutes for the videotape record, which must be considered the primary document. Any separation of signs from speech distorts, and I examine a transcription and translation of the speech component first, not because of any implicit hierarchy of importance, but because I assume most readers will be more familiar with this medium. Informed by this, we can then add an analysis of the signed component to see exactly how signs work in conjunction with speech. For a full appreciation of the whole, however, one must go to the Labanotation texts where speech and signs are represented together. This is because the rhythm of speaking and silence coordinates closely with the rhythm of signing and stillness.

Earthboy's narrative takes us on a journey that starts in the north and traces the boundaries of an area of country that is roughly circular (see Fig. 3.1). Traveling counterclockwise, we go roughly southwest and then south, around to the east, and then north again. Earthboy tells us that the Assiniboine who live "here" (Fort Belknap today), lived all over this territory during the "intertribal wars," as he chose to name the time

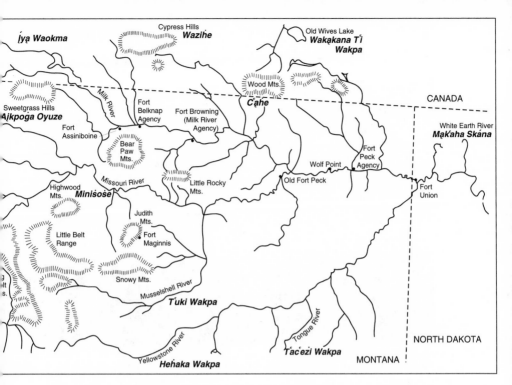

Figure 3.1. Map of Assiniboine Territory/ *'Nak'ota Mąk'oc'e'*.

period. Assiniboine people knew where the boundaries were and knew that beyond them was enemy territory into which only war parties would venture. Earthboy names the places which he calls the "boundary markers" of this territory, and many of these places have a story attached to them that is referred to in the names themselves. Only brief mention will be made of these names here; detailed discussion will be deferred until the next chapter in order to concentrate here on indexical features of the narrative.

The place called *Wazihe*, whose etymological meaning, if any, was not clear to Earthboy (but may refer to *wazi* 'pine ' + *he* 'ridge'), is a ridge in a group of hills now called the Cypress Hills in English. This is the place where the Assiniboine received the Crow Belt Dance from the Sioux. Nearby are the Wood Mountains (*C'ąhe*) and Old Wives Lake (*Wakąkana T'i Wakpa* 'river by the old lady's place'). Although not mentioned in this version of the narrative, this place too evokes a story, of how an old woman's singing foretells the fortunes of war.

The next place is *Íyą Waokma* 'Picture Rock' or 'Writing-on-Stone', a rock outcrop that became a source of spiritual assistance, and, like the

Photo 3.1. Storm clouds gather over *Wazíȟe*, the pine-covered ridges of the Cypress Hills, Saskatchewan.

Photo 3.2. *Íyą Waokma* 'Picture Rock' or 'Writing-on-Stone', where weathered rock formations line the Milk River Valley.

Photo 3.3. James Earthboy surveys the landscape around Fort Belknap Reservation looking toward the Canadian border from the top of Snake Butte.

Photo 3.4. Snake Butte, a few miles south of Fort Belknap Agency, rises like a sentinel above the rolling plains.

old lady's singing, helps foretell what is to come. The morning after prayers and offerings have been made, the rock will show what one wishes to know through petroglyphic writings on its face.

Aíkpoġa Oyuze is the next boundary marker, today called the Sweetgrass Hills in English. The Assiniboine name refers not to sweetgrass but to a variety of aromatic cedar that was first chewed and then spat out and rubbed over the body or shirt as a perfume. Here the name does not evoke a story but—like Old Wives Lake and Writing-on-Stone—encodes the action associated with the place.[9] "Cedar Gathering Place" is what the name says. From here, Earthboy directs us toward "the direction of the sun at noon" (south) until we meet a large river called Muddy Water. It is so named because that is how it appears much of the year as sediment and the spring thaws create swirling floodwater.[10] This is the Missouri River in English.[11] Beyond this, still traveling south, we come to *T'uki Wakpa* 'Clam River' which is called Musselshell in English for the edible clams that can be found there.

Farther on is Elk River[12] (*Heňaka Wakpa*), called Yellowstone in English after the color of the rock along its banks in places.[13] Going east a long way from here "to where the sun comes up" is Tongue River (*T'ac'eži Wakpa*), a name that comes from a Crow story of buffalo tongues that rotted there.[14] From there we reach White Earth River (*Mąk'aha Skána*), named after the white alkaline powder of its banks that was used for cleaning buckskin clothes and healing broken bones. We then travel back over the "mysterious line" to the Cypress Hills, thus completing the circle.

When contrasted with the area described in this account, Fort Belknap appears as a diminutive rectangle, a mere postage stamp in the center of this former territorial claim. Figures 3.2 and 3.3 show the impositions of the last century upon this territory and highlight the contrast between the Euro-American map and the Native American one. Figure 3.2 illustrates how the large tracts of land agreed upon in the first treaty of 1855 have been reduced to small rectangular patches. Figure 3.3 shows how today, straight lines cross in all directions in defiance of natural forms. The Canadian boundary, established in 1818 without regard to indigenous territories, cut across the northern part of Earthboy's circle and separated groups of Assiniboine relatives from each other. Movement across the border was increasingly restricted after it was

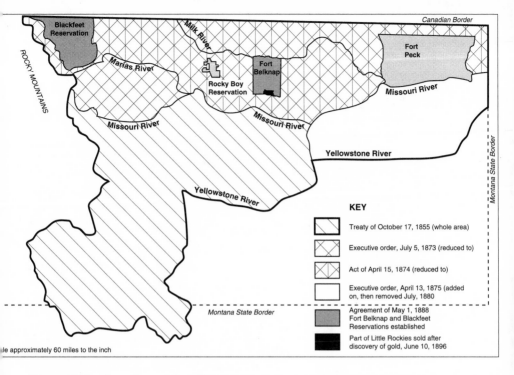

Figure 3.2. Land treaties and Assiniboine territory.

formed, and a person was thereafter either a Canadian Indian or an American Indian as far as white authorities were concerned. The Assiniboine word for this boundary, *C'ąku Wak'ą*, translates into English as "mysterious (or holy) road," an apt label for such a powerful yet invisible structure.

The Canadian border cut into the circle of Assiniboine territory by slicing off the top end. Then came the Great Northern Pacific Railroad in 1887, equally unbending in its commitment to join east and west, linking Chicago to Seattle but providing little for life on either side or in between except stopping points for ever-increasing numbers of white homesteaders. Most of the towns that sprang up along this line had their names picked off a spinning globe by a rather unimaginative post office worker back east, whose job it was to label places he had never seen. Thus we find Malta next to Harlem, (Le) Havre, Glasgow, and Zurich. These towns lie along Route 2—a practical but impersonal designation of an equally uninspiring straight line that hugs the railroad track.

Fort Belknap Reservation boundaries were established in 1887, the year the railroad began its operations, and the "surplus" land was thrown

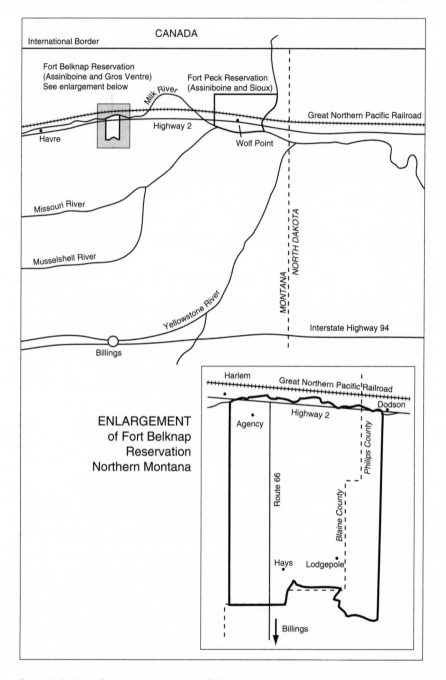

Figure 3.3. Map showing impositions of the present century.

open to settlers, many of whom were already living along the river, in May of 1888. The name "Fort Belknap" comes from an earlier trading post and Indian Agency nearby, named after William Belknap, then secretary of war under President Grant.[15]

That the name of the reservation should come from a former U.S. government secretary of war seemed a cruel irony, and I imagined that this would probably be viewed as a humiliating insult to the residents of Fort Belknap. This was not the case, however. Most people I spoke to were, genuinely I think, unaware of the source of the name, and those who were saw it in contemporary terms as a marker of their *lack* of conflict with the U.S. Army during the nineteenth century (in contrast to their former enemies, the Sioux) and perfectly in accord with their military loyalty to and service in the American armed forces throughout the twentieth century, which proudly continues the "warrior" tradition for many men, but also women, today.

County boundaries came later and cut the reservation in two from north to south, between Philips County and Blaine County, the first named after a wealthy and powerful cattle rancher in the region, the second after a Maine politician who was the presidential candidate of the Republican party in 1876, the choice of an admiring resident of the nearby town of Chinook after much political wrangling over boundaries, none of which included Indian concerns.[16]

Another straight-line highway runs from north to south through the reservation connecting Route 2 to Route 87, which runs south to the city of Billings 250 miles away. Within the reservation, this highway replaced the winding wagon road from the communities of Hays and Lodgepole at the south end of the reservation to the administrative center of the Agency at the north end.

The natural features of this territory are the rivers that meander like green veins through the dry summer grasslands on which islands of rounded hills rest patiently, and sloping buttes rise like sentinels above the endless rolling plains. These have been altered, significantly and irreversibly, by the crisscrossing straight lines of the Euro-Americans: international boundary, railroad, reservation boundary, county lines, highways, and power lines. In 1922, the land within the reservation also was fenced into barbed-wire parcels to be owned by individuals when the Dawes Act of 1887 was finally enforced.

While these impositions and their history are very familiar to Earthboy, it is the ideal conceptual form of the prereservation historical period that remains salient, the most meaningful. The changes, which might be a source of resentment and anger to some, are regretted but fail to dim the importance of the circular form and the names of the territory for Earthboy. It is marked by history and legend, kept alive through oral narratives passed on to him. Earthboy tells his story placing himself "here," at Fort Belknap, but "here" in this context is not simply the zero point of the deictical coordinates of the speech/signed event. It indexes the center of an ideal circle, literally the center of his meaningful geographical, historical, social, and moral world.[17] To retain this conception demands considerable commitment by Earthboy to a retention of Assiniboine identity and meaning.

Other narratives and other place names, many of which overlap, accomplish similar ends for other Assiniboine people. Only some small fraction of the collective sense is contained in one person's viewpoint, and I do not imply that all Assiniboine people would view this territory or use these symbols in the same way. Narratives of this kind are creative indexes because they point to the location of the speaking/signing self in a network of relationships with the places referred to and named, they describe key events that brought those relationships into being, and above all they set up potential meanings that not every Assiniboine has to achieve or understand in the same way.

Another account that marks the boundaries of Assiniboine territory was written by an Assiniboine man from the neighboring Fort Peck Reservation, which is shared (reluctantly) with Sioux people, former enemies of the Assiniboine. (The relationship between Sioux and Assiniboine at Fort Peck in many ways parallels that between the Assiniboine and Gros Ventres at Fort Belknap: there is a similar concern with who was there first.) The Fort Peck Assiniboine says about the same territory:

> The Assiniboines came into Montana in the late 1600's and early
> 1700's. They controlled an area starting in Manitoba, Canada
> across from Minot, North Dakota, south down the Mouse River,
> until they came into the United States and westward to the White
> Earth River, south to the Missouri River west to the mouth of the

Yellowstone River, up the Yellowstone River to Pompey's Pillar, north up the Musselshell River to the Missouri River, west up the Missouri River to Fort Benton, North westwardly up the Marias River, up to the Sweet Grass Mountains in Alberta Canada and east to Manitoba. The Sioux never did come into Montana until 1876 after the Custer Massacre when they were running away from the Cavalry. (Undated manuscript, Fort Belknap Education Department Media Archives)

The area of land covered is roughly the same, but note the differences because of the use of standard English and a written rather than oral performance. Neither the style of language used nor the names from the map are Native American. The creative indexing going on here is the rendering of an account that denies legitimacy of residence to the Sioux.

THE SIGNED COMPONENT

What is distinctive about the oral narrative from a non–Native American English speaker's point of view is the frequency of deictic words such as "this way," "over there," and "from there," all of which have no definite reference beyond the context of the speech event. If we only pay attention to the *spoken* component of such deictic expressions in this story, however, we are left outside much of the meaning because there is little or no information as to where "over there" or "this way" might be. Equally problematic is that even if we see the story being told—or study a videotape—over and over again, all we can see are a series of pointing gestures that seem to move all over the place. We remain outside of the cultural resources that inform Earthboy's actions as he performs those pointing gestures, and we have no access to the full semantic content of the performance.

In order to examine how such symbols are performed, the gestures that accompanied the telling of Earthboy's narrative were transcribed in Labanotation, and they have a story of their own to tell (see below). The process of creating the transcription itself and subsequent analysis showed that crucial to an understanding of the narrative is knowing which of the cardinal directions the gestures are oriented toward. Regardless of the storyteller's facing this will be constant. In this case,

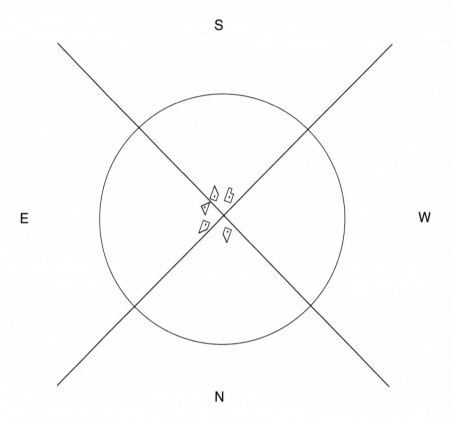

Key

forward

forward-left diagonal

side left

back-left diagonal

back-right diagonal

Figure 3.4. The four quarters and Earthboy's spatial orientation.

Earthboy was sitting facing southwest. Because on this day things were very busy at Earthboy's home with a new baby expected, we had come to the large tribal building to continue our work. Although we were deep inside a building with stairs and long corridors, and down in an unfamiliar basement room with only tiny ceiling-level windows, actual geographical direction remained a constant orientational feature for Earthboy. An awareness of Earthboy's spatial orientation is necessary for an understanding of the indexical components of both words and signs in the text. This is why at the start of the movement text there appears the key signature w⊕ɛ. This tells the reader that a constant spatial orientation is in effect during the whole event, much like a key signature in a musical score indicates a constant harmonic structure for a composition.

As with the spoken text, I will focus here only on the use of referential indexing in relation to direction, deferring discussion of other aspects until later. Throughout the narrative a correspondence was retained between the direction of gestures and the actual cardinal directions. Even such apparent universals as geographical direction are part of semantic fields whose meanings are by no means universal.[18] What at first seemed to be anomalies fell into place once I learned that the cardinal directions are conceived of as quarters, as shown in Figure 3.4, in contrast to Western notions of four directional arrows emerging from a central point.

Throughout the narrative, Earthboy situated himself in the center of a circle divided into the four quarters of north, south, east, and west, facing southwest. This particular cultural conception of geographical location and direction as a constant spatial orientation is also written into the start of the notated text ɛ⧇w . Figure 3.4 diagrams this as if seen from above.[19] From this perspective we can see that Earthboy starts the journey (sentence 6) at *Wazíhe* going toward *Íyą Waokma*, and his indexical gestures are directed forward ⸢⸣ toward the southwest or "where the sun goes down." In sentence 11a, where he says in speech, "farther this way, where the sun goes down but more this way" (or "this side of where the sun goes down"), it is only through his arm actions that we know he means to the left of the previous direction, a little to the left of southwest (*iyohnatac* 'in between'). Subsequent actions are performed into the space between forward and diagonal-left-forward from Earthboy's perspective as we travel south-southwest. As we travel on, gestures are directed toward diagonal-left-forward ⌐ which is *wiyotahą* 'where the sun is at noon' or southward (sentence 13). Actions (with the right hand) are then directed toward Earthboy's left side (sentence 17) ⌐ as we travel east to *T'ac'eži Wakpa* 'Tongue River' and into the back left diagonal ⌐ (sentence 18) indicating travel still toward "where the sun rises" or east, but moving slightly north as we go from Tongue River to reach *Mąk'aha Skána* 'White Earth [River]' on the Missouri (sentences 19 and 20).

In order to complete the journey and get back across the Canadian border, Earthboy directs us from there northwestward over his right shoulder (sentence 21) or into the back-right-diagonal ⌐ until we arrive at *Wazihe* again. Only at this last point, in order to avoid an awkward reach out of the usual signing space into the area directly behind him, does Earthboy break this consistency with the cardinal directions. Deixis becomes indexically creative, as he shifts the frame of reference to a body-centered orientation to indicate traveling with a forward ⌐ gesture, as if he himself is now facing the direction of travel (sentence 23).

Had his chair been facing in an alternative direction when he told the story, Earthboy's arm and hand gestures would have traveled in different directions than they did in order to maintain the connection to the cardinal directions. Where he breaks this consistency to use a body-centered frame of reference (sentence 23) his gestures would have kept their relationship to his torso whichever way he was facing.

The Labanotation text shows all this clearly because it is written from the mover's perspective, not the observer's—one reads as if performing the actions as one reads along.[20] In order to make the movement score more ethnographically accurate, I have taken advantage of the flexibility of the Laban staff (the columns for writing) and symbol set, and the descriptions of the gestures have been written as far as possible according to the storyteller's conceptions of his actions. That is, instead of noting simply that the hand moves toward a direction that is forward-left-diagonal of the body, which is a structural description of the action, I have added an ethnographic component by noting that the hand moves toward south $\forall$ (e.g., sentence 13 Labanotation text). In this way, taking advantage of the flexibility of description that the Laban script affords, it was possible to record *actions*, not simply gross physical movement (see also Appendix B).

Looking more closely at the variety of demonstratives that appear in this narrative, one sees that Earthboy usually uses the space nearest to his body to indicate "here" (*nen*, e.g., sentence 1). He thus places himself, with both speech and gesture, at the "zero point" or "origo" of the deictic space. Pointing to a space farther away with the finger directed diagonally downward usually indicates "there" or "that" ▌ (*że, żen, żec'a*) as shown in sentences 7b and 14b. A puzzling contradiction occurs in sentence 24a, however, when this same gesture is accompanied not only by the spoken word "there" (*że*) but also by "here" (*nen*). This deictic shift is not an error but a creative index. Earthboy has at this point in his narrative temporarily moved the circle of territory from its placement around him into the space in front of him. This gesture ▌ now marks the center of it. By saying the word "here" (*nen*) simultaneously, he achieves a deictic shift of self back into the center of the circle.

Now approaching the end of the narrative (sentence 24a), Earthboy joins all the boundary markers into this circular form in front of him as he says, "So—that much of it is here, that land where the Assiniboines live." The final words of the story, "That land was ours," are accompanied by the PST sign LAND, a spreading gesture made with both hands, palms turned upward. The movement fills the space inside the circle Earthboy has just described. The final gesture is a grasping or closing of the right hand into a fist, palm facing the chest, that pulls from the center of the circular space toward the body (sentence 27). The sign is a polysemic one that in this case provides amplification of the spoken word "theirs" because it also means POSSESSION, MINE, and TO HOLD.

Earthboy in two senses consistently placed himself at the center of the territory that surrounded him. Geographically he was actually situated in the approximate center of this circle of territory, but also maintained an accurate correspondence to geographical reference through his gestures, by using his personal space in a way that placed him at the center of the space internal to the story. Earthboy's body was the center of an imaginary circle created around him for the telling of the story, and we moved to each location according to where he placed his gestures in this circular space as we moved around the boundaries of the territory. Through referential gestures that radiated out from his body, he used deictic categories to create a geographical, historical, and moral space: a framework for meaning through movement and speech that was centered in his sense of his own embodiment.

The use of a constant frame of reference like geographical direction also means that members of the audience do not have to do any imaginary reversals of left/right, front/back in order to understand the gestural indexes: no matter which way *they* happen to be facing, the geographical directions remain the same, so the reference is clear as long as the frame of reference itself is shared, which it normally is among Assiniboine people. The audience is drawn into a shared spatial orientation that makes "your" deictic space continuous with "mine."

The inclusion of the gestural component in what counts as the narrative has not only provided references for the spoken demonstratives therein, it has also provided access to a fundamental organizing principle of language-in-use here, one in which embodiment is central. That is, the action and location of the body itself play an explicit role in the use of deixis, and expressions are predicated upon body movement. Gesture and speech do not merely coincide but integrate to provide equally available resources for the creation of meaning.

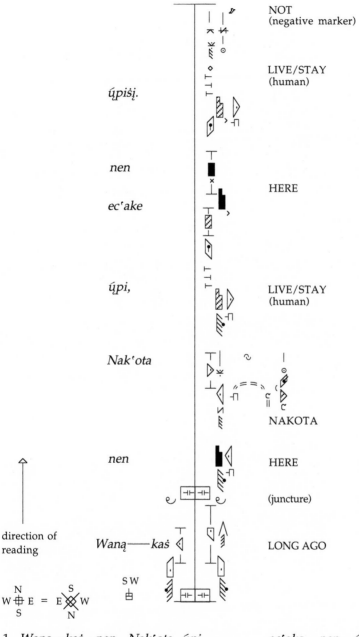

úpiśį. NOT (negative marker)

LIVE/STAY (human)

nen

ec'ake HERE

úpi, LIVE/STAY (human)

Nak'ota

NAKOTA

nen HERE

(juncture)

direction of reading

Waną——kaś LONG AGO

S W

N   S
W ⊕ E = E ⊗ W
S   N

1. *Waną—kaś, nen, Nak'ota úpi,   ec'ake   nen   úpiśį.*
   Long ago   here Nakota they live/ be always   here they live not
   Lo—ng ago, the Indians that live here now, did not always live here.

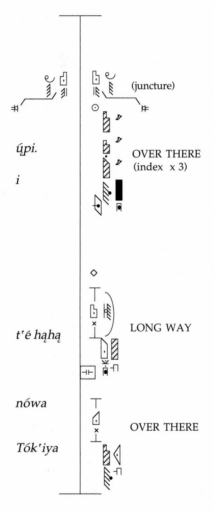

2. *Tók'iya nówa   t'é hąhą   i   úpi.*
   Everywhere   long way   there at   they live
   They lived at many far-off places.

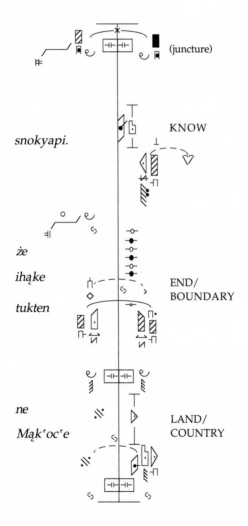

3. *Mąk'oc'e   ne, tukten   ihąke że,   snokyapi.*
    Land/country this which/then end   that   they know
    They knew the boundaries of this country.

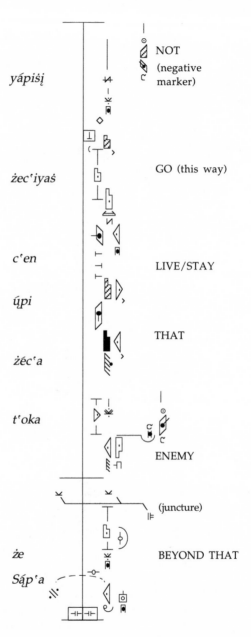

4. *Sáp'a   že,   t'oka   žéc'a   ũpi   c'en,   žec'iyaś   yápiśị.*
   Beyond that enemy that kind they live   so   not that way   they do not g
   Beyond that lived those who were enemies so they did not go there.

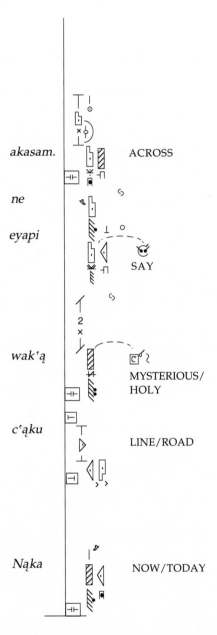

akasam.	ACROSS
ne	
eyapi	SAY
wak'ą	MYSTERIOUS/ HOLY
c'ąku	LINE/ROAD
Nąka	NOW/TODAY

5a. *Nąka,   c'ąku   wak'ą   eyapi   ne   akasam,*
    Nowadays line/road mysterious/holy they say this   across
    Nowadays, beyond what they call the "mysterious line" [Canadian border],

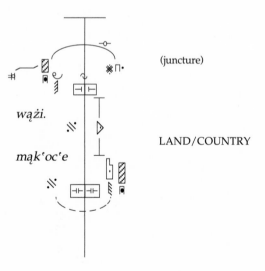

(juncture)

wąži.

LAND/COUNTRY

mąkʻocʻe

5b. . . . *mąkʻocʻe*   *wąži.*

. . . land/country   one

. . . there is a place.

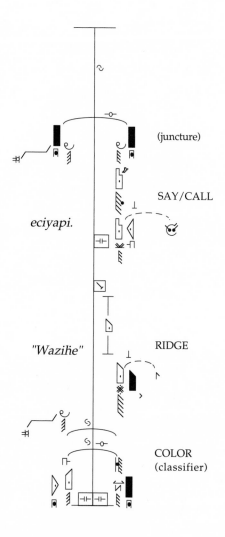

6. *"Waziħe," eciyapi.*
   Waziħe   they call it
   They call it *"Waziħe."*

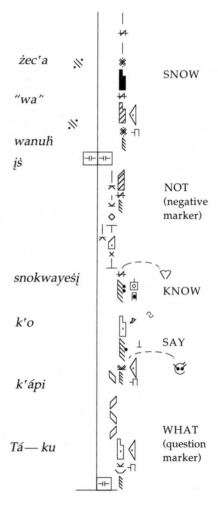

7a.
Tá—ku	k'ápi	k'o	snokwayeśį	įś	wanuħ	"wa"	żec'a
What	they mean	also/too	I do not know	but		snow	that kind

Wha—t the meaning is I do not know, but "wa" means "snow,"

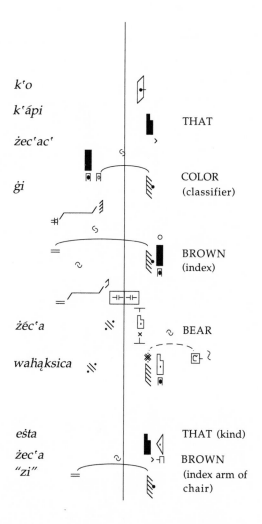

7b.   ... *"zi"*   *żec'a*   *eśta,*   *wahąksica*   *żéc'a,*
   ... yellow/brown that kind maybe grizzly bear that kind
   ... *"zi"* means yellow/brown and *"wahąksica"* a grizzly bear,

   ġi   *żec'ac'*   *k'ápi*   *k'o*
   brown   that kind   they mean   also/too
   it's brown perhaps that is what they mean

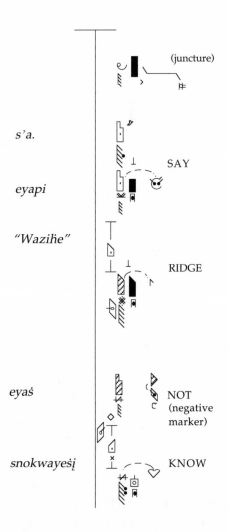

7c. ... *snokwayeśį eyaś, "Wazilĥe," eyapi   s'a.*
    ... know not   just   *"Wazilĥe"* they call it   usually
    ... I do not know, they usually just say *"Wazilĥe."*

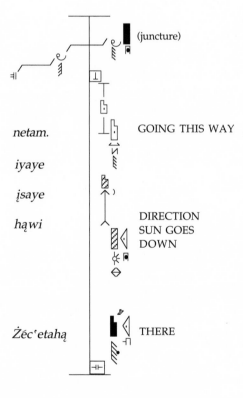

netam.   GOING THIS WAY

iyaye

įsaye

hąwi   DIRECTION
                              SUN GOES
                              DOWN

Żéc'etahą   THERE

8. *Żéc'etahą,   hąwi įsaye   iyaye netam.*
   From there sun out of sight   goes this way
   From there, one goes over this way where the sun goes down.

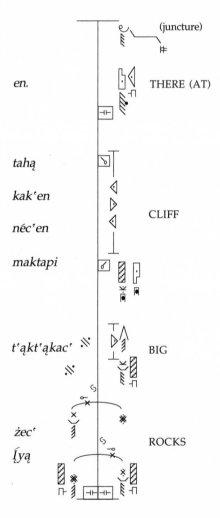

en.

taha̧

kak'en

néc'en

maktapi

t'a̧kt'a̧kac'

żec'

Íya̧

(juncture)

THERE (AT)

CLIFF

BIG

ROCKS

9. Íya̧   żec', t'a̧kt'a̧kac' maktapi néc'en kak'en taha̧, en.
   Rocks there big cliff [cut edge] this   over there   at
   There are large rocks that form a cliff, over there.

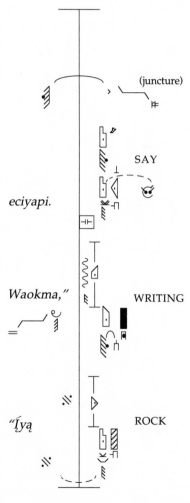

10. *"Įyą   Waokma,"   eciyapi.*
    Rock/stone picture/writing on they call it
    "Writing-on-Stone," they call it.

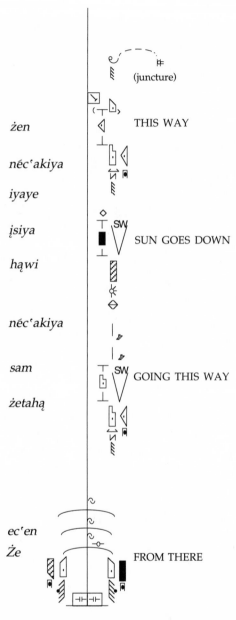

żen   THIS WAY

néc'akiya

iyaye

įsiya   SUN GOES DOWN

hąwi

néc'akiya

sam   GOING THIS WAY

żetahą

ec'en

Że   FROM THERE

11a. *Że ec'en,   żetahą   sam néc'akiya, hąwi įsiya iyaye néc'akiya żen,*
      Then   from there farther this way   sun   goes down   this way   there
      Then from there, farther this way, where the sun goes down but more this v

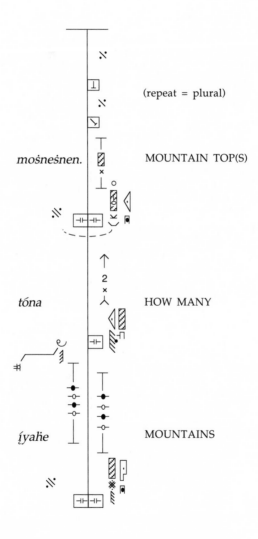

mośneśnen.   MOUNTAIN TOP(S)

(repeat = plural)

tóna   HOW MANY

įyaḣe   MOUNTAINS

11b. ... *įyaḣe,*   *tóna,*   *mośneśnen.*
    ... mountains how many/some come to a point
    ... there are mountains, that come to a point.

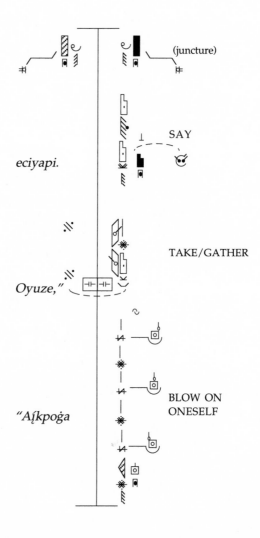

12. *"Aįkpoġa*   *Oyuze,"*   *eciyapi.*
     To blow it out on [cedar]   place where one gathers   they call it
     "Cedar Gathering Place," they call it.

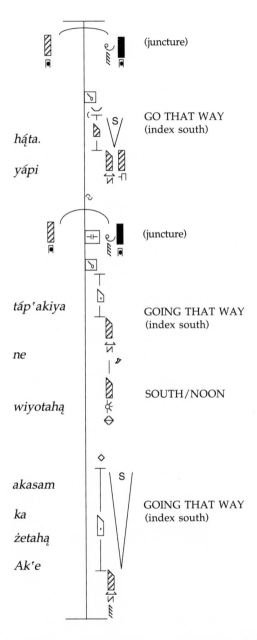

Ak'e   żetahą   ka   akasam, wiyotahą ne   táp'akiya, yápi   hą́ta.
Again from there over there across   south   this beyond   going toward when
From there again, when they go over there, going across toward the south.

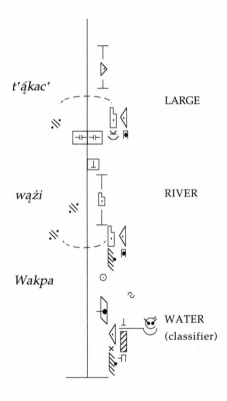

14a. *Wakpa   wą́ži   t'ą́kac'*,
     River   one   large
     Over there is a large river,

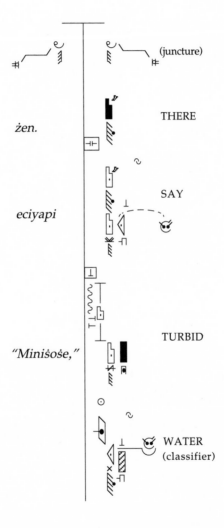

(juncture)

żen.

THERE

eciyapi

SAY

"Minišoše,"

TURBID

WATER
(classifier)

14b. ... *"Minišoše,"*   *eciyapi   żen.*
     ... muddy/turbid water they call that
     ... "Muddy Water," they call it.

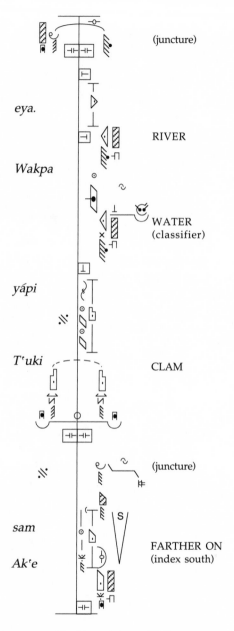

15. *Ak'e   sam,   T'uki   yápi   Wakpa eya.*
    Again farther clams they go river   say
    Farther that way, is Clam River they say.

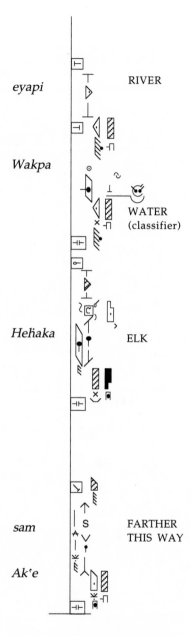

eyapi   RIVER

Wakpa

WATER
(classifier)

Heȟaka   ELK

sam   FARTHER
THIS WAY

Ak'e

16a. *Ak'e*   *sam,*   *Heȟaka Wakpa eyapi,*
      Again   farther   Elk   River they say
      Farther on Elk River is over there,

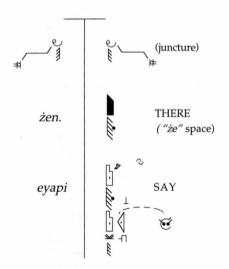

(juncture)

żen.

THERE
(*"że"* space)

eyapi

SAY

16b.   *... eyapi   żen.*
       ... they say   there
       ... they say.

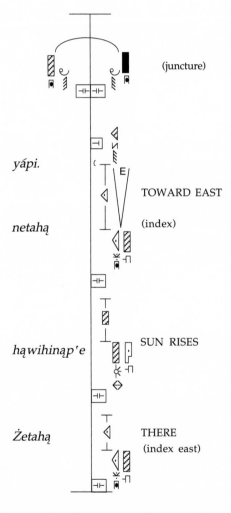

17. *Żetahą   hąwihinąp'e netahą   yápi.*
From there   sun rises   from here they go
From there they go toward where the sun rises.

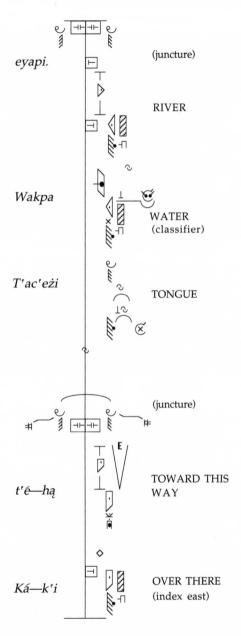

18. *Ká—k'i,   t'é—hą,   T'ac'eżi Wakpa eyapi.*
    Over there long way Tongue River   they call it
    Fa—r over there, a lo—ng way, is what they call Tongue River.

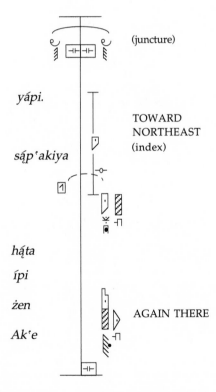

yápi.

są́p'akiya

hą́ta

ípi

żen

Ak'e

(juncture)

TOWARD
NORTHEAST
(index)

AGAIN THERE

19. *Ak'e żen ípi   hą́ta, są́p'akiya yápi.*
    Again there they at when go beyond they go
    When you reach there, you go farther still.

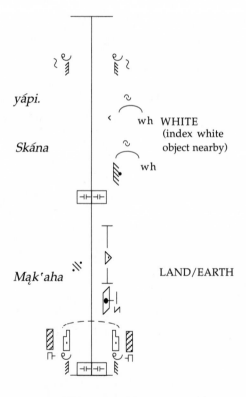

20. *Mąk'aha Skána yápi.*
    Earth   White they go
    To White Earth [River] they go.

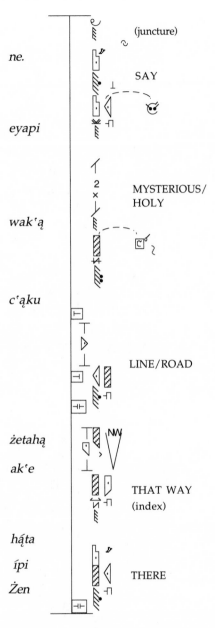

ne.

(juncture)

SAY

eyapi

MYSTERIOUS/
HOLY

wak'ą

c'ąku

LINE/ROAD

żetahą

ak'e

THAT WAY
(index)

hą́ta

ípi

Żen

THERE

Żen	*ípi*	*hą́ta,*	*ak'e*	*żetahą,*	*c'ąku*	*wak'ą*	*eyapi*	*ne.*
There at	they	when again	from there	road/line	mysterious	they say	this

After you get there, again you go from there, to what is called the "mysterious line."

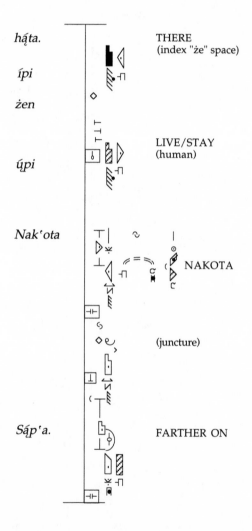

hą́ta.   THERE
                           (index "że" space)

ípi

żen

ų́pi   LIVE/STAY
                           (human)

Nak'ota   NAKOTA

                           (juncture)

Są́p'a.   FARTHER ON

22. *Są́p'a.   Nak'ota ų́pi   żen   ípi   hą́ta.*
    Farther. Nakota they live there   they are at when
    Farther on, when you get there it is where the Assiniboines live.

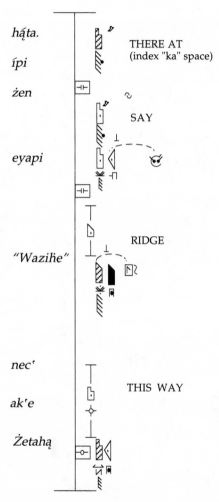

háta.   THERE AT
                         (index "ka" space)
ípi

żen

                         SAY

eyapi

                         RIDGE

"Waziħe"

nec'   THIS WAY

ak'e

Żetahą

23. Żetahą   ak'e nec',   "Waziħe,"   eyapi   żen   ípi   háta.
    From there again this way "Waziħe" they say there they at when
    From there, going this way again, you arrive at the place called "Waziħe."

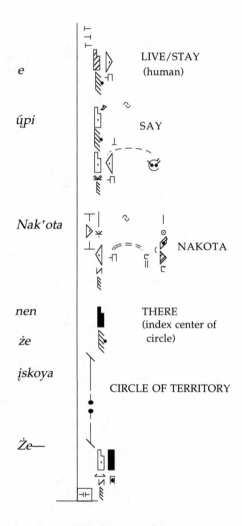

24a. Że—   įskoya   że nen, Nak'ota   úpi e,
     So   that much   that here Nakota   live
     So— that much of it is here, that land where the Assiniboines live

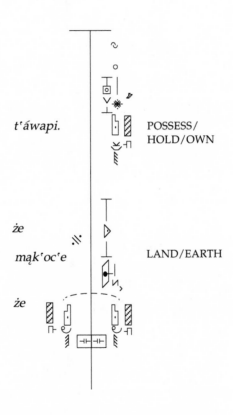

t'áwapi.　　　POSSESS/
　　　　　　　HOLD/OWN

że

mąk'oc'e　　　LAND/EARTH

że

24b.　... *że*　*mąk'oc'e*　*że,*　　*t'áwapi.*
　　　... that　land　　that　　theirs
　　　... it belongs to them.

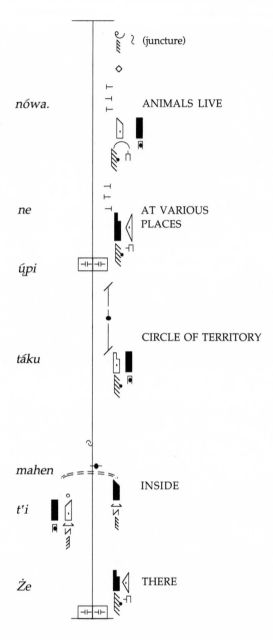

nówa.   ANIMALS LIVE

ne   AT VARIOUS PLACES

ų́pi

táku   CIRCLE OF TERRITORY

mahen   INSIDE

t'i

Że   THERE

25. *Że   t'i mahen,   táku   ų́pi   ne nówa.*
    There living inside things they live this all
    Inside there, all kinds of things lived.

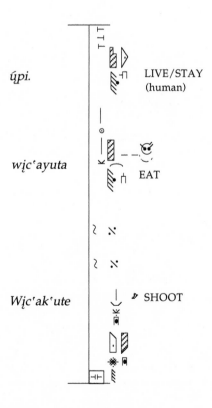

úpi.

LIVE/STAY (human)

wįc'ayuta

EAT

Wįc'ak'ute

SHOOT

26. *Wįc'ak'ute   wįc'ayuta   úpi.*
 Shoot them   eat them   they live
 They lived by shooting them and eating them.

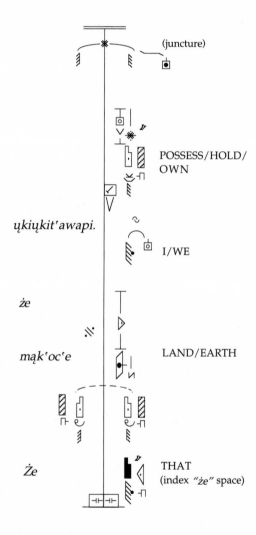

27. *Że   mąk'oc'e że   ųkiųkit'awapi.*
That land   that belong to us
That land was ours.

Chapter 4

NIGHT HAWK

He's worried about his rights.
They are clear: the air.
Night holds just one secret.
He doesn't know it
so he cries air, the air.

I know finicky secrets.
In the mountains, for instance,
a man lives close to his eyes.
For another, he speaks
with his hands. And another:
man is afraid of his dark.

JAMES WELCH (1976)

MORAL AND ETHICAL SPACES: NAMING PRACTICES AND VISUAL IMAGERY IN NAKOTA AND PST

In the last chapter I concentrated on how the indexical components of Earthboy's narrative of Assiniboine territory, with its naming of places, located the actor in a multidimensional space—a space not only geographical and historical but also moral and ethical. The discussion continues here in order to explore more fully the profoundly moral and ethical dimensions of this territory. I examine how spoken and signed languages integrate through naming practices, and explore other uses of language about territory and landscape that locate the actor in various moral and ethical spaces.

The practice of naming places and the spatial organization of territory involve indexing the kinds of relationships believed to exist between humans and the natural world. Unfortunately, a widespread stereotypical notion exists today about American Indian peoples and their relationship to nature. It is one that has become more and more popular among non–Indian Americans in times of perceived environmental crisis, and, like all stereotypes, it is partly true but also misleading. Platitudes about "respect" for "nature" and "harmony" with "mother earth" abound but are misleading because they fail to suggest anything of the nature of the relationship, which, as Native American novelist and poet Scott Momaday has suggested, is intricate (1976:79).

Momaday has summarized some of the features in common across tribal groups in order to formulate a Native American attitude toward the environment. He suggests:

> The native American ethic with respect to the physical world is a
> matter of reciprocal appropriation: appropriations in which man

invests himself in the landscape and at the same time incorporates
the landscape into his own fundamental experience. . . . This
appropriation is primarily . . . realized through an act of the
imagination which is moral and kind. . . . His heritage has always
been rather closely focused, centered upon the landscape as a
particular reality. Beyond this, the native American has a particular
investment in vision and the idea of vision. (1976:80–81)

This idea of reciprocal appropriation, which Momaday considers
fundamental to Native American philosophy, is illustrated (in a culturally appropriate manner) with a story:

There was a man living in a remote place on the Navaho reservation who had lost his job and was having a difficult time making
ends meet. He had a wife and several children. As a matter of fact,
his wife was expecting another child. One day a friend came to
visit him and perceived that his situation was bad. The friend said
to him, "Look, I see that you're in tight straits, I see that you have
many mouths to feed, that you have no wood and that there is
very little food in your larder. But one thing puzzles me. I know
you are a hunter, and I know too, there are deer in the mountains
very close at hand. Tell me, why don't you kill a deer so that you
and your family might have fresh meat to eat? And after a time the
man replied, "No, it is inappropriate that I should take life just
now when I am expecting the gift of life." (1976:82)

It is this kind of moral act of the imagination that constitutes the
Native American understanding of the physical world. What is morally
appropriate occurs within the context of a relationship between how a
person thinks of himself or herself and the world around. "There is in
the Indian world view this kind of understanding of what is and what is
not appropriate. It isn't a matter of intellection. It is respect for the understanding of one's heritage" (Momaday 1976:83). That which is appropriate within such a context is that which is deemed to be natural.

Momaday expands upon the importance of vision and draws a distinction between the Indian way of seeing and that of non-Indians. Using the analogy of looking through the viewfinder of a camera that op-

erates by means of a split image, he says that focusing is a matter of trying to align two planes of a particular view: when we look at the world around us, we see it with the physical eye—as it appears to us in one dimension of reality—but we also see it with the eye of the mind. The Indian, Momaday suggests, has achieved a particularly effective alignment of these two planes of vision and sees the landscape in both ways, thus realizing a whole image from the possibilities within his or her reach.

From this analogy we can attempt to understand the nonseparation between sacred and secular in the Native American worldview. Religious ideas are involved here in that perfect alignment creates a moral universe: "The appropriation of both images into one reality is what the Indian is concerned to do: to see what is really there, but also to see what is *really* there" (Momaday 1976:84). This metaphor promotes a profoundly different philosophy from that of Euro-Americans regarding relationships between humans and the rest of the natural world; herein lies no theory of the alienation of nature from the world of humans brought about by the self-consciousness achieved in Adam's postcreation act (Deloria 1973:104).

There is a relationship between "seeing what is really there" and "talking" that helps formulate the role of sign talking in Plains cultures. It is highlighted in the following statement by Walking Buffalo, an Assiniboine (Stoney) leader from Canada:

> Did you know that trees talk? Well they do. They talk to each other and they'll talk to you if you listen. Trouble is, white people don't listen. They never learned to listen to the Indians, so I don't suppose they'll listen to other voices in nature. But I have learned a lot from trees: sometimes about the weather, sometimes about animals, sometimes about the Great Spirit. (Quoted in Deloria 1973:104)

The same attitude is true for many Assiniboine people at Fort Belknap today. The "voices in nature" to be listened to include the appearance and the calls of animals or birds at particular times and places, and they are frequently read as indexes to appropriate moral action that needs to be taken, or as offering assistance in times of trouble by conveying messages across time and space impossible for humans.

For example, on one occasion a companion related a story about a recent event, a medical emergency. Confusion had existed at the time about how to let a mother down at the Agency know about an accident that had placed her son in the hospital there. In the rush to follow the ambulance, a small deer had leapt out of nowhere across the path of the car and disappeared just as quickly. "So I didn't have to worry," said the narrator, bringing the story to its conclusion. Completely puzzled by such an abrupt end to the story, I tentatively asked her for an explanation for what she, from "the native's point of view," took very much for granted. The appearance of the deer in that manner, she explained, was a sign that the message had already been carried via the swift-footed deer, this attribute of the animal acting as a metaphor for the required speed of the message.

Numerous other examples could be cited. The role of animals as spiritual helpers and sources of religious power that can be gained in dreams or visions is important for an increasing minority at Fort Belknap today who have returned to traditional religious practices.[1] The natural world is part of the human: one is not looking *at* nature, one exists in it. The two are intricately intertwined, through traditional myths and religious practices as well as daily experiences such as that related above. By virtue of this creative indexing, features of the local landscape and its inhabitants acquire value and significance no less than utterances. If trees talk, then "talking" and the "voices in nature" are to be understood as including visual communication of all kinds and not literally as "speech."

Smell also enters this domain. A most distinct aroma associated with Native American religious events of all kinds is that produced by burning sweetgrass. This special grass is picked and braided for use in ceremonies and is often given as a gift, or in payment for religious services. I currently have two braids of sweetgrass on my shelf and sometimes, for no apparent reason, the smell permeates the room quite strongly. One day, I happened to mention this fact to my adoptive Montana mother at Fort Belknap when we were talking on the telephone between Indiana and Montana. Her reply was given in the soft, patient tone she might use when explaining the obvious to a child: "That's how they let you know we're thinking of you," she said. "They have no other way, see." "They" in this context referred to the unseen powers of the superhuman world that for Native Americans are so much a part of nature (making the Western natural/supernatural distinction highly problematic).[2] The spirits were, in this instance, causing the sweetgrass to release its perfume.

What is involved here is a theory of causality in which smell can be the carrier of quite specific meaning: smells can also "talk." In English we speak of the ways in which particular smells can "evoke particular memories." Embedded in such a statement is a theory that places the power of causality with the smell itself, which then passes to an individual agent whose memories of the past can be evoked "inside the head": we are *re-minded*. In contrast, the Assiniboine theory holds that smell is a medium that can be used actively by the superhuman powers to bind existing personal relationships across time and space. It emphasizes an ongoing and shared present rather than an individual and no longer active (except "in the mind") past.

Nature, then, is to be understood through an active "listening," an interactive dialogue between all the senses, particularly sounds and vision, that engages the moral imagination. Sign talking is therefore only one kind of "talking" through vision, as speech talking is only one kind of "talking" through sounds. With this understanding in mind, further exploration of the place names involved in Earthboy's description of Assiniboine territory will illustrate the ethical nature of that space.

Several of the place names discussed in Chapter 3 (such as "Old Wives Lake," "Writing-on-Stone," "Cedar Gathering Place") take their names from specific events, remembered or legendary, that have been woven into narratives. Although these narratives are not explicitly included in Earthboy's rendering, it is because of them that each place when named is an "allusion to narrative" (Kendall 1980:261) that recalls for Earthboy and his listeners the tribal knowledge and attachment to this land as well as the meaning of those events. Such names are "abbreviations for histories" (Kendall 1980:261) and the linguistic signs for them have highly situated meanings requiring exegesis in addition to translation.[3]

For example, the place called *Wazíħe* (near Maple Creek in the Cypress Hills) is where the Assiniboine received the Crow Belt dance (*p'eži mįkna wac'į* 'grass + gird around the loins + dance') from the Sioux, a ceremony that was performed by four warriors when the first thunder of spring was heard, or when the first green grass started to come up after the long winter. The story of how this was obtained and the ceremony itself (no longer performed) both confirm many religious, social, and moral principles of Assiniboine culture.[4]

These include the appropriate way to meet strangers and exchange gifts; how to go about buying the rights to a ceremony; that a warrior never retreats (which is why men who dance in what is today called the "men's traditional" style should never dance backward); the sacred number four; the prohibition of sexual activity before ceremonies; humor as an intricate part of religious events; the telling of war stories; the honoring of older men; and so on.

Also included in Earthboy's memory of this event are reasons why many sacred ceremonies were "pushed aside" to become dances more social in function than explicitly religious. Around 1870 to 1890 when the reservation was becoming a reality, Earthboy explained, the elders felt that with so many social changes going on the younger generation in time would fail to observe the correct taboos, and so they agreed to change the nature and function of the dance.[5] Such evidence provides an important cautionary against too simplistic an interpretation of culture change of this type as being solely the result of white hegemony. The latter reduces the Native American to victim rather than skillful and pragmatic negotiator through difficult choices (see Fowler 1987 for discussion of such negotiation at Fort Belknap).

The place name, as well as referring to a physical place, indexes any or all of these meanings for Earthboy each time it is used; it is not only an allusion to history, then, but an allusion to social and cultural practices also.

SPEECH, SIGNS, AND NAMES

Speech and gestural signs cooperate semantically and syntactically in the naming of the places in Earthboy's narrative. There is a striking similarity to the way in which place names—as well as personal names, tribal names, and many other words—are formed in spoken Nakota and the sign language. For example, I mentioned previously that the names of places in the Nakota territory narrative all refer to some action or event that happened there, or to some striking visual characteristic of the place. This makes them extremely susceptible to representation with a visual medium such as the sign language, but it is important to note that the spoken language also utilizes this visual imagery and action in the naming. Nouns are frequently not simply a name for a thing, but a description of what that object is used for, a reference to the action involved. This creates a high degree of semantic isomorphism between PST and Nakota.

For example, the place name *Aíkpoġa Oyuze* literally means "a place where one gathers 'blow it out on'[cedar]" (*a* 'on' + *íkpoġa* 'to blow out' + *oyuze* 'place where one takes'). The sign which names this place reenacts part of this action, using the hand to suggest the action of blowing out the chewed cedar perfume across a shirt. *Minišoše*, the Missouri River, is a compound word with two parts, 'water' + 'muddy or riled' (*šoše* can also be used to mean murky or muddy in the context of cooking, as when the juices of the meat make the boiling water murky). The PST sign is also a compound sign with two parts whose order of performance follows the spoken form. First is the generic sign for WATER (which acts as a classifier for any kind of water or drink).[6] Following this is a sign in which the hand (or two hands), with fingers spread and palm down, moves forward, the fingers leading away from the chest with a side-to-side wavy motion that indicates the swirling or riled nature of the water as it flows. This sign can also mean RAPIDS. Earthboy could have added a third component here by following the WATER classifier with a sign that specifies RIVER. He omitted this here presumably as a redundancy, a practice mirrored in spoken Nakota where the word for "river" is often omitted from the vocal name when context allows.

Likewise, the names of rivers such as the ELK, TONGUE, and CLAM provide visual or active referents. The PST sign for ELK refers to that animal's distinctive antlers; for TONGUE the signer touches her or his own tongue with an index finger; and for MUSSELSHELL the distinctive action of the clam's mode of locomotion is enacted, the signer using both hands as if they were the two sides of the shell. *T'uki* is the name of the clam itself, and this would be the translation given in a dictionary, but Earthboy's description of what the name "means" also includes the movement the clam makes as it crawls along; part of the identity of "clam" is this way of moving.

WHITE EARTH RIVER presents a challenge because it demands the representation of a color. Both the sign for RIVER and the word *wakpa* are again omitted as being understood, and *Mąk'aha Skána* 'land/earth

+ white + diminutive' appears in signs that again follow the noun + adjective order of the speech. First is the sign for EARTH or LAND ⟶ a spreading of upturned palms from the center of the signing space out to either side, followed by an index finger pointing to or touching something white in this case a cigarette that happened to be lying to one side. Colors are generally represented in this way, by pointing or touching something of the relevant color in the immediate vicinity, another example of deixis being indexically creative. Two exceptions are BLACK, which is represented by touching the hair with a pointing index finger and RED, which is indicated by touching the cheek with the inside surface of all the fingers (etymologically a reference to the former use of red face paint). As an indication that reference is to the color and not some other attribute of the object or the object itself, a signer may rub the back of one hand as a classifier to indicate COLOR prior to pointing to an article.

NAMES OF PLACES WITH PEOPLE

Widening the discussion beyond this particular narrative to the names given to places of human habitation such as villages, towns, or other reservations, one finds that when speaking Nakota, the names of places are phrases that name *the people* who live there. This is done instead of adopting a name for the physical space in which they reside—a name like "New York" for example—that refers to the urban area regardless of who lives there. Thus, if I were talking about going to the town of Browning on the Blackfeet Reservation, I would say, "Pikana úpi ekta mnį́kta," literally, "I will go to the place where the Piegan [one of the three Blackfeet divisions] stay." If going to Hays at the south end of Fort Belknap Reservation, one might say, "T'okt'i ekta mnį́kta" ("I am going to the place where the Gros Ventre [t'oka 'enemy'] live"). In PST signs, exactly the same mode of expression is used, and is accomplished through the use of a distinctive tribal sign that identifies a group of people through a particular feature of their visual appearance, their way of life, or a visual translation of their spoken name. Examples include:

By visual appearance:
KIOWA: HAIR CUT AT ONE SIDE; ARAPAHO: TATTOOED ON THE

CHEST; NAVAHO: BLANKET PEOPLE; NEZ PERCE: PIERCED NOSES; CREE: A BRAID FALLING DOWN THE RIGHT CHEEK.

By way of life:
ARIKARA: CORN SHELLERS; ASSINIBOINE: [one band of] CANOE PADDLERS; CREE: [one band of] RABBIT SKINNERS.

By visual translation of their spoken name:
CROW: BLACK BIRD; BLOOD [a division of the Blackfeet confederacy]: BLOOD/RED; FLATHEAD: HEAD FLAT.[7]

To refer to a particular people in PST signs, one uses the tribal sign together perhaps with the sign for GO, an indexical gesture performed from the actor's locus toward the actual geographical direction in which those people live. If context requires that one distinguish the fact that one is talking about a group of people rather than the activities of shelling corn or paddling a canoe, then a classifier PEOPLE or (the latter also meaning a MAN) will precede the tribal sign.

If a place is not distinguishable by tribe, as became the case when the permanent residences of the "white man" began to spring up a hundred years ago in this area, then names in Nakota describe actions or events associated with those places. For example, names have been assigned to the following towns in the area of Fort Belknap:

HARLEM: *T'iota* 'many houses' (*t'i* + *óta* 'to live/place of living' + 'many/lots of'). Also a generic name for "town" if no other name is given. An alternative is *Mazot'i* 'store' (*máza* 'metal/manufactured goods' + *o* (locative) + *t'i* 'house'). *Máza* is a root that refers to any kind of metal, a material distinctly associated with the coming of the Euro-American. It has come to act as a prefix that denotes many objects of the Euro-American's world—e.g., *mázaska* 'money'—and as used here in *mazot'i* to refer to any kind of manufactured goods to be found in a store. The PST sign for town is an iconic representation of the pattern of logs on the corners of a log cabin created by interlocking the spread fingers of both hands, fingers pointing diagonally forward.

CHINOOK: *T'i Ska Óta* 'many white houses' (*t'i* + *ska* + *óta* 'to live/

Photo 4.1. The PST sign TOWN/HOUSE(S) is iconic of the distinctive corners of a log cabin.

house' + 'white' + 'many'). The PST sign is also a compound WHITE HOUSES + MANY.

HAVRE: *Paha Sápa* 'Black Butte' (*paha* + *sápa* 'hill/butte' + 'black'), named after a prominent butte on the west side of the present town. This Nakota name for the landmark preceded the development of the town. The PST sign is a compound in the same order: BUTTE + BLACK (index finger touches hair).

GREAT FALLS: *Mini įħpaye* 'waterfall' (*mini* + *įħpa* + *ya* 'water' + 'to fall' + adverbial suffix (\continuative). The PST sign is WATER (classifier) + FALLS + BIG.

DODSON: *Mąkʻaosapa Oyuħpa* 'the place where they drop the coal' (*mąkʻa* + *o* + *sápa* + *o* + *yúħpa* 'earth' + nominative prefix + 'black' + 'into' + 'to make fall'). "Trains stopped there and they took coal off— they freight them out to the mountains, so they call that town 'the place where they drop the coal'." The PST sign can be glossed as the compound EARTH + BLACK + DROP.

MALTA: *Kʻoka Akasam* or *Kʻokamowįcʻąku* 'a crossing', 'cut across road', 'road goes by them' (*kʻoka* + *akasam* 'in front of' + 'across'; *kʻokam* + *o* + *cʻąku* 'in front of/across' + 'in' + 'road'). This marks a railroad crossing with an underpass: "they cross over it as well as underneath." The PST sign combines two movement paths, one going from left to right across the signing space and another at right angles to it going forward and passing underneath.

SACO: This is the Cree word for "crossing."

ZORTMAN: *Mazokʻe* 'where they dig the gold' (*maza* + *o* + *kʻa* 'metal of any kind' + 'in' + 'dig'). The PST sign is a compound of METAL + YELLOW + DIG.

There are two points in common between this use of speech and gesture in naming places of human occupation and the naming of natural geographical features such as those mentioned earlier. First, a concern with relationships, through actions and history in the former case and with people in the latter, and, second, a salient visual imagery that permeates both PST and spoken expressions.

PERSONAL NAMES

Further examples of the semantic isomorphism between PST signs and speech due to visual imagery can be found in personal names also. Euro-American bureaucratic requirements imposed a naming system quite alien to Indian peoples a century ago, and people were arbitrarily assigned first (notably "Christian") names and family names, only some of which were English translations of their former names. Despite this humiliating intrusion, most Assiniboine people today have at least two names, a "white man name" and an "Indian name" (and most have at least one nickname). It is in Indian names, which retain former naming practices, that once again we find not only vivid visual imagery but relationships to such things as personal and family histories, actions, events, and religious power in the natural world. For example: *Mat'o Witko* 'Crazy Bear'; *Mína Yuhena* 'Holds-the-Knife'; *T'okahe K'ute* 'First Shoots'; *Hípʻena* 'Sharp Tooth'; *At'o Waśte* 'Good Tattoo'.[8] It is easy to imagine how, given the visual references available, such names could readily be made with signs. This variety of personal names provides actors with different reference points to choose from in different contexts. An Indian name will be used in ceremonies and in prayer, but for most people, unless Nakota is spoken at home, it tends to be known by many but used by few. A person's Euro-American name is used in school and for other bureaucratic purposes. A popular topic of conversation among some older women when they get together, however, is to identify and talk about who is related to whom, what their Indian names are, where the names came from (was a name the grandfather's name, an index of some special characteristic of the person, an animal power?), who gave the names, and so on. Indian names act as performatives here, generating a seemingly endless conversation that builds the social person and binds connections between people, histories, and events in the community at large.

An indication of the "cultural revival" under way at Fort Belknap today—as people call the return to some "traditional" ways—is that some teenagers and adults are going through naming ceremonies in order to obtain an Indian name, a practice that had been in decline. An Indian name today is beginning to be viewed as a marker of a distinct ethnic identity to be proud of, rather than something of which one should be ashamed. A name is to help you in times of difficulty, to pray with, to connect you to the power of the spirit world more easily and to those relatives who have gone before. If a young traditional dancer (male) wants to paint his face as part of his regalia, he must have an Indian name.[9]

Only Indian names and nicknames can be represented in PST, because of their salient visual imagery. PST has no equivalent to what in ASL is called the "finger-spelling alphabet," with which names of places and people can be spelled out using handshapes that each represent one letter of the Roman alphabet. Finger spelling borrows from the visual appearance of written English, not from spoken English. This development in ASL mirrors the lack of visual imagery associated with most personal and place names in English.

Nicknames are an important topic in their own right as indexes of the social person in different contexts but will not be discussed here except for brief mention that at Fort Belknap they are a constant source of humor and teasing, frequently changing according to interpersonal relations between namer and named, and reputation, and serving as subtle creators of the social person by their pejorative uses which highlight social norms (see Harré 1984:101; R. Rosaldo 1984).

NAMES AND TIME

The same principles of maintaining a relationship to actions or events via the use of names, together with the predominant use of visual imagery, apply not only to names of places and people but also to names given to periods of time. The phrases that name portions of a year are not so much labels of "time" in the way that "January," "February," and so on are in English (the etymology of which is submerged and not known to most users) but are descriptions of the natural changes to be seen in the landscape throughout the year: the state of the grass, berries, and animals, or the temperature. In other words, time passing is encoded through words/signs that describe space, that is, the changes in appearance of physical spaces.

Rose Weasel had this to say about the times of the year:

> They did not know these [English] names; just that "the leaves or grass is yellow," "now the buds are coming out," "the cherries are ripe." They did not know how the months were named. "Now it's getting cold" they said. "Winter is coming now" they said, "it is cold." They just said, "It is the middle of winter," "the middle of the cold." "Now we have passed it," from then "now we are getting toward spring" they said.[10]

This statement and the Assiniboine names themselves suggest a much more fluid conception of boundaries around units of time and time passing than that marked in English. The passing of each month is observable through the changing phases of the moon, hence the Nakota word *hąwi* 'moon' (night + sun) is also used for "month." However, the names, which are descriptive phrases rather than single words, do not seem to have been fixed beyond having the same references, and there are variations to be found today among consultants who attempt to align the Assiniboine names with those of months in English. As Ardener (1989:136) notes, learned consultants often exhibit an excusable failing in such situations by attempting to make their own terminological system developed in specific and highly local conditions match a "standard" of supposedly higher status.

What is consistent, however, is the description of passing time in terms of visual changes in nature and their effects. For example, "February" or "March" is *wįc'išta yazą hąwi* 'they have sore eyes moon'; "April" is *t'apeha hąwi* 'moon when the frogs come out'; and "June" is *wípasoka' sápsapa hąwi* 'the moon when the juneberries are ripe'. Once again it is easy to see how such names can be made with PST signs because they include salient visual references.

Plains Indian history has little use for numbers because time passing is primarily a matter of events; what is most important is *what* happened, not when in any numerical sense. Some Plains tribes marked the passing of each year (or winter) by assigning a name that recalled an important event. Some of these year labels were recorded graphically on hides that have become known as "winter counts" (see Mallery 1886, 1893; Mooney [1898] 1979; Howard 1960, 1976, 1979; and discussion in DeMallie 1982, Pt. 3). Although it is not known whether this was an Assiniboine graphic practice, the creation of history through the naming of past "winters" in the same way through words and signs certainly was. It continues today as Nakota speakers remember time as events, as Earthboy did when he used the term "intertribal wars" to indicate the time period of his narrative, or in such phrases as "during the war," "the year Mount St. Helens exploded," or "the year of the drought." A pictograph is a condensed graphic description of an event that serves to bring to memory through a visual image the name of the year in question. A PST sign achieves the same goal but uses the body in motion to make the reference to history.

VISUAL IMAGERY AND ACTION AS CREATIVE PRINCIPLE

Contemporary additions to Nakota vocabulary also illustrate this principle for the structuring of linguistic signs. For example, *iyec'įkayen* 'car' means literally "it goes by itself" (auto-mobile, in fact). The PST sign involves an iconic representation of the action of the hands on a steering wheel for both the verb TO DRIVE and the noun CAR. *Mazap'api* 'telephone' means "hit the wire," a description of the action of a telegraph key. Explanation of this name invokes a joke about the old days of telegraph signals when Native Americans would see a soldier climb a pole, connect his transmitter to the telegraph line, and send messages. The "old-timers," so the story goes, thinking all that was necessary was to "hit the wire," would try the same.

This is one example of a popular genre of jokes involving "old-timers" and misunderstandings of English. One that depends upon sign language is told of an old lady who went to the store to buy beans but did not know the English word. After several failed attempts to make the storekeeper understand what she wanted, she indicated the size by using the last digit of her little finger in the PST sign for BEAN, followed by the sign for BAD performed next to her rear end accompanied by an onomatopoeic representation of flatulence. The storekeeper guessed immediately what she meant!

Other words and signs of contemporary origin include *mini įhpiġa* 'boiling water' (PST sign = WATER + BOILING) for "beer" or "soda." Likewise *minip'eta* 'fire-water' is the well-known designation for "whiskey." "Bracelet" is *nąpe c'ask* 'tied up hand', and "Easter" is *wįtkaśaśa* 'paint eggs red'. Once again these are all actions or qualities highly accessible to visual representation and so readily encoded into gestural signs.

NAMES AS INDEXES

In all these domains, a name serves as a living symbol, an index of something much more than itself. This is recognized explicitly in the linguistic signs (vocal gestures and manual gestures) themselves, whether what is indexed is a narrative, a visual image, a history, a series of actions or events, a relationship, or a particular group of people.

In Nakota, the naming of things in the world as objects is not separated from their use, their actions, and their attributes in a host of contexts—indeed the distinction between nouns and verbs may be only a function of linguistic analysis. The building up of compound words in both speech and gestural language reflects this blurred boundary in distinctly similar ways.

All the above examples share an insistence upon marking the relationship to place, person, or event through naming practices. Perhaps this may be seen as part of the same principle that makes kin relationships between people so central to Assiniboine and all Plains cultures. Further examples of this concern with relationship and place can also be perceived in the complex vocabulary surrounding verbs of coming and going, in which there are eight verbs that change according to whether one is coming or going from home and where one is speaking from, a topic to be taken up in more detail later.

I have suggested and given a few examples of the semantic isomorphism that exists between spoken and signed expressions. The predominance of visual imagery (both active and static) as a basis for representation in naming is clearly common to both the spoken and the signed languages. The spoken representation of a visual image is necessarily arbitrary, but not so a representation in the sign language.

In my field notes at one point I have written in large letters: "As I am learning more Nakota I seem to be able to understand the signs more easily," but the statement is followed by some rather large question marks. In retrospect, it seems that only in the context of holding on to a somewhat erroneous model of PST and spoken Nakota as two separate languages could such a question even have occurred. In the light of further knowledge, and in particular a growing awareness of the high degree of semantic isomorphism, the reasons why such simultaneity of learning should have occurred have now become fairly obvious.

Also, on occasion, when Earthboy and I were working on the transcriptions of videotaped performances, I would get confused because his slower repetition of the Nakota spoken words used in the story often did not coincide with what I could hear on the tape. Because I taped the transcription sessions too, I was able to listen again and think about what was going on. I later realized that the discrepancies arose because he was including meaning that in his storytelling was encoded only in the signs. This indicated his own sense of the unity of meaning here, rather than any idea of two separate languages going on at the same time. He was not "hearing" one language and "seeing" another: both were integrated so that when he repeated to me what he had "said" on the videotape, he included a translation of a sign into spoken Nakota if its meaning had not appeared in words in the original telling. Because I was only writing down the words and translations of the words, he presumably did not want meaning to be left out. In making my transcriptions, I had to change my method and work on words and signs simultaneously rather than first of all transcribing the spoken component and then going back to work on the signs. In this way we were also better able to discuss interrelationships of meaning as they occurred.

Just as we can, with Momaday, posit the extension of a concern with the moral nature of relationship beyond the immediate sphere of kin relations into the natural world, so also perhaps can the importance of vision in Plains Indian culture extend beyond an explicit religious event to a fundamental languaging process.

ON AND OFF RESERVATION: LANGUAGE AND TERRITORY

The degree of ease or discomfort felt by Fort Belknap residents in places outside the reservation boundaries varies enormously according to age and education as well as according to individual experiences with non-

Indians and prejudice. Often Nakota is used in a humorous way as a buffer against the foreign nature of the Euro-American's world. For example, one elderly Assiniboine man referred to a cafe in the nearby town of Chinook named "The Cozy Corner" as "The Friendly Cafe," making a pun on the Nakota word for "friend" (*kona*) while at the same time indicating that it was a place Indian people need not feel "shamed" to go into (i.e., they were not likely to be discriminated against or made to feel out of place).

Likewise, when driving to the store in the nearby town of Harlem one day, this same man and I happened to follow a Toyota truck with its name written across the tailboard. "That's a real town truck," he said, making reference to the similarity between "Toyota" and *t'iota*, the Nakota word for "town" (and also testing my knowledge of Nakota by seeing if I would get the joke). When we came to Napa Auto Parts, he could not resist a pun on *nap'a* 'beat it/run away/escape'. "They don't want you to shop in there, they're telling you to beat it," he said.

This happens in English also, as in a joke that interprets the road sign "Watch for falling rock" as an instruction to look for a lost warrior (named Falling Rock) who never returned. In all these examples, language is activated to familiarize the strange, to impart something of "our" identity onto "their" ground. It provides the means by which deeply felt alienation can be actively and artfully resisted, in this case through humor, by those without power (see also Basso 1979).

Irony as well as humor is frequently used to characterize traveling in what is still generally perceived as "white man's territory." For example, the designation by the American government of the Native American situation during the last century as "the Indian problem" was appropriated creatively for the following situation. A friend observed that he and his family often see Indians stopped at the side of the road with the hood up on their broken-down car. He explained that "they get a little money and go buy a car—they never look under the hood, they just buy it if it looks good." Laughing, he stated that whenever he and his family pass such foolish consumers they always say, "Aha, Indian problem!" In typical fashion, humor creatively indexes their own awareness of a history in which they have been unable to affect non-Indian constructs of their relationships with the non-Indian world.

Typical of ironic humor was this comment by a young man in response to learning that I was "studying Indian culture" (as the unusual presence of an English woman in the community was frequently explained by my hosts). He said, "Yeh, I'm really losin' my culture; ya know, I saw a covered wagon the other day and I didn't know how to react!" Everyone dissolved into laughter, of course, the irony and reference to Hollywood stereotyping plain to all.

Beyond the surface humor, however, this use of the words "culture" and "Indian problem" indicates that Native Americans have been forced to learn that their own cultural practices are seen as special in the eyes of a non-Indian majority. Until the encounter with the Other, cultural practices simply define the form of life the members of the culture live without any particular consciousness that it is simply one form of life among many. Once the encounter has been internalized, however, the culture faces the question of its identity, which means endeavoring to see itself from without. The perceived judgments and standards of the Other, through which a culture undertakes to arrive at self-understanding, become a mirror through which to view itself (Danto 1990).[11] In this case, humor and irony index various degrees of awareness and discomfort with perceived virtues and shortcomings that are evaluated against such a standard.

When dealing with racial prejudice against Indian people in the area—prejudice that is frequently real, but just as often perceived as such prior to any evidence—the same kind of humor will be employed. When being injected at the hospital where the white nurse had difficulty with the needle, a friend told the nurse, "Hey, that's buckskin, you know."

Poet and novelist James Welch, however, has a less lighthearted way of dealing with the prejudice he felt, as illustrated in some biting lines from a poem called "Harlem, Montana: Just off the Reservation":

We need no runners here. Booze is law
and all the Indians drink in the best tavern.
Money is free if you're poor enough.
Disgusted, busted whites are running
for office in this town. The constable,
a local farmer, plants the jail with wild

raven-haired stiffs who beg just one more drink.
One drunk, a former Methodist, becomes a saint
in the Indian church, bugs the plaster man
on the cross with snakes. If his knuckles broke,
he'd see those women wail the graves goodbye.

Goodbye, goodbye, Harlem on the rocks,
so bigoted, you forget the latest joke,
so lonely, you'd welcome a battalion of Turks
to rule your women. What you don't know,
what you will never know or want to learn—
Turks aren't white. Turks are olive, unwelcome
alive in any town. Turks would use
your one dingy park to declare a need for loot.
Turks say bring it, step quickly, lay down and dead.

Here we are when men were nice. This photo, hung
in the New England Hotel lobby, shows them nicer
than pie, agreeable to the warring bands of redskins
who demanded protection money for the price of food.
Now, only Hutterites out north are nice. We hate
them. They are tough and their crops are always good.
We accuse them of idiocy and believe their belief all wrong.

Harlem, your hotel is overnamed, your children
are raggedy-assed but you go on, survive
the bad food from the two cafes and peddle
your hate for the wild who bring you money.
When you die, if you die, will you remember
the three young bucks who shot the grocery up,
locked themselves in and cried for days, we're rich,
help us, oh God, we're rich.

                                                        (WELCH 1976:30–31)

Although much could be said about this powerful and bitter poem,
I here want merely to draw attention to the way in which Welch uses the

typical name-calling of racists—"redskins," "wild," and "bucks"—to reverse the direction of prejudice back onto those who perpetrated it.

I soon learned that to speak Nakota in town was not acceptable, as friends would look around uncomfortably to see if anyone had noticed and only make replies in English or in an embarrassed whisper. An elderly consultant complained that her daughter was "shamed" to take her into the supermarket because she would embarrass her by "talkin' Indian" (in both signs and words). Using PST among a non-Indian public also fits into this negative picture, since "talking with your hands" is interpreted by non-Indians as stereotypical Indian behavior, an inability to articulate oneself with words and therefore a marker of either stupidity or "primitiveness," a persistent survival of Tylor's times. Self-understanding through this stereotype has created a mirror that makes sign talk and spoken Nakota carry the same negative weighting from the daughter's perspective, being equally "Indian" and equally embarrassing in the "wrong" context—among "white people." On the reservation, however, for the same daughter such expert knowledge in the family is a source of considerable dignity and pride, but again this is at least partly constructed through a mirror provided by the attention of anthropologists.

I began to realize that for many people at Fort Belknap, the places where as an Indian one can feel comfortable exist as a series of islands, analogous perhaps to the way in which the ancient rocks of the Little Rocky Mountains, the Bear Paw Mountains, and the Sweetgrass Hills rise up like islands in the sea of rolling grassland. Other Indian reservations, or cities like Great Falls and Billings that have Indian communities, are pockets of familiarity and comfort separated by large tracts of unpredictable, potentially hostile territory.

Chapter 5

*Does the sign-post leave no doubt open about the way I have to go?
But where is it said which way I am to follow it, whether in the
direction of its finger or (e.g.) in the opposite one? And if there were,
not a single sign-post but a chain of adjacent ones or chalk marks on
the ground—is there only one way of interpreting them?*

LUDWIG WITTGENSTEIN (1958:39)

GETTING TO THE POINT: SPATIAL ORIENTATION AND DEIXIS IN PST AND NAKOTA

The system of spatial orientation and use of deixis in Earthboy's narrative about Assiniboine territory are shared by his community. They are shared not only in the sense that all adhere to similar principles of spatial organization (regardless of whether they know the sign language or not) but also because the whole system operates successfully due to a sense of shared localized relationships. Actors in this social space share personal histories, and such localized biographies are consistently brought to bear in their use of language. Such use simultaneously creates and confirms the local nature of those biographies. We have here not Bernstein's "restricted code" of language use but a language community in which a rich local knowledge of persons can be presumed to such an extent that deictic modes of expression provide unambiguous reference for its members. It is also a language community in which speech and gesture carry equal validity as ways of "talking" and thus achieving such reference.

Earthboy's narrative illustrated how the four cardinal directions, north, south, east, and west, permeate the use of the body and space in the context of storytelling performances. This chapter continues that theme by investigating how this symbolic form plays a role in structuring the lived experience of everyday action and interaction.

FRAMES OF REFERENCE: THE FOUR DIRECTIONS

The cardinal directions are collectively known as *t'ate tópa* 'the four winds' or *t'ate oye tópa* 'the four tracks of the winds'. In Assiniboine religious thought it is from the four winds that various kinds of spiritual assistance or "power" come. Each term would appear to connote a general direction from which certain things come toward a person in contrast to the Euro-American conventional image of the four directions as lines moving outward from a given point, as shown by the pointing arrows on most geographic maps (see Fig. 5.1). An additional difference lies in the conception of the cardinal directions as four quarters—that is, as a circle sectioned into four quarters. Each direction therefore comprises an area, in contrast to the single directional line of Euro-American convention. All four directions (in addition to sky and earth) within the circle are of significance in religious ceremonies in both ritual action and spoken prayer, as well as playing a prominent role in danced movements and the organization of performance spaces for dancing.

In the Nakota language, *wíhinąp'e* 'east' refers to the sunrise—literally it means "the sun comes up"— and it is the direction from which the grandfather spirits come. In the prereservation period, when the bands were scattered to hunt, east was the direction in which the tipi would often be faced, so the morning sun could be greeted with prayer. Indeed, one of my Nakota teachers complained about the orientation of her new frame house because the builders had ignored her request that it be faced toward the east.

Wiyotahą 'south' refers to noon, literally "the sun in the middle." South is a particularly salient direction for the Assiniboine: the doors of two ceremonial structures, the sun dance lodge and the sweat lodge, for example, face the south. Some people today assign south as the direction in which the creator or *wak'ą t'ąka* lives and the direction people go after death. There are variations upon this. Others conceive of death involving a journey from east to south to west, as with the passage of the sun during a day, and some consider west to be the direction taken by departing souls after death (these contemporary conceptions can be compared with historical statements in Maximilian [1843] 1906:446; Henry, cited in Coues [1897] 1965:521; Lowie 1909:41). One person explained to me why south is said to be the direction we are always facing. At noon when the sun is in the south, your shadow is directly behind you—whether you turn your back on the sun or not, your shadow still looks the same way. [1]

Wiyohpeya 'west' refers to "the sun going down." It is the home of

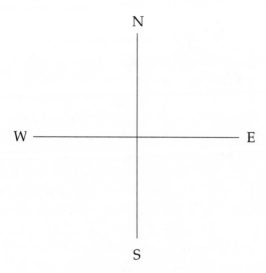

Euro-American cardinal directions

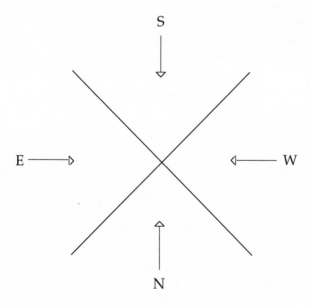

Assiniboine cardinal directions

Figure 5.1. Two different cultural conceptions of the cardinal directions.

the eagle who "lifts prayers to heaven" and other "winged ones," the birds of the air (*wakiyą*), especially the thunderbirds whose spiritual assistance is frequently sought, but whose displeasure and power is made manifest in destructive lightning and thunder. *Waziyata* 'north' refers to "where the snow comes from," the home of the old man who "lives in the cold and makes the cold and rarely takes pity on anyone."[2]

Although these terms to describe the four directions exist in the spoken language, it is significant that they are rarely if ever used in everyday contexts. Consultants who were fluent speakers of Nakota had to search their memories for the names, and conceived of the words as being appropriate in three contexts: pertaining primarily to religious concepts and ritual actions involving the four winds; referring to the four seasons and passing time; and relating only to far distant places and peoples. Another term for south, for example, was *maśta mąk'oc'e*, literally "hot country," which might be used of someone traveling to Arizona but not for someone traveling south within the reservation or state of Montana. Two variant terms for north—*waziyam* and *wiyohąpą*—refer to places where other Assiniboine people live: the Red Pheasant Reserve and the Santaluta/Regina area, both in Canada. To say "Did you come from the North?" (*wiyohąpą etaha yahi*) is to ask whether you came from Canada. The spoken language terms themselves therefore do not seem to involve either local geographical space or immediate orientation space. How then is information about such local spaces organized?

I found that despite a lack of vocal reference in everyday contexts, the cardinal points nevertheless provide a constant frame of reference that all use, whether they speak Nakota or English only, and regardless of whether they know the sign language or not. It is through indexical spoken expressions and gestures that this frame of reference is utilized.

Today, even though few people are fluent in the sign language proper, there remains a use of gesture that is coincident with it and undoubtedly stems from a very different view of language than that held by Euro-American people. For example, I found that speech and gesture are equally important in giving route directions, regardless of whether Nakota or English spoken language is used.

In asking how to get from the Agency buildings on the Fort Belknap

Reservation to the nearby town of Harlem, I received the following reply in English from an Assiniboine person:

> You go out of here this way, turn this way again and you'll come to
> the highway. Go this way again, over the river and you're gonna
> go that way into town.

Obviously if one were to take notice of only the spoken component involved in this utterance, the information would be somewhat ambiguous. What is of equal importance in understanding these directions,
however, is the accompanying gestures of the arms and hands, as shown
in the movement text in Figure 5.2.

This is in marked contrast to the directions of a non-Indian Harlem
resident who said:

> Well, go out of these doors to the parking lot, then take a left past
> the Headstart Building till you get to the road, and take a left
> again. You'll get to Highway 2. Go west on 2 about three miles and
> Harlem's right there on your right. There's a sign right there says
> "Harlem."

The only gestures accompanying this were a hand directed toward the
doors in question ⸘ \Ꝃ and a raised hand at the end, indicating the road
sign, placed as if in front of the speaker.

In contrast to the Assiniboine case, the Euro-American example encodes directions by making reference to landmarks such as doors and
signposts, buildings and a numbered highway, as well as directional
terms such as left and right. In the route directions given by an
Assiniboine person, indexical expressions such as "here," "this way,"
and "that way" are accompanied by gestures that point to the actual
geographical directions involved. The indexicals and gestures provide
information just as accurate as that encoded in the Euro-American case
but in a different manner.

Assiniboine people always seem to know where the actual cardinal
directions lie, even if deep inside a multirooted building in a room
without windows (which was the case when these directions were given).

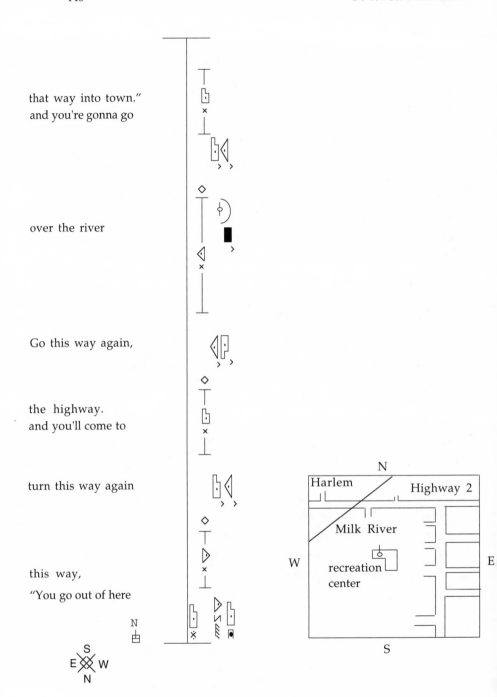

Figure 5.2. Route directions given by Fort Belknap resident.

Consequently, when giving directions, the cardinal points provide a constant frame of reference that everyone uses, even though the actual words "north," "south," "east," and "west" are not used. This implicit awareness of geographical direction means that people draw upon a map that is constant regardless of which direction the speaker happens to be facing at the time. In this way spoken indexical expressions plus the gestures of hands that point to actual geographical directions are sufficient, and no one (except perhaps the anthropologist) gets confused.

Whereas the Assiniboine person's description mentions only "town," the Euro-American directions use a proper name, Harlem. In all four of the Assiniboine possibilities—"town" in English, *t'iota* 'many houses' or *mazot'i* 'the store' in Nakota, and WHITE MAN'S HOUSE in PST— the names require local knowledge to be unambiguous. All this is not meant to imply that Assiniboine people never use the name Harlem when speaking in English, but unless context demands an explicit distinction— say between Harlem and another nearby town such as Malta—the norm is "town" in all three languages.

BODY FRAME OF REFERENCE

The spatial frame of reference discussed so far is one organized around an external and constant frame, that of the four directions E⊗W . A second frame of reference is also available in this community. In Labanotation terms this is called a "body frame of reference" -◇- which means that spatial orientation (including what counts as front/back, left/right, up/down) is judged from the body of the actor rather than from any external spatial frame. In the next movement text (Fig. 5.3), a person using Plains Sign Talk and Nakota gives directions for how to travel from the town of Harlem to Lodgepole, a community at the other end of the reservation. On this occasion, she was sitting with her back toward the actual direction involved (south) and so chose to orientate herself as if she was facing the direction of travel and taking the journey herself.

This allowed her to perform clearly the signs for each feature on the journey starting with "town." Her description here is not tied to actual geographical direction but is a 180-degree reversal of it, although internally consistent once begun. It is feature-orientated and so in some ways similar to the Euro-American case above. It contrasts with the latter,

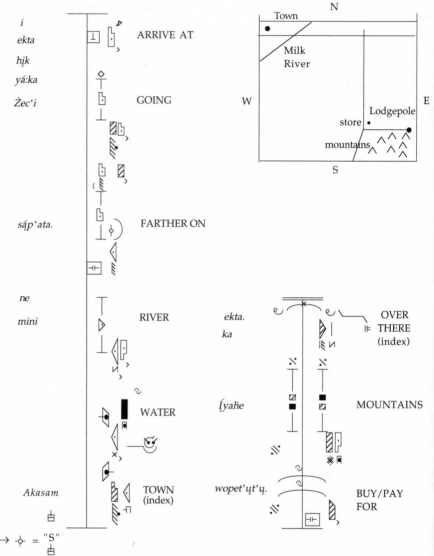

Figure 5.3. Route directions from Harlem to Lodgepole in Nakota and PST.

however, because again the gestures are indispensable to meaning. In Figure 5.3, signs from the lexicon of PST that can be glossed in English as TOWN, RIVER, STORE, and MOUNTAINS are used along with indexicals such as STRAIGHT THIS WAY, THIS SIDE, and OVER THERE. The directions begin with yet another way of referring to the town of Harlem in spoken Nakota and PST, as *akasam* which means "across." The explanation for this lies in the fact that one must go across the Milk River to get to Harlem from the Agency. The river is also a distinct cultural boundary between Indian and white communities. One is therefore going across in more ways than one. The movement text shows that although the route directions began with the word *akasam*, this metaphor was not repeated in signs performed at the same time; rather, the standard sign for TOWN, as described above, was used.

GESTURE AND SPEECH IN SPATIAL ORIENTATION

An Assiniboine passenger riding in a car, where visual field is restricted, will probably still gesture and say "go this way" or "go that way" rather than use American English alternatives that do not require a gesture, such as "take a right here" or "go east until you get to the highway." British English equivalents would be different again, involving such expressions as "turn right at the Red Lion" and "take the York Road."

These last three brief examples demonstrate three different possibilities for organizing spatial orientation:

1. The Assiniboine case. Indexicals and gestures are both necessary and sufficient for accurate interpretation. They are used in a constant frame of reference orientated to the four cardinal directions.

2. The non-Indian American English case. Some indexicals, but primarily a combination of directional words (such as right/left, east/west) and landmarks are used; some gestures are involved.

3. The British English case. A feature-orientated description is based upon landmarks and proper names with directional words such as left/right; it requires no gestures. (Once again we find shades of Tylor!)

FRAMES OF REFERENCE AND ANTHROPOLOGICAL DESCRIPTIONS

A further example serves to illustrate the power of the Laban script for anthropological descriptions of this kind. Writing can be accommodated to the frame of reference being used by the mover. Earthboy's narrative in the previous chapter illustrated how the logic of the constant spatial frame relating to geographical direction is employed in a storytelling performance.[3] While working on the text of another story, I was puzzled as to why on one occasion the signs for MORNING and AFTERNOON were performed as shown in Figure 5.4a and on another occasion were performed as in Figure 5.4b. (The first finger and thumb create the shape of a circle, with all other fingers curled in. The hand moves in a curving arc of the whole arm, upward or downward, the whole sign being an iconic representation of the sun rising and lowering in the sky.)

While the handshape and arm action remained the same in both performances, the space in which the arm moved was quite different. On the first occasion the storyteller raised her right arm on the right side of her body and lowered it to the left side; on the second occasion the sun rose directly in front of her and set behind. Later on, the puzzle was solved through the realization that in the first instance (Fig. 5.4a: E = right, W = left) the storyteller was facing almost due north, so east (the direction of the rising sun) was to the storyteller's right side and west to her left. On the second occasion (Fig. 5.4b: E = forward, W = backward), she had been facing east.

This situation makes a difference to the transcription of those signs if it is to be ethnographically accurate. What is constituent to the sign is not the visible forward middle $\boxed{\cdot}$ or side middle $\triangleright$ direction of the arm in relation to the torso, but the spatial orientation system which informs us that from the mover's perspective what is meant here is the arm goes toward geographical east and rises $\bigvee$ $\overset{E}{\underset{\perp}{\boxtimes}}$ (see Fig. 5.4c). The earlier descriptions are not wrong, but a transcription that is ethnographically more informed and therefore preferred is the one given in Figure 5.4c. Instead of the full structural description, or a shortened version, describing curved fingers and opposing thumb as shown on the left and center in Figure 5.5, I have used the Labanotation symbol for "in the shape of" $\diamondsuit$ and added a small iconic representation of the sun so that the nota-

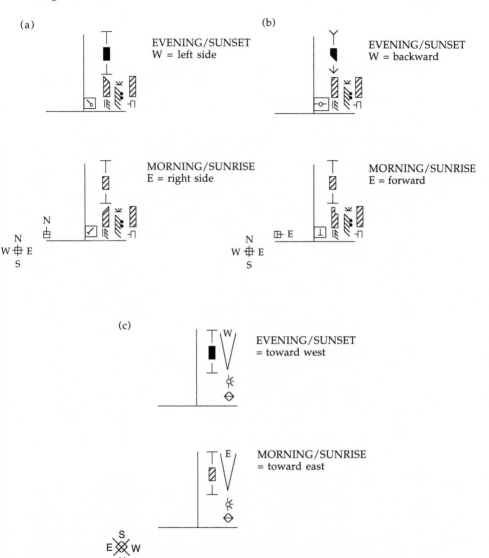

Figure 5.4. Assiniboine spatial orientation and PST signs for MORNING and EVENING: (a) left/right; (b) forward/backward; (c) east/west.

tion reads "in the shape of the sun," which is what is constituent to this sign. I have called such an ethnographically informed description an "ethno-graph."

The aim throughout the creation of a movement text is to identify such constituent features and describe accordingly. It is precisely this

full structural   abbreviated   ethno-graph
description   description

Figure 5.5. Different levels of description using the Laban script.

possibility that Williams (1988) intends when she says that a Labanotated text *is* the ethnography. That is, the writing of a movement text cannot be purely descriptive any more than a standard ethnographic text can— both are beset with theoretical choices and problems of translation and interpretation. As with a standard ethnography, one builds one's inter- pretations over time and makes choices about descriptions with increas- ing knowledge. With a movement text, one is aiming at a performable script that encodes the kind of indigenous understandings of actions that I have described above, rather than a record of gross physical movement.

DEIXIS AND THE LANGUAGE COMMUNITY

The intimate social space of a reservation community permits the use of indexicals in speech and gesture well beyond this kind of general spa- tial orientation and giving of route directions. It extends into the fre- quent use of pronouns and demonstratives in many contexts, so that proper names of places and people are avoided wherever possible. For example, whereas in British English I might say, "Would you tell Pat that Mary has taken the red pickup truck to go to Harlem," a Fort Belknap resident would say, "Tell her that my daughter has taken that truck to go down there." The persons involved ("her" and "my daughter"), the particular truck (the red or brown one?) and destination ("down there"), would all be identified correctly by the listener from knowledge of pre- vious events and by a quick elimination of alternatives.

This use of language invests heavily in both deictic and anaphoric reference, so much so that these localized orientations cannot be under- stood from the immediate conversational context alone. Anaphoric ref- erence, which allows speakers to use pronouns and demonstratives to refer to a previously mentioned noun instead of repeating a name (e.g., "Tom has the food, *he* will bring *it* later") extends far beyond the context of one conversation. Context in this case has to be expanded indefinitely to include local knowledge of specific relationships, and implies a whole realm of social connectedness.

The phrase "down there" is part of yet another set of resources for spatial organization. Spoken in Hays at the south end of the reservation, "down there" refers to the Agency at the northern end. This way of talking contrasts with Euro-American expectations that north is "up" and south is "down," an expectation that comes from—and probably contributed to—standard Euro-American map-making conventions. Instead, the Assiniboine convention is organized along an up-down axis according to the altitude of the land and the flow of the Milk River and several smaller creeks. One goes "up" to Hays or "up" to the mountains from the Agency, and "down" to the Agency and Harlem from the mountains. To say "farther up we have the Blackfeet" refers to the Blackfeet Reservation, which is west of Fort Belknap but at a higher elevation on the edge of the Rocky Mountains. One also goes "down" to Fort Peck, the neighboring Assiniboine and Sioux reservation two hundred miles downstream along the Milk River.

This works as follows. When inquiring about an upcoming hand game to be held in the small community of Frazer on the Fort Peck Reservation, a person might say simply, "Are you going down below Saturday?" and rely on the listener to fill in details about the particular event in question, as well as exactly where "down below" is. Those interested in hand games would be informed about such an important local event and would have no trouble identifying what was meant. Local knowledge of persons would also mean that the inquirer would be known to the listener as a supporter of such events.

Person reference in the form of pronouns also draws upon similar local knowledge, whether one is speaking in Nakota or English. In English, for example, if a married woman in conversation uses "he," it can safely be assumed, in the absence of further contextual information, that she is referring to her husband. Beyond that, kin terms will be used to identify who is being talked about, as in "my eldest son," "my daughter," "my nephew," and so on. People will be addressed by kin terms also, as in "Sister, pass me that." Such emphasis constantly foregrounds the relationship between speaker and addressee in a way that the use of proper names does not.

When conversational practices constantly foreground kinship relations in this way, *not* being related creates problems for successful interaction. The way in which my own arrival and continued presence in the community was explained illustrates just how creative the solutions to this problem can be.

CREATING A BIOGRAPHY

When I first arrived in Montana, it was just in time to attend an important and only recently revived annual ceremonial event, the sun dance on the Fort Peck Reservation. I parked my small city car hesitatingly among the pickup trucks and campers that were all drawn into a circle. The human presence seemed dwarfed by the vast expanse of the prairie grassland stretching for miles with the horizon visible 360 degrees around. The circle of vehicles in turn surrounded a circular arbor made of cottonwood trees and brush where, I assumed, events were to take place. I set about putting up my tent and soon discovered that I had forgotten a mallet. Looking around, I found a stone that would knock the tent pegs into the hard baked earth, but it was hard on my hands. An elderly Indian man who had been watching me from his pickup truck now strolled over, quietly and without comment handing over a mallet. He said nothing, simply offered the hammer. I thanked him profusely and we both laughed at my predicament.

Upon hearing my English accent, he was pleased to continue the conversation, because he, like many Native Americans, had served in the American armed forces during the Second World War and had spent some time in England. Fortunately for me, the English had been kind to him and he recalled some fond memories of those days. He wanted to introduce me to his wife and so we walked back to his camp and shared some tea. Over the course of the next few days we spoke occasionally in passing, but when the sun dance itself was over and the final feed and giveaway were completed, the veteran soldier came over again to tell me that at his home on Fort Belknap Reservation, two hundred miles west, they too would be having a sun dance in a couple of weeks' time. I would be welcome to stay with them if I wished.

I doubt that he ever really expected me to turn up, but I did and ended up staying not only for the sun dance but for two more weeks that included the annual summer powwow. Throughout this time we all camped in a beautiful meadow hidden deep inside the Little Rocky Mountains by a narrow winding canyon. During this time I met many other members of the family and the community, and as an English-woman I am sure I was as exotic to them as they were to me. Having a vehicle, I was also a useful extra source of transport for going to the store for groceries.

It was on one such occasion that I was driving along with my host's wife when she said with a smile, "Ooh, I'm gonna have a lot of visitors when you've gone." "What do you mean?" I replied in a puzzled tone. "Well," she said, "they're all gonna want to know who you are, you have been here with us a long time now." She paused in thought for a few moments before exclaiming with great enthusiasm, "I know, I'm gonna say that you're my husband's [illegitimate] daughter from England and you've come to find out who your real father is!" She was obviously delighted with her solution to the problem of how to account for my continued presence to her neighbors. Her statement left me some-what stunned and a little apprehensive as to what implications "illegiti-macy" might have for me. At the time, however, I thought it was prob-ably a joke and thought no more about it.

Soon after this, I left to continue my exploratory visits to reserva-tions in Canada but returned to Fort Belknap to visit just once more before the end of the summer. Upon my return, I found that my hostess had indeed told some of her neighbors the story, and several people I did not previously know were most friendly. At first we used to laugh about this—it was our little secret—but it wasn't long before her chil-dren were calling me their "British sister" and I had the nickname "BeeBee" (British Brenda). The following year when I returned, having decided to embark upon long-term field research, my "brother" and his wife had a giveaway at the powwow in honor of their little girl, in the process of which, and unbeknownst to me, they announced to the whole community that his parents had taken me as a daughter. The whole thing was made official and public by the action of placing a dance shawl around my shoulders. What is striking about this is that obviously the "truth" of the situation from a non-Indian American viewpoint is simply not relevant. What my hostess had succeeded in devising, with remarkable aplomb, was a strategy that not only served to fit me into the kinship system but also provided me with a biography that could be shared. I could now count as a "real" person and not simply a visitor or stranger. Her solution provided a framework within which other people in her community would feel comfortable because they would know how to interact with me: according to the norms of interaction associated with various kinship relations and according to this personal history that gave me an identity. It was the reality of a warm social relationship and the importance of providing me with a shared biography that counted as "truth." My "Montana mother" gained considerable respect for her generous attitude toward an offspring of her husband's wartime transgressions. She was always eager to point out, however, that they had not been married at that time and so her husband was not being unfaithful. All in all, everyone stood to gain from her version of events.

BIOGRAPHY, STORY, AND DEIXIS

The story of how we met has since become a family story that the grandchildren love to ask about. It has turned into a humorous account of how I was trying to knock tent pegs in with my bare hands! In other contexts too, however, I found that "telling stories" (*owoknaka*) is a constant strategy for confirming relationships. According to Euro-American expectations, a story—say, about a funny thing that happened when we went to Havre the other day—is reportable only "for a day or two at most after the event as a story about what happened" (Linde 1987:345). In contrast, at Fort Belknap such a story retains an extended reportability as an account of our relationship, something we share and remind ourselves about frequently that foregrounds our relationship in the telling and that anyone in the vicinity can share with us. Such stories are not self-presentations but the presentation of selves in relationship. Because we all share so much of the detail already, deictic and anaphoric expressions abound. Not only stories of recent events (*owoknaka*) but the Inktomi (trickster) stories (*ohųkaka*) also are talked about in this manner whenever a particular context fits. The full story need not be told; vignettes and reminders of the humorous parts are sufficient and act as metonyms so that listeners recall the whole and make the connections.

This use of indexical expressions, often but not always accompanied by gesture, is a distinct characteristic of language use at Fort Belknap regardless of which languages are being used. It serves to emphasize constantly both membership in the community and connected local histories via the use of local knowledge about persons, places, and events. Unfortunately many non-Indian educators fail to understand this and find Indian children "inarticulate" in school (cf. Labov 1968; Heath 1983). What is often referred to somewhat derogatorily by educators as "Indian English" or "reservation English" differs from more standard American English, at least in part, precisely because of this predominance of deictical terms expressed in both speech and gesture.[4] Silverstein (1987) has noted how establishing standard monoglot English as the purest, most natural English is a very effective way to discount the value of any non-standard English. Gesture, which does not even count as language in this view, is not on the whole part of an acceptable code of interaction in a school environment that promotes non-Indian norms and values regarding speech and comportment—unless, that is, PST itself is being highlighted as an acceptable performance of a Plains Indian identity (see Introduction). This cuts off an important ingredient of normal interaction for Plains Indian children, as they are expected to stand or sit still and look at the teacher rather than employ their own cultural norms wherein gestures are frequently used in interaction and eye contact is avoided out of respect for elders.[5]

POINTING

Gestures such as those involved in route directions and spatial orientation are usually glossed in English by the word "pointing," but little attention has been paid to potential complexities and cross-cultural differences in what seems, on the surface, to be the most simple, direct, and probably universally understood means of denotative reference. In PST, pointing gestures that look the same predominate as pronouns, adverbs of time and space, and demonstratives. Grammatical organization and understanding, however, depend upon conventions and contexts that distinguish different kinds of pointing. Before proceeding to a closer examination of these organizational features in Plains Sign Talk and Nakota, brief mention of some Euro-American presuppositions about pointing will serve to clarify some of the issues involved.

In the epigraph at the start of this chapter, Wittgenstein's statement questions a general assumption that the meaning of pointing is transparent and probably universal. Just as we might reasonably question which end of a signpost we are meant to follow, we can also ask how we can know which end of an arm to follow in a pointing gesture—and indeed whether the arm is acting as an indicator of direction or doing something else. For example, the elbow could be the active part doing the pointing. We have sufficient ethnographic evidence about the semantics involved in taxonomies of the body and its parts to know that such things differ enormously across cultures, and La Barre (1947), Pouwer (1973), and Williams (1980b), among others caution against making assumptions about actions that look the same.

Even if pointing in the sense of directing attention to a particular place or object is the intended aim, it cannot be assumed that the body part used will be the hand. A preferred alternative to a pointing index finger in many Native American communities, for example, is the use of the lips, a gesture which is often invisible to non-Indians and therefore a source of confusion (cf. La Barre 1947; Sherzer 1973; Van Winkle 1983). The performative value of this gesture lies in its potential for discretion as a smaller and less obvious gesture, often serving to preserve a degree of intimacy between speaker and addressee that would be lost if a finger-pointing gesture or speech were used instead. For example, one of my Nakota teachers had a fifteen-year-old granddaughter whose boyfriend, of whom she did not approve, kept arriving to visit. The grandmother never refused the youth entry to her house or said anything, but as he passed by she would sign her disapproval to his back in my view alone, saying HIM/THAT ONE (lip gesture) + BAD (a quick spreading of the fingers, tips and palm directed toward the person or thing). The same lip gesture also serves a pragmatic function in myriads of circumstances whenever both hands are otherwise engaged in a task such as preparing food, washing dishes, holding a child, working on a car, or beating a drum.

While it might seem to be the case that pointing to an object with an extended index finger is transparent in its meaning, without contextual information the act is, in fact, entirely ambiguous: how does one distinguish between pointing to the shape rather than to the color, the texture, or the smell, for example (see Wittgenstein 1958:36)? In PST, there is a special sign that acts as a classifier for COLOR. It is often used prior to

Photo 5.1. Rose Weasel touches her nose in reference to I/ME/MYSELF.

pointing at an object when it is the color that is being denoted rather than the object itself or some other attribute.

Neither is it necessarily the case that pointing is unambiguously interpreted as an intended directional guide for one's gaze. For example, the Chesareks (1988), educators from the Crow Reservation in Montana, report a school situation in which a non-Indian teacher used a pointer on the blackboard. Non-Indian pupils looked at the end of the pointer. Indian pupils, in contrast, looked at the face of the teacher, ignoring the pointer. To these Crow students, who live in a culture where the act of pointing directly is considered rather rude, it was not at all obvious what the pointer was for.

Neither is a pointing gesture as a referral to self unambiguous. In Japan (and sometimes among Plains Indians), for example, a reference to self is achieved by touching an index finger to the nose rather than the chest, a gesture that according to Western convention would probably be interpreted as a reference to the nose itself. In PST, a flat hand placed against the center of the chest, which a Euro-American might interpret as a reference to self, is a PST sign that means PEOPLE.

An examination of the way in which deaf children acquire first- and second-person pronouns provides further evidence of the conventional nature of pointing. Bellugi and Klima (1982), citing the work of E. Clark (1977), discuss the difficulty that hearing children have in learning that terms like "I" and "you" involve shifting reference. Children at first assume that "I" is an alternative to a person's name and that "you" is a reference to themselves. Later the child learns a stable self-other reference through the use of shifting pronominal terms. Studying the language acquisition of deaf children with deaf parents, Bellugi and Klima expected that given the apparent directness of first- and second-person pronominal signs in ASL (an index finger pointing toward the actor's chest and toward the addressee, respectively), there would be no evidence of the problems caused by spoken language shifting terms. They were therefore surprised to find that with two-year-old deaf children, mothers used name signs in addition to, or instead of, pronominal forms. When asked why, deaf parents reported instances of misunderstanding on the part of the child. If the mother signed, for example, I WASH YOU, the child attempted to wash the mother as if misunderstanding the mother's pronoun references. Bellugi and Klima concluded that the deaf child overlooks the simplicity of reference of the pointing gesture because pointing signs in ASL share formal properties (of handshape, location, and movement) with other ASL signs; there is nothing in their form that singles them out as different. The child in the early stages of acquiring signs assumes that the pointing sign (ME) directed to his or her own chest is a formal name, perhaps an alternative name for MOTHER. Evidence suggests that the acquisition of deictic terms in deaf children parallels that of hearing children: the apparent directness of reference does not seem to lead them more quickly into mastery of such forms; they ignore the apparent iconicity available to them (Bellugi and Klima 1982:309).

As in the case of ASL, pointing in PST is a conventional feature of a system, a part of the grammar of the language that performs several syntactic and semantic functions. When signs and speech are being used simultaneously, however, deictic expressions in spoken form do not always coincide with a pointing gesture; the relationship is more complex than this.

For example, one can say in words "This woman [was] over there" while signing WOMAN + SITTING. The sign for the verb TO BE SITTING would be inflected to include the spatial location "over there," that is, the sign would be performed in the "over there" space (see example in Chap. 6, sentence 6). There is no need for the addition of a pointing gesture to indicate the space in question. Instead, the action of an object or person being referred to can be represented in a verb sign that is itself inflected and located in the desired space.

In most English-speaking communities, in response to a question such as "Where did you put the scissors?" one can answer equally well by pointing to the table instead of—or in addition to—giving a vocal reply. The act of pointing in this case is a direct alternative to the act of speaking the words "Over there on the table" and the two are synonymous: "here pointing is part of the language game" (Wittgenstein 1958:169). The problem that stems from this simple observation is that the vocal component of such a response is labeled "verbal" and acknowledged to be part of a complex symbol system we call spoken language, but the gestural component is defined only in terms of what it apparently is not—that is, as "nonverbal"—or it is at best given a peripheral status, as in the term "paralinguistic."

The anthropological problem lies in the fact that while Anglo-Saxon and derived cultures make only minimal use of such body movement in everyday interaction, such is obviously not the case among the Assiniboine and probably many other cultures in the world. For example, in the Fort Belknap community it would be perfectly reasonable for both the question and the answer to the scissors question to be encoded in gesture rather than speech if there were any noise going on, if other people were conversing in the room, or if there were any distance between speaker and hearer such that voices would have to be raised. It would not be uncommon for speech and action to be used simultaneously if such conditions were not the case. This raises questions as to whether or not current definitions of language adequately accommodate these kinds of ethnographic facts.

Pointing or indicating, when encoded in spoken language form, is achieved through syntactical features relevant to the context of utterance, such as demonstratives, pronouns, and adverbs of time and space. These devices point to, or locate, persons, places, and times and relate them to the spatio-temporal context of the speech event itself. These features were introduced in Chapter 1 as indexical features of language, or shifters, to use Jakobson's term ([1957] 1971). "Deixis," the technical term in linguistics that refers to these features, is a Greek word that means "pointing" or "indicating" (see Lyons 1977:636).[6]

It is only in a metaphorical sense, however, that the concept has been used by linguists, the act itself being excluded from subsequent Western definitions of language and language-in-use. While deixis in spoken language is considered a verbal surrogate for pointing, in a sign language such as PST (and also ASL; see Bellugi and Klima 1982:299) it *is* pointing.

DEICTIC SPACE/TIME IN PST AND NAKOTA

Nakota deictic space can be thought of as falling into three zones horizontally (see Fig. 5.6). Demonstrative pronouns, for example, express proximal, distal, and extradistal areas, or, as Franz Boas put it, "here, there, and there visible so that it can be pointed at" (Boas and Deloria 1941:2). If we set aside standard spoken language categories such as demonstratives, pronouns, and adverbials and categorize according to spatial criteria, we see that in the Nakota deictic space these three zones are remarkably consistent (see Fig. 5.7). Proximal space is marked by a series of words all beginning with *ne,* and all terms dealing with near space use this root. Likewise, all gestures referring to near space either with or without vocal accompaniment are performed closest to the body itself. References to "here" or "this" do not always require a gesture for locating (as "over there" does), however, because the body itself marks the reference point.

Distal or "there" space consistently uses terms beginning with *že* and corresponding PST signs refer to and reach into a space farther from the body than the *ne* space. The extradistal or far but visible space uses

HERE (Near space and time)		THERE (Medium distance away)		YONDER (Far but visible space)	
ne	this, this one	*że*	that, that one	*ka*	(that) over there
nejs	this, this one	*żéjs*	that, that one (it)	*kájs*	that over there
nen	here	*żen*	there	*kan*	over there
nec'i	here, over here, this	*żéc'i*	there	*kák'i*	over yonder
nec'iya	this way, toward this place, over here	*żec'iya*	that way, in that direction, over there	*kakiya*	yonder, toward yonder place
nec'iyatahą	through here, from (over) here	*żec'iyatahą*	from (over) there (*ya*/*u*—going/coming)	*kakiyatahą*	from yonder, over there in that direction
nec'en	here, over here, thus, this way, like this, in this manner	*żec'en*	then, so, after that	*kák'en (ken)*	over there
netam	over here, this way	*żetam*	over there, that way	*katam*	over that way
nec'etuh	so, this way	*żec'etu*	like that		
nec'a	then (near time), this kind, one like this, similar to	*żec'a*	that kind, thus		
		żec'a u	so it was (thus it used to be)		
nena	these here (plural of *ne*)	*żena*	those	*kana*	those there
netamya	go this way	*żetamya*	go that way		
netam u	come this way	*że u*	thus (use), that kind		
netahą	from here (this time/place)	*żec'enżehą*	then		
		żehą	that, then		
netu	right here	*etahą żehą*	from then, after that		
netun(a)	near here	*żehąta*	then, after that (time)		
ąpa ne(n)	today, this day	*żehąc'ehą*	then, in those times		
estena nen	soon	*żetahą*	from there (that time/place)		
n(e) iyuha	all of these	*żena (k'o)*	those (too)		
nehąkamnįkte I'm going this far		*żehąkamnįkte* I'm going that far			

Figure 5.6. Deictic terminology in Nakota.

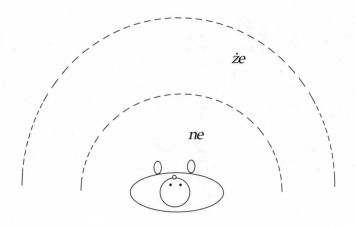

ka

że

ne

ne   - near space/time (here/now)

że   - farther space/time (there/then)

ka   - far and visible space/time

(also *t'ehą* far nonvisible distance and
wanąkaś time beyond memory)

Figure 5.7. Deictic zones in Nakota and Plains Sign Talk.

ka, although PST signs relating to this group do not necessarily reach out of the comfortable signing space in front of the torso during performance, because this is a relative rather than an actual positioning. Figure 5.6 shows the consistency of this structure in spoken language terms when applied to demonstratives and adverbials of space and time. Given this consistency, it is hardly surprising to find that these three zones of horizontal space are maintained in the gesture system.

This zoning should not be understood as referring to absolute distances; these are relative terms, just as "this" simply refers to something nearer than "that" does in English. The same kind of flexibility occurs with *ne* and *že* as they are used to indicate nearness of time. Something mentioned in near time will be "this," as opposed to something mentioned in further away time, either later or earlier, which will be referred to as "that."

Additional work is required of these two terms in Nakota because third-person pronouns are unmarked, and so *ne* and *že* often act like pronouns in the sense of indicating "this one" or "that one." (They are also sometimes accompanied by *įš*, which seems to act as a definite article, creating *ne įš* and *že įš.*)

Spoken Nakota, like English, often combines space and time, and this too is paralleled in gesture. Thus, *étu* 'close' refers to both near space and near time, and the PST sign is performed in near space and moves toward this zero point of the deictical coordinates, the here and now of the body itself. The same gesture means *ésten* 'soon/right away'.

Likewise the word *t'éhą* 'far away' refers to either a long time or far distance, and there is one gesture that can be used for both. (There is also an additional variation that refers to long distance only, see Chap. 3, sentence 18.) In these cases the *ka* or far space in the general signing space is not used, perhaps because *t'éhą* refers to invisible rather than to visible distance. The same gesture is also used with the word *wanąkaš* meaning "a long time ago," and in storytelling it is often used in a similar manner to the way "once upon a time" is used to begin European stories. A shortened version of this gesture is often used as a past time or completed action marker. These forms thus offer a fourth category to Nakota deixis, one that does not participate in this zoning of space. It is a category dealing with far distance that is not visible and time that is beyond memory.

PST, like spoken Nakota, is a language in which verbs are not marked for tense and so the time of an action or state is not indicated. The "when" of events can be dealt with instead through separate words or phrases such as "yesterday," "today," "tomorrow," and "soon," all of which are deictic because they locate time in relation to the here and now (the space/time) of the actor. Spoken verbs, but not PST verbs, can be marked in one of two ways that in the past have been labeled as past/present and future tenses (e.g., Buechel 1939:31). Today, linguists recognize this two-part distinction as a concern with aspect rather than tense: what is important is whether the job is completed or in progress, not when it was done. Verb forms mark completed or ongoing action or states in one form and potential or hypothetical action or states in a second form through the addition of the enclitic *kta* (Taylor and Rood 1972:3–11). PST does not encode this distinction in the same way, but maintains an emphasis upon aspect as completed and incompleted action.

Some of the ways in which dealing with "time" in Nakota differs from Euro-American conceptions can be illustrated by comparing PST with ASL, the sign language used by many deaf communities in America. ASL provides a useful contrasting case because it illustrates visually concepts relating to time held by American culture and English speakers generally.

When we locate time in space, we say the future is "ahead of us," or "in front of us" and the past lies "behind us," whereas the present is "here." In ASL, signs relating to the future are performed in front of the signer's body; those dealing with the past are located behind, over the shoulder of the signer, and those relating to the present are level with the signer's body. This is frequently referred to as the "time line" by ASL researchers, and time signs or time indicators have relative locations on this time line that agree with their meaning (Baker and Cokely 1980:176). The direction of movement of each time sign indicates its relation to present time, so, for example, FEW DAYS FUTURE goes forward in space, whereas FEW DAYS PAST goes backward, and the greater the distance from the body the greater the distance in time from the present (see Fig. 5.8). ASL may appear iconic and occasionally transparent to the casual observer, precisely because it is a visual realization of the same kind of spatio-temporal conceptions that occur in spoken English (see also Friedman 1975 and Farnell 1985). Time is taken to be iconic by speakers of English, that is, we assume there really is such a thing as time and that it naturally consists of past, present, and future. ASL achieves a double iconicity in this sense by actually placing time as a line in the signing space.

In contrast to ASL, PST employs no line of "time," and completed,

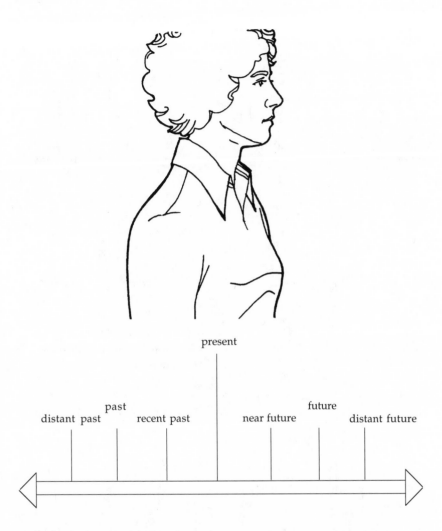

Figure 5.8. The "Time Line" of American Sign Language (ASL): signs that refer to present time are located close to the signer's body. The direction of movement of each sign indicates its relation to present time. Signs that refer to future time move forward, while signs that refer to past time move backward. From Baker and Cokely 1980:176. Used by permission of Gallaudet University Press.

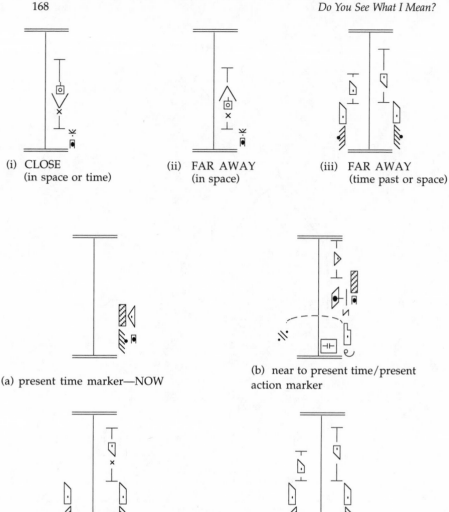

(i) CLOSE
     (in space or time)

(ii) FAR AWAY
      (in space)

(iii) FAR AWAY
       (time past or space)

(a) present time marker—NOW

(b) near to present time/present
     action marker

(c) past time marker—SHORT TIME AGO

(d) past time marker—LONG TIME AGO

Figure 5.9. Some time/space markers in Plains Sign Talk. Note that (i) and (ii) are a minimal pair, differing only in the direction of the movement toward or away from the signer. The PST sign TODAY is formed with (a) and (b). Either (b) or MORNING (sun rises east), followed by (a) indicates TOMORROW, and (b) plus (c) combine to designate YESTERDAY.

Photo 5.2. This series of still frames show aspects of the PST sign LONG TIME AGO. The distance the left hand travels diagonally back away from the right indicates the length of time or distance away from the present.

ongoing, and potential action are referenced rather than the "when" of events. There is a NEAREST TO PRESENT TIME/ONGOING ACTION marker that is specified with a raised index finger and I have glossed it as NOW, but it can also mean HERE and ONE (see Fig. 5.9). Used on its own it can refer to TODAY/PRESENT ACTION, or a second sign can be added that cannot be glossed accurately in words but would appear to represent NEAR TO PRESENT TIME/PRESENT ACTION over a longer period of about a DAY. The hands spread apart in front of the torso with the palms upward, laying out an area for action, as it were. The compound sign therefore has the sense of THIS (NOW/HERE) + DAY. This NEAR TO PRESENT TIME/ONGOING ACTION sign appears alone, however, in the translation of the English and Nakota words for "tomorrow." Here it would appear to mean the next appropriate occasion to do something rather than the English conception of tomorrow as a fixed twenty-four-hour period that follows today. As in the spoken language, potential action is being marked, not "future time." "Tomorrow" can also be represented in signs by a compound of MORNING (sun rises—homonymous with EAST) and NOW/HERE/ONE, meaning the next morning. The same NEAR TO PRESENT TIME/ONGOING ACTION or DAY sign also occurs in the sign for YESTERDAY together with the short PAST TIME/COMPLETED ACTION marker mentioned above.

As mentioned earlier, time and space frequently coincide in Nakota as they do in English, and so length is a metaphor for duration (i.e., a short time ago, a long time ago). In PST a diagonal line marks this conception, a short path of movement indicating a short time ago or recently completed action, a longer movement path indicating a long time ago or a far distance away. These are, however, linked to completed action, to events that happened then or there.

A minimal pair distinguished by direction and length of movement occurs in the signs for CLOSE/SOON (space and time), which comes toward the body of the signer, and FAR DISTANCE (space only), which utilizes the same handshape but moves away from the body, the length of the movement indicating the distance.

Preliminary analysis of data suggests that in contrast to spoken Nakota grammar—which, as mentioned above, has an unmarked verb form to represent present or completed action and a marked form for potential/hypothetical action (the enclitic *kta*)—PST marks completed action with the TIME PAST/COMPLETED ACTION marker (that always starts an utterance) and leaves present and potential action unmarked. If conversation and the wider context leave the distinction unclear and a distinction is necessary, then an explicit marker such as a sign for TODAY, TOMORROW, MORNING, or EVENING can be used.

The position and movements of the sun define both cardinal directions and times of day in spoken Nakota and PST. Thus signs for MORNING, NOON, and EVENING are homonyms of the signs for the directions EAST, SOUTH, and WEST. That fact brings us full circle back to the four directions and to a place where this chapter might conclude.

I have explored how a symbolic form like the four directions acts as an implicit yet potent organizing principle that permeates many aspects of everyday life for members of the Fort Belknap community. It acts as a potential resource for meaning making and illustrates a structuring of lived experience that occurs through the use of indexical expressions, both gestural and spoken. I have implied that a focus on indexicality allows us to include such forms within processes of social action and interaction rather than being relegated to the status of static cultural symbol on the one hand or internal cognitive structure on the other. Such forms are, rather, resources for action that give particular cultural shape to deixis—to spatial organization, spatial orientation, and social interaction—through frames of reference both bodily centered and constant. I also took Wittgenstein's suggestion seriously and explored how a deictic gesture such as pointing, frequently assumed to be an unproblematic universal, works as a conventional feature of a specific grammar that performs several syntactic and semantic functions. As with place names and visual imagery, again it seems to be the case that spoken Nakota and PST both provide resources which, while not identical, integrate to achieve successful deictic reference.

Chapter 6

The central issue [in deixis] is thus not whether meaning is left to context, but how it is and how it is reintegrated.

ROBERT J. JARVELLA AND WOLFGANG KLEIN (1982:1)

STORYTELLING AND THE EMBODIMENT OF SYMBOLIC FORM

Alongside Highway 2 between the reservations of Fort Peck and Fort Belknap lie two very large solid pieces of stone, called "medicine rocks" by some.[1] For non-Indians the roadside point of interest is a highway tourist stop and a hot springs camping resort. For Native Americans the rocks are of sacred significance and it is appropriate to stop when passing and offer a prayer, leaving behind some tobacco (a cigarette perhaps) or money.[2] One rock has the shape of a buffalo, and is known as Sleeping Buffalo Rock; the other, of indeterminate shape, has ancient petroglyphs carved into the stone that include a representation of a right hand and a circular design.

So far, it is the four cardinal directions that have formed a focus for my discussions of deixis and spatial orientation, but it must now be emphasized that these are inseparable from, and one aspect of, an all-encompassing circle. The resultant combined form is that which is represented on the rock. As a design element, it is realized in myriads of different visual forms and colors in the intricate beadwork of women's and men's dance costumes and regalia, such as a quilled or beaded hair ornament attached to an eagle feather or on a fur- or hide-covered ring sometimes held by men while dancing. It is also a form that appears in Plains visual graphic art, a published example of which can be found in Standing Bear's drawing "Black Elk under the Tree of Life" in Neihardt ([1932] 1972).

A succinct description of the symbolism of the circle among the Oglala Sioux, which largely coincides with Assiniboine conceptions, was given by Tyon to Walker:

Photo 6.1. A petroglyph on Sleeping Buffalo Rock illustrates the four directions within the circle.

The Oglala believe the circle to be sacred because the Great Spirit caused everything in nature to be round except stone. Stone is the implement of destruction. The sun and the sky, the earth and the moon, are round like a shield, though the sky is deep like a bowl. Everything that breathes is round like the body of a man. Everything that grows from the ground is round like the stem of a plant. Since the Great Spirit has caused everything to be round mankind should look upon the circle as sacred, for it is the symbol of all things in nature except stone. It is also the symbol of the circle that marks the edge of the world and therefore of the four winds that travel there. Consequently it is also the symbol of the year. The day, the night, and the moon go in a circle above the sky. Therefore the circle is a symbol of these divisions of time and hence the symbol of all time.

For these reasons the Oglala make their tipis circular, and sit in a circle in all ceremonies. The circle is also the symbol of the tipi and of shelter. If one makes a circle for an ornament and it is not divided in any way, it should be understood as the symbol of the world and of time. If however, the circle be filled with red, it is the symbol of the sun; if filled with blue it is the circle of the sky. If the circle is divided into four parts, it is the symbol of the four winds;

Photo 6.2. A woman's "shawl" on "fancy" dancer at Fort Belknap powwow, July 1990, displays the symbol of the 'four directions within the circle' beaded with shiny sequins on the dance costume.

if it is divided into more than four parts, it is the symbol of a vision of some kind. If a half circle is filled with red it represents the day; filled with black, the night; filled with yellow, a moon or month. On the other hand, if a half circle is filled with many colors, it symbolizes the rainbow. One may paint or otherwise represent a circle on his tipi or his shield or his robe. The mouth of a pipe should always be moved in a circle before the pipe is formally smoked. (Tyon, quoted in Walker 1917:160)

Given the widespread importance of the circle in many Native American cultures, it is not surprising to find that the circle, like the four directions, is well represented in storytelling performances among the Assiniboine, and also permeates many spheres of everyday contemporary life, including social interaction.

For example, children in the bilingual program in the third grade at Hays School on Fort Belknap Reservation (the only curriculum space in which aspects of Native American traditions manage to intrude) created an art display with "The Circle" as a theme, among which were the following captions:

Earth is round.

Sky is round.

Sun comes forth and goes down in a circle, Moon does the same as Sun, both are round.

Seasons form a circle in their changing.

Stars are round.

Sun-Dance Lodge is also a circle.

The Flowering Tree was the center of the hoop. The circle of the four quarters nourished it.

Life of man is a circle from childhood to childhood.

Birds make their nests in a circle.

Wind whirls.

Tepees are round and are always set in a circle.

Prayer circles made of stones, with a cross in the middle, are very old.

East gave peace and light; North gave strength and endurance; South gave warmth; West gave rain.

It would be a mistake to think of this paradigmatic symbol as merely a static visual image with some religious associations. Instead it is a dynamic one, central to ritual action and dance forms, but dynamic also in the sense that it has many layers of meaning and is open to a host of imaginative interpretations and applications, one aspect of which can be seen through its employment in oral narrative.

In order to continue the investigation into the embodiment of deixis through gesture, this chapter looks at how the grammatical structure of PST and the storytelling context both utilize and creatively contribute to the semantics of such a paradigmatic structure. I have chosen to examine two narratives, performed with both PST signs and speech. The Labanotation text of the first narrative has been omitted here but can be examined together with the videotape record of the performance on the CD-ROM that has been produced in conjunction with this book.[3]

The first narrative is an Assiniboine story about the division of winter and summer months, and comparison with some features of the Judeo-Christian origin story highlights certain fundamental differences in worldview and social structure. It is one of many tales among the Assiniboine that involve a "trickster" character whose name is Inktomi. The PST sign for this name is synonymous with LIAR, a visual representation of the stereotypical "you speak with forked tongue" metaphor. This sign can mean *iyąktomic* 'you're telling a lie', or *knaya* 'you fooled him'. Outside of storytelling, this action sign can be used as an aside during arguments when it seems to provide a more subtle retort than calling someone a liar in spoken words. This is more than simply code-switching from words to signs: it is a manipulation that is part of the code of language-in-use itself (Herzfeld 1982:209). In a different context, the same action sign—or the spoken name "Inktomi"—can be used in a joking fashion by either perpetrator or victim whenever a person has tricked or is trying to trick another, or by observers when someone is playing the fool. The essential difference in the latter context is that it

Photo 6.3. A still frame taken from video catches Earthboy making the sign INKTOMI. This sign is synonymous with LIAR: a visual metaphor that refers to speaking sideways and with a "forked tongue" if not telling the truth.

will be performed in such a way as to be seen or heard clearly by the addressee. Obviously it is not the lexical item itself but the manipulation of its use in either medium that indicates the degree of social harmony or lack of it.

This use of signs as a more appropriate alternative to speech in certain contexts may be connected to religious beliefs. According to Assiniboine theology, benevolent spirits do not like loud noises or loud people, and quiet behavior and silence are valued in order not to drive such spirits away. Regardless of an individual's knowledge of, or adherence to, this belief, the sound level of Assiniboine conversation is usually softer than that of non-Indian Americans. It is noticeable too that some consultants drop the volume of their speech considerably when switching from English to Nakota. There is no doubt that the use of signs instead of speech contributes to this preferred quiet aesthetic (cf. Basso 1969). It may have been a factor in the past that led to the use of signs at large public gatherings in order to avoid raising the voice— although, on a practical level, sign talking carries much farther than sounds in the open air.

In Assiniboine mythology, Inktomi was responsible for creating the earth with the help of various animals after a flood.[4] While certainly involved in the creation and ordering of the natural, social, and moral worlds, Inktomi is not an omnipotent or omniscient being, nor an ultimate cause, like the Judeo-Christian God, but rather a funny and foolish character who is always getting into trouble through trying to outwit the other animals (cf. Radin 1959). Inktomi is only too prone to human foibles and failings but a creature whose identity has neither clearly human form nor that of any particular animal (in contrast to similar tales among other tribes—the Cheyenne, for example, where Coyote takes on the same role).[5] Inktomi is, however, able to change into many different forms in order to trick people. In the narrative told here, Inktomi is given a (male) human form, information that is only apparent through the PST signs, a point to which I will return below.

This particular story takes place at a time before the existence of any people on the earth, and Inktomi is suffering from the constant heat during a very hot spring. He calls all the animals (the four-leggeds) and the birds (the winged ones) to come and settle the matter of how many months of cold and how many months of hot weather there should be. The animals arrive, seating themselves around a large circle, and the discussion begins.

Problems arise because the animals from the cold country want the weather cold, whereas the animals from the hot country want it to remain hot. Inktomi tells them that there are twelve moons and he suggests six hot and six cold, but asks what it is that they want. They debate over the outcome and cannot reach a decision. A little frog sitting next to Inktomi interrupts to say that seven moons shall be his. After seven months of winter he will croak and it will then be spring. Inktomi ignores the frog, telling him he is nobody. The animals and birds continue to debate the issue and still fail to reach a decision. Inktomi suggests

Photo 6.4. "The seventh moon shall be mine," says the frog. This still frame captures the handshapes used in the number SEVEN.

that there should only be as many months of winter as there are hairs on his scabby buffalo robe, but that is not accepted either.

The discussion continues, without resolution. The little frog pipes up again, saying the seven moons will be his, and Inktomi tells him to be quiet and sit there! More debating and quarreling go on and again the frog makes his plea. Inktomi, impatient by now, looks at him and cracks him over the head, knocking him out. The poor frog holds out seven fingers as a final plea before he loses consciousness. Inktomi relents and feels sorry for what he has done to the frog, saying, "You are pitiful, but you beat me," and he gives him the seventh moon. So that is why nowadays, from the time when there are no leaves, one can count seven moons and then the little frog will call to bring the summer.

Įktomi, T'apeħana Mnoketu Kaġapi	Inktomi and the Frog Make the Seasons
Mąk'oc'e Hokśina woknaka	Told by James Earthboy

1. Waną—kaś

   wįc'aśta takuni mąk'a akan
   úpiśį.

2. Įktom įsnana
   nen ų́ka.

3. Maśta mnoketu ne
   tohani inażiśį.

4. Wa įs tákuniśį ka.

5. E'ec' wókc'a yąka:ka.

6. "Ne
   waśteśįc'," eyaka
   "eyaś nína k'áta."

7. "Hąke įś
   osni ų́kś waśtektac'," eyaka.

8. Żéc'en pą́ka.

9. "Táku wamąk'aśka t'éhąn
   yaµpi ne
   u po," eyaka.

10. "Nąku tákukiyą yaµpi nejś
    iyuhana u po," eyaka.

11. "Néna wóµknakapiktac',"
    eyaka.

12. "Tákuwążi µknuśtąpi
    wac'įkac'," eyaka.

13. Żé'ec' awįc'akip'e yąka:ka.

1. Lo—ng ago

   there were no people on this
   earth.

2. Inktomi lived
   alone here.

3. The heat of the summer
   was never-ending.

4. There was no snow there.

5. So he sat thinking.

6. "This
   is no good," he said,
   "it's really hot."

7. "If it was half-cold
   it would be good," he said.

8. So he called loudly.

9. "All you animals that live far
   away
   come here!" he said.

10. "Also, you birds
    all of you come!" he said.

11. "We will discuss these things,"
    he said.

12. "One thing we want to settle,"
    he said.

13. Then he sat waiting for them.

14. Żé—'ec' tákunowa
    [wążikżina] hípi káyąka.

14. The—n everything began to
    arrive [one by one]
    and sat down over there.

15. Táku įś kiyą úpi iyuha įś
    iyahąpi ka.

15. All the winged creatures landed
    there.

16. T'ą̇—ka mimeya kák'ita
    yąkapika.

16. In a la—rge circle over there
    they were sitting.

17. Że įś Įktomi
    náżįka
    "súkapina," wíc'akiyaka.

17. Inktomi
    stood up.
    "Little brothers," he said to
    them.

18. "Ne ą́pa ne
    tákuwążi ųknuśtąpi
    wac'įkac'," eyaka.

18. "On this day
    we want to settle one thing," he
    said.

19. "Apa
    osni mąk'oc'e úpi en
    waśte ákinapic'," eyaka.

19. "Those of you

    who live in the cold country
    you are happy there," he said.

20. "Apa įś
    maśta mąk'oc'e
    en yaųpi en
    waśte ákinapic'."

20. "Those of you
    who live in the hot country
    you are happy there."

21. "Tuk'a żéc'en túkteśįc',"
    eyaka.

21. "But then there will be nobody
    [here]," he said.

22. "C'okankan tuktaś," eyaka

    "c'okam

    osni

    osnįktac'."

22. "Half and half, which shall it
    be," he said
    half-

    cold

    it will be half-cold."

23. "Hąke įś ak'e k'átįktac',"
    eyaka.

23. "Then half of it shall be hot
    again," he said.

24. "Ne hąwi ne
    ak'enųpac'," eyaka.

24. "These moons,
    there are twelve," he said.

25. "Že tóna osnįkte
omiyecinakapikta," eciyaka.

25. "How many shall be cold, you
will tell me," he said to them.

26. "Tóna įš
hąwi k'átįkta
omiyecinakapiktac',"
eyaka.

26. "How many
moons shall be hot, you will tell
me,"
he said.

27. E—'ec'
táku wamąk'aška kan
kįyą úpi néįš.

27. So—
over there were the animals
and the birds.

28. "Misųka

hąwi žénąke šten

maštac'
hąwi tóna įš osnįktac',"
eyaka.

28. "My little brothers

if that many moons

are hot
how many moons will be cold,"
he said.

29. Apa
osni mąk'oc'e éc'i úpi éc'i
waniyetu e t'é—hą c'įkapika
eyaka.

29. Some of them
who lived in the cold country
[north]
said they wanted winter for a
lo—ng time.

30. Žéhą apa
mašta mąk'oc'e en úpi že
"Hiya," iyapika.

30. Then those
who lived in the hot country
"No," they said.

31. Žéc'etu šten.

31. "If it is going to be that way."

32. "Tóna
mašta mąk'oc'e ekta uk'ųpi en
nutįųtapiktac'," eyapika.

32. "Those of us who live in the hot
country
will starve to death," they said.

33. Žec'en ak'inicapika.

33. So they were arguing over it.

34. Ne Įktomi yąke kakna néna
t'apehana wąži yąka t'okam.

34. Inktomi was sitting alongside
them all
while in front of him sat a little
frog.

35. "Mic'in
    tóna hąwi iyuśna nówa
    miye mit'awaktac'," eyaka.

36. "Hąwi įc'iiyuśna hą́ta
    wahotų hą́ta żen
    mnoketuktac'."

37. Įktom ak'itaka, "O tákeyeśį
    wo," eya.

38. "Ne nitakuniśį ne apapi ne
    anawįcawahųkta."

39. Żé'ec' wamąk'aśkana
    tákukiyą ų́pi ak'inįcapika.

40. "Néc'etu śten," eyaka Įktomi
    "tá—kunih ųknuśtąpikteśįc',"
    eyaka.

41. Śina wą́żih yuha
    t'at'ąka ha żéc'ac'.

42. Owa tók'iya nówa skuskuka

    hi żé'ec' cónąka
    cónąkah ha įk'oyaka

    Įktomi żeyaka.

43. "Ne
    śina mit'awa ne

    hi że ótaśįc'," eyaka.

44. "Hąwi że żénąka hą́ta
    mnoketuktac'," eyaka.

35. "My older brother
    when it is seven moons
    it will be all mine," he said.

36. "When it is the seventh moon
    when I call
    then it will be summer."

37. Inktomi looked at him
    "Oh shut up!" he said.

38. "You are nobody, I will listen to
    the others [around this
    circle]."

39. Then the animals
    the birds
    were arguing.

40. "If it is going to be this way,"
    said Inktomi
    "we will not settle a—nything,"
    he said.

41. He had a robe
    the kind made of buffalo fur.

42. In places all over it there were
    bare patches,

    "On the hide there is only a
    little bit
    a little bit of hair,"

    Inktomi said.

43. "This
    robe of mine

    does not have much hair," he said.

44. "When there are that many
    moons
    it will be summer," he said.

45. Nąka apa

    wamąk'aśka ceyaka, "Hiya,"
    eyaka.

46. "Mic'in
    że hi że ha ótac'," eyaka.

47. "Żéhąka osni hą́ta apapi
    nówa
    nutiųt'apiktac'," eyaka.

48. "Mnoketu né'e hą́ska hįk
    waniyetu ne
    p'téc'ena ųkś waśtektac',"
    eyaka.

49. Żéyapi żéc'en.

50. Osni mąk'oc'e ekta táku úpi,
    "Hiya," eyaka.

51. "Żéc'e túkteśį," c'eyaka.

52. "Osni hąwi żé'e hą́ska śteń
    tayą́ktac'," eyaka.

53. Żéc'en ak'e t'apeńana ne
    "Hiya," eyakayac'.

54. "Hąwi iyuśna śten
    mit'awaktac'," eyaka.

55. Żé'ec' Įktomi żeyakaya,
    "Takeyeśį yąka wo," eyaka.

56. É—c'en ak'e wamąk'aśkana
    tákukiyą úpi
    ak'inįcapika.

45. Now some

    of the animals cried out, "No,"
    they said.

46. "My older brother
    that hide has a lot of hair on it,"
    they said.

47. "If it is cold that long some of
    us will all
    starve to death," they said.

48. "If the summer was long
    and the winter short
    it would be good," they said.

49. Then those over there said.

50. Those who lived in the cold
    country said, "No."

51. "It cannot be that way," they
    cried.

52. "If the cold moons are long it
    would be good," they said.

53. Then again the little frog
    was saying, "No."

54. "When it is the seventh moon it
    shall be mine," he said.

55. So then Inktomi said to him,
    "Be quiet and sit there!" he said.

56. So— again the animals
    the birds
    were arguing.

57. Įknuhanaȟ akʼe tʼapeȟana ne
    żeyaka,
    "Hą̇wi iyuśna hą́ta
    miye mitʼawaktacʼ," eyaka.

57. Suddenly again
    the little frog said,
    "When it's the seventh moon
    it shall be mine," he said.

58. Įktom akʼitaka pʼaenapʼaka
    kasuta įȟpaya.

58. Inktomi looked at him
    hitting him on the head
    knocking him down stiff.

59. Tʼapeȟana ną̇pe ne iyuśna
    pazo.

59. The little frog's hands showed
    seven [fingers].

    [laughter]

60. Įktom akʼitaka. "E— únisike
    no mayaktenacʼ," eyaka.

60. Inktomi looked at him. "O—h
    you are pitiful
    but you beat me!" he said.

61. "Hą̇wi iyuśna cʼicʔuktacʼ,"
    eyaka.

61. "I will give you the seventh
    moon," he said.

62. Żécʼen ną̇ka.

62. So nowadays

63. Waȟpe tákunišį żetahą̇
    yawapi hą́ta
    hą̇wi że
    iyuśna hą́ta ne
    tʼapeȟana ne hotų̇ hą́ta
    mnoketucʼ
    żécʼetu hų̇stacʼ.

63. If you count from when there
    are no leaves
    that moon
    when it is the seventh one
    when the little frog calls out it is
    summer
    that is the way it was, it is said.

    [laughter]

The story thus accounts for the present division of the year into winter and summer, and does indeed mark distinct natural occurrences. The cottonwood trees, which in this area of the dry Plains are confined to creeks and the banks of the Milk River, all turn yellow and drop their leaves rapidly sometime in September, thereby heralding the onset of the long bleak winter months and the start of the traditional Assiniboine year. One of the first distinctive signs of spring once the snow and ice have melted is the chirping of tiny frogs in every little pond, temporary lake, and irrigation ditch. As with so many stories of the Inktomi genre, natural features and beings that inhabit the natural world are made a part of culture; that is, they are made familiar, ordered, and accounted for. A relationship with the rest of the natural world is recreated via this story each year when one hears the frogs calling. In Nakota the name of the moon that corresponds to March in the Euro-American calendar is *t'apeȟana hawi* 'frog's moon', and the PST sign is correspondingly a composite sign MOON + FROG.

Beyond this explicit theme, however, the tale provides a "charter" for appropriate social action, to borrow Malinowski's ([1948] 1954) phrase, although it must be mentioned that most of the Inktomi stories provide examples of what *not* to do. One learns via a negative and usually humorous example not to make the mistakes Inktomi has made, as illustrated here by the inappropriately intolerant attitude Inktomi shows toward the frog.

I want to draw particular attention to the circle that the animals form as they gather, an action sign that is so clearly described in space during Earthboy's narration. It creates an arena for face-to-face discussion among equals, a democratic process in which Inktomi takes part and attempts to gain consensus. This arrangement mirrors the ideal political forum of prereservation Assiniboine culture, when leaders had authority only insofar as they were good orators and able to persuade others to accept their point of view. Lowie tells us:

> The authority of a chief, as among most of the Plains tribes, was dependent on his personal characteristics, such as bravery, liberality, or the possession of *wak'ą* power. He erected his lodge in the center of the circle, and directed the movements of the camp. Only on the march and during the great tribal hunt was there a strong

executive force, vested in the *agitcita* [*akic'ita*], or soldiers, braves
in the prime of life, who, under the direction of the chief superin-
tended the camp from a large lodge (*wiyot'ipi*) in the center of the
circle. (Lowie 1909:35)[6]

This description provides us with an image of a social structure that
is a series of nested circles, beginning with the camp circle made up of
individual circular family lodges, in the center of which is a central lodge
that is also the council chamber, a circular political forum.

In contrast to the egalitarian and democratic relationship between
creator and the animal kingdom idealized in the Inktomi narrative, Figure 6.1 diagrams some essential contrasts between classifications in the
Judeo-Christian worldview and those of the Assiniboine. The Judeo-
Christian model presents a vertical schema in which the world was created by, and is under the auspices of, an omniscient and omnipotent
deity, an ultimate cause as well as a humanized benevolent father figure. Inktomi is no such authority, and although in part a creator, he plays
no role in religious practice.[7] Instead it is *wak'ą t'ą́ka*, a term often translated as "Great Spirit" but more accurately as "large mystery/holiness,"
that today is sometimes deemed to be the same as the Judeo-Christian
God. *Wak'ą t'ą́ka*, however, is a mysterious power without any manifest form (see DeMallie 1984:81; Walker 1917, 1980).

The Judeo-Christian tradition provides a model that creates a sharp
division between the natural world and the supernatural, the world of
matter and the world of the human spirit or soul. The natural world
contains both animals and humans, but humans, by virtue of a soul have
a special transcendental status, having been made "in God's image."
Language is a marker of this status and distinguishes humans from all
other animals. God gave humans a divine charter to rule over and use
the rest of the natural world for their own purposes.[8] In contrast, the
Inktomi story presents a worldview in which Inktomi (who is at least
partly responsible for the way the world is) and the animals are equals
in a circle. While Inktomi has some authority and does make the final
decision, he does so only after much debate and after failing in his responsibility to acknowledge the contribution of one of his little brothers, the frog. The solution is arrived at in response to a pitiful creature,
the wronged frog, thereby also emphasizing a religious belief that only

Judeo-Christian model

GOD
Omnipotent
Omniscient
"Father"

_____

Human
"In God's image"
Transcendent soul
Language

Vertical
hierarchy

_____

animal
No soul
No language

"Chain of being"

Assiniboine Model

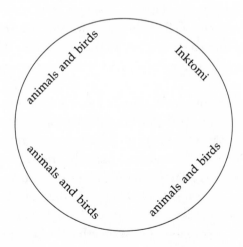

Figure 6.1. Assiniboine and Judeo-Christian models of relationships between the natural and human worlds.

when the supplicant is most pitiful will requests be answered, a fundamental rationale for the bodily suffering associated with the sun dance, for example.

Assiniboine conceptions—currently adhered to by a growing minority in a period of religious revitalization—involve a natural world that is infused with spirits whose power can assist or destroy and who often enlist the help of, or actually take the form of, animals. In the Assiniboine model, animals enjoy status equal (and occasionally superior) to that of humans as inhabitants of this world. Like the human *nagi* 'ghost/soul/spirit', they also travel after death to the other world.

Animals were able to talk in human fashion at the time of the narrative, but they now rarely have need for human language except when communicating explicitly with humans as spiritual helpers, although "talking" can take many visual forms also, as discussed earlier. Instead of language being a special attribute of humans that places them in a superior position relative to the rest of the animal kingdom, the view held by many Assiniboine people is that animals do not have language because they do not need it. They can communicate perfectly well without it. It is only imperfect humans who need such a device and who have to cope with ambiguity and misunderstanding because of it. Animals, who survive perfectly well on this earth without language, clothing, or fire are therefore to be respected, learned from, and appealed to for assistance, rather than controlled and used indiscriminately for human purposes.[9]

This narrative gives some indication of the significance of the circle (*mimeya* 'in a circle') as an appropriate form through which to express ideal political and social interaction, as well as being symbolic of an equal relationship between humans and animals, creator and created. Having established the large circle in the signing space, Earthboy henceforth used it for the arrangement of characters in the story. It thus provided an organization for referential gestures throughout the narrative and gave precise form to pronoun use and verb inflections in PST.

Before examining in detail some of these grammatical devices it is appropriate to mention briefly some other ways in which the idea of the circle enters into daily lived experience. Its importance for describing the nature of human relationships and a sense of loss due to the altered shape of contemporary living spaces can be seen through the following statement by another of my Assiniboine teachers, Emma Lamebull:

> After the white people came, they said, everything changed, you
> know, they're sitting there [the oldtimers] telling stories, they said
> everything changed, they said. Long ago, they said, everything we
> did in a circle, like in a tipi we always sat in a circle and looked at
> each other's faces. When we ate we sat in a circle. When we talked
> and visit each other, tell stories, we sat in a circle, and when we
> looked at each other [we] could tell when this person was feeling
> bad, what his feelings were 'cause you could see their faces. And
> after the white people came, well then they took our kids to school
> and instead of looking at each other, they're looking at the back, at
> the back of heads—you don't see their face no more, you don't
> know if they're feeling bad or, if they don't feel good you can't
> comfort them because you can't see their faces. And then the
> teacher stands up there, teaching you, and instead of trying to
> make you learn lessons, they teach you your lessons but they learn
> you how to compete—they learn you to be higher than this one—
> you study harder and you get A's and they do things for you
> because they learn you how to compete. Even these animals, we
> learn too, they learn their children to kill them when they need it—
> when they need to eat. When the white people came they turn that
> into competing—they wanna see who killed the biggest elk or the
> biggest buffalo or the longest fish, you know, and . . . they get
> recognized for doing the biggest things they killed you know, they
> don't think of the animal itself, what they're doing to them, and
> they learn the people how to compete against one another. And you
> see they turned our kids, teaching them like that and they said its
> sad the way some kids they don't even care now, or pay attention.
> It's hard to make them mind because now they went and bought
> homes like this one and they said, their brother's got TV and he's
> got his own room, sister's got TV and she's got her own room,
> parents got their own room—no more circle, they broke the circle.

Thus the circle was, and still is—though perceived as diminished through
architectural and social change—a powerful form for the organizing of
social relations and interaction in a very practical sense. It symbolizes

not only community and caring but a face-to-face noncompetitive ideal social world.

Some of those social changes are indeed highlighted by the shape of public gatherings. For example, at public events such as winter dances, family or community feeds, and hand games, people will always arrange chairs so that a circle is formed even though those events may take place in a rectangular recreation hall or gymnasium. Religious buildings such as the sun dance lodge and the sweat lodge are temporary structures built with local natural materials; the sun dance lodge is erected every year, while the sweat lodge is semipermanent or built as required by participants. These have been unaffected by the design of permanent structures built according to Euro-American engineering methods and materials.

In marked contrast to these kinds of long-standing public events that utilize the circle are others that have come about as a legacy of non-Indian impositions upon social structure. For example, political reorganization following the adoption of the 1934 Indian Act has led to a format similar to that of the state and federal systems: Native American representatives are now elected to serve four-year terms as politicians and bureaucrats on the tribal council. An entirely different use of these same rectangular halls can be found at political meetings or open committee meetings. On these occasions, chairs will be arranged in rows facing the front, where speakers will sit facing their audience.

That a similar arrangement is common at funeral wakes may seem to be a striking departure from the circle essential to traditional events, but funerals are a considerable departure from earlier customs. In prereservation Assiniboine culture, the dead were placed upon high scaffolds or in trees out on the prairie. Later the bones would be collected and buried, except for the skulls, which would be placed in a circle out on the plain (De Smet 1905:1141, quoted in Lowie 1909:42). It was only upon the insistence of the Catholic Church and an Indian agent in 1905 that interment came to be the norm (see also Rodnick 1938:12). So funerals, although certainly distinctive from those of non-Indians in ways too numerous to mention here, have taken on the spatial arrangement provided by the Christian church and funeral homes: rows of seats facing the "front" (i.e., a place rather than a surface or relationship).

In the storytelling context, the circular form is involved as an intricate component on three quite different levels: (1) as part of the narrative content of the story, (2) as a structuring device for the organization of characters and events, and (3) as a grammatical component of PST. All three levels can be examined using a short extract from the beginning of a narrative told by Mrs. Rose Weasel.

Unlike Earthboy's family experience, in which deafness played an important role in his learning of PST, Rose Weasel learned signs as a young girl sitting on the lap of her grandmother watching and listening to stories being told among friends, relatives, and visitors. Now eighty-four years of age, Mrs. Weasel still delights in telling these stories whenever an occasion presents itself, increasingly rare in these days of television and video. She is clearly delighted at my request to film her storytelling and by the following day has suggestions about designing the performance space especially for the camera. The living room sofa now sports a cheerful star quilt and there is a vibrant red blanket with beaded rosettes to hang on a wall and so provide an interesting backdrop. Her hair is neatly braided, and she looks particularly endearing in a new print dress, white shell earrings, and high-top moccasins that bear the bold design of the rose that is her namesake. Even though it means telling "nighttime" stories in the daytime, she assures me with a girlish laugh that violating the rule will probably only mean that I will get lost on the way back to town.

Her best audiences are her two daughters and son, who have heard these stories consistently since childhood, but other important listeners are close friends like Juanita Tucker (ninety-four years old). While daughter Josephine organizes her mother, I drive off to fetch Mrs. Tucker for a special visit. After some intense discussion about which story it should be, eventually we are all ready. "*Wana* [now]," says Josephine, "*Wana?*" says Mrs. Weasel, and her clear eyes sparkle as these aged but wondrously elegant hands begin to weave their delicate tones in space, merging with the colors and shades of her spoken voice.

Like the Inktomi genre, this is a nighttime story (*ohųkaka*), one with many episodes, and I shall focus on just the first section here. Normally (outside the ethnographer's gaze) it is the kind of story just perfect for a long Montana winter evening when the children are restless and need to be settled for sleep. Or perhaps some relatives have dropped by for a visit and the news and gossip (*owoknaka*) have been exhausted for now. Whether snuggled under the blankets in the first case, or gathered around

Wíyą Hokšipinųpa Wic'ałpi P'a en Yuk'apin

An excerpt from "The Woman and the Twin Boys Born with Stars on Their Foreheads"*

Nąpe Wak'ą Wíyą woknaka

Told by Rose Weasel

1. Žéįš
   oyate ka t'ípi hųšta
   kan.

1. So
   the people were camped over
   yonder they say
   over yonder.

2. Ka
   ne wíyą
   ne k'oška ne
   t'ąk'una kic'išnana t'i
   you know.

2. Over there
   this woman
   this young man
   and his sister lived alone
   together
   you know.

3. Įš nec'etu hénąk'aš.

3. It must have been this way.

   Iye ka k'oška ka t'i c'en.

   That one there, the young man
   lived over there.

4. Įš ne
   wíyą ne
   sųkaku
   sųkaku wok'u:ka.

4. So this one
   this woman
   her younger brother
   she was giving food to her
   younger brother.

5. Táku špayą hą́ta k'u hįk
   žéc'en k'oška ne yuta:ka.

5. When the food was cooked she
   gave it to him
   and the young man was
   eating it.

6. Wíyą néįš kak'i.

6. The woman was over there.

7. Atohą įš akic'ic'itapišį k'o
   žéc'en nų́pakiya wota:kapic'.

7. They were facing but did not
   look at each other
   then both were eating.

---

*On the CD-ROM that accompanies this book, WIYUTA: Assiniboine Storytelling with Signs, the title of this story has been abbreviated to "The Star Children."

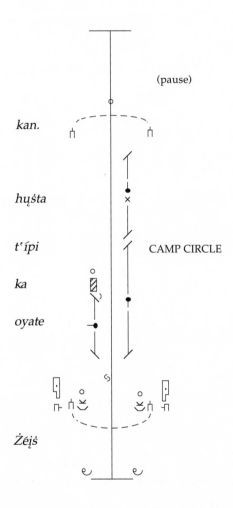

1. *Zéįš,   oyate ka   t'ípi   hu̧śta   kan.*
   That one tribe   over there they live it is said   over there
   So, the people were camped over yonder they say, over yonder.

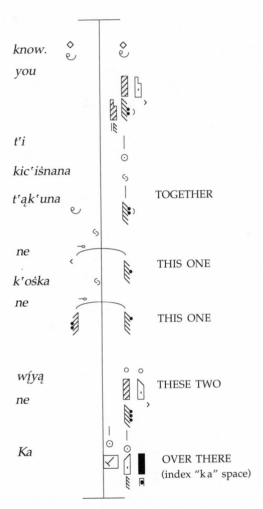

2. *Ka,   ne wį́yą,   ne k'oška   ne, t'ą́k'una*
   Over there this woman   this young man   this   sister
   Over there, this woman, this young man and his sister

   kic'išnana   t'i, you know.
   alone together live you know
   lived alone together, you know.

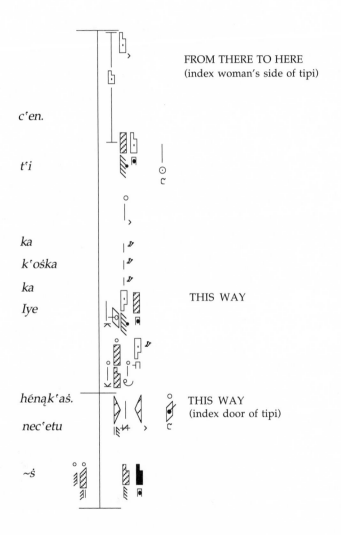

FROM THERE TO HERE
(index woman's side of tipi)

c'en.

t'i

ka

k'ośka

ka

Iye

THIS WAY

hénąk'aś.

nec'etu

THIS WAY
(index door of tipi)

~ś

3.　*~ś nec'etu　hénąk'aś.　　　Iye　ka　　k'ośka　　ka　t'i　c'en.*
　　This way　　must have been.　He　over there　young man　there　live
　　It must have been this way.　That one there, the young man lived over there.

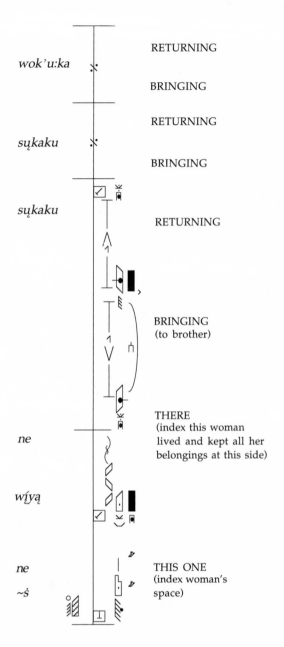

4. ~*ś ne,   wį́yą   ne,   sų̨kaku,   sų̨kaku   wok'u:ka.*
   This one woman this   younger brother   younger brother giving him food
   So this one, this woman, her younger brother, she was giving food to her
   younger brother.

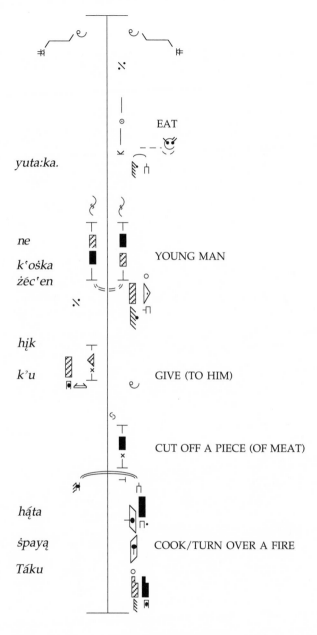

	EAT
yuta:ka.	
ne	
k'oṡka	YOUNG MAN
żéc'en	
hįk	
k'u	GIVE (TO HIM)
	CUT OFF A PIECE (OF MEAT)
hą́ta	
ṡpayą	COOK/TURN OVER A FIRE
Táku	

Táku ṡpayą	hą́ta k'u	hįk	żéc'en k'oṡka	ne	yuta:ka.
Something cooked	when gave him	and	then young man	this	eating

When the food was cooked she gave it to him and the young man was eating it.

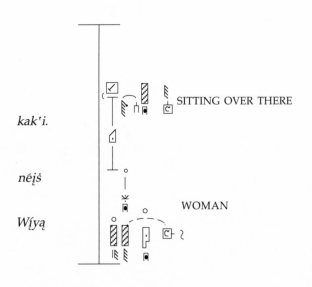

kak'i.

néįś

Wíyą

6. *Wíyą   néįś   kak'i.*
    Woman this one over there
    The woman was over there.

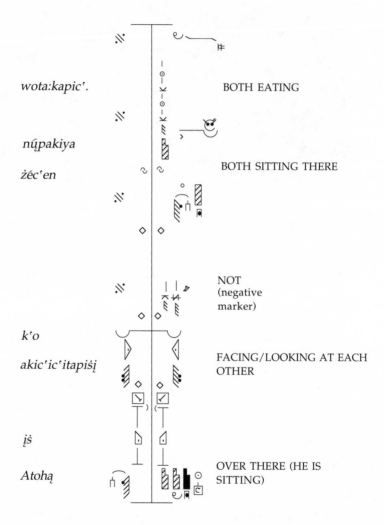

wota:kapic'.		BOTH EATING
nų́pakiya		
žéc'en		BOTH SITTING THERE
		NOT (negative marker)
k'o		
akic'ic'itapiší		FACING/LOOKING AT EACH OTHER
įš		
Atohą		OVER THERE (HE IS SITTING)

7. *Atohą įš akic'ic'itapiší   k'o, žéc'en nų́pakiya   wota:kapic'.*
   Facing   not looking at each other too   then   both doing   eating
   They were facing but did not look at each other, then both were eating.

Photo 6.5. Rose Weasel is here caught in the action of describing the CAMP
CIRCLE at the start of her story.

the kitchen table in the second, everyone settles down to watch and listen as the story begins. Mrs. Weasel first draws a large circle in the space
in front of her as she says:

"Žéįs,   oyate   ka   t'ípi   hųśta   kan."
So, the people were camped over yonder they say, over yonder.

Mrs. Weasel often begins a story with a large circular gesture like this. It
is an action sign that describes the camp circle of the people who live
"over yonder." More than this, however, through the metaphor of the
circle she is creating the social and moral space within which her characters will interact and the story will unfold. She is also circumscribing
the limits of her signing space, clearing or setting her spatial stage, as it
were.

Having set her stage by creating the camp circle, Mrs. Weasel continues by introducing two characters, a young woman and a young man,
sister and brother, who "live alone together." This state of affairs would
be unusual in Assiniboine society; both parents must be dead and nei-

ther of the children yet married. The ideal relationship between a brother and sister is one of mutual respect. A sister supports her brother's activities and celebrates his successes just as much today as in pre-reservation days when a sister made beaded moccasins for her warrior brother, danced in his honor, and celebrated the birth of his child by making a beaded cradleboard for it. A brother should act in such a way that his sister can be proud of him and in return he should show respect for his sister. It is a breach of etiquette, for example, for a man to be joking and teasing with his friends about sexual matters if his sister is within hearing distance, and vice versa. "If brother's friends came over, he wouldn't start anything if she were there, but if his friends did, she would leave." A sister should be willing to feed her brother on a fairly regular basis and look after him if necessary. Mrs. Weasel does not need to be explicit about the character of this relationship in her story, because such knowledge is familiar to the audience, but it is important for understanding what she says and does next.

In sentence 2, she gestures toward her right-forward-diagonal $\triangleleft$ as she says "over there." This gives a specific location in the previously circumscribed camp circle to the tipi home of the characters she is about to introduce (Fig. 6.2). She then touches her thumb and then the first finger of her right hand to designate the brother and sister. These two fingers close to touch each other as she tells us that the brother and sister lived together. She does not choose to use the standard PST signs for WOMAN and YOUNG MAN here, in part because having said the spoken words it is not necessary but also because the point is to emphasize their equal status as siblings, not the gender difference, plus the fact that they lived together.

At the same time as she says "It must have been this way" in sentence 3, she gestures to her right and then behind her. The camp circle previously circumscribed has now been telescoped into the circle of a single tipi. The audience must imagine or realize that Mrs. Weasel has now placed herself in the center of the space internal to the story and inside the tipi home of the characters. The gesture to her right locates the tipi doorway. This coincides with geographical south, because Mrs. Weasel is facing east to tell the story on this occasion. Having orientated the home itself in relation to geographical space, she then explains the organization of the living space inside the tipi. The young man's living

Photo 6.6. This series of still frames shows the diagonal path in the signing space that connects the respective locations of the sister and brother when the sister is FEEDING HIM.

space is behind her to the left (west) of the tipi doorway, the young woman's living space she locates in front of her on the right (east) side of the tipi (Fig. 6.3).

In sentence 4, although in words she says "this one, this woman," Mrs. Weasel adds information through action signs that tell us the woman lived and kept all her belongings on this side of the tipi. She accomplishes this by moving her right arm into the location of the signing space and making small actions with her hand that indicate a group of objects or belongings are scattered around that particular place. She then traces a diagonal line with the same arm, fingers leading, from this place toward her left shoulder. This action describes the coming and going of the sister as she feeds her brother. The repetition of this diagonal action marks this as a continuative state of affairs in PST and this is confirmed by the spoken verb form *wok'u:ka* 'feeding him'. *Ka* following an elongated vowel acts as a continuative, so *wok'u:ka* translates best as "giving him food" in the continuative sense (*wóta* 'to feed/food' + *k'u* 'to give' + *ka* 'continuative'). The continuation is also mirrored in her repetition of the word *sųkaku* 'younger brother' as she repeats the action.

In sentence 5, Mrs. Weasel uses signs from the standard PST lexicon for ROASTING/COOKING MEAT ON A FIRE, CUT OFF A PIECE, GIVE, and EAT, and performs each of these actions as if doing it herself. She is therefore taking an agentive role in portraying actions in the story, even though not using the first person and playing the role of the character doing the action. She also uses the PST sign for YOUNG MAN at this point to make it clear who is eating. I should emphasize here that

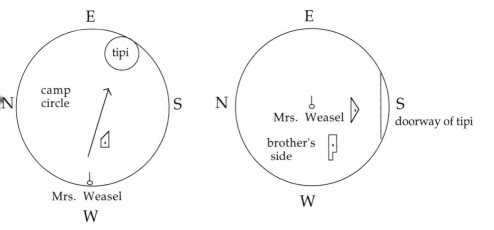

Figure 6.2. The space internal to the story: Mrs. Weasel creates a camp circle within the signing space and identifies the location of one tipi.

Figure 6.3. Mrs. Weasel now uses the signing space as if she is in the center of the tipi home.

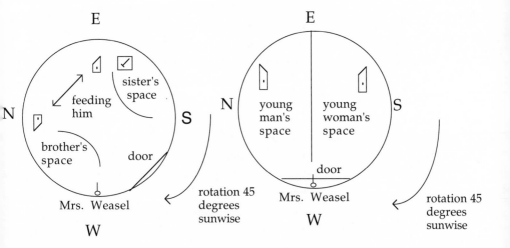

Figure 6.4. Mrs. Weasel rotates the tipi 45 degrees.

Figure 6.5. A second rotation of 45 degrees and the storyteller has her characters symmetrically placed to continue her story.

the third-person pronoun is unmarked in Nakota; therefore the English translations given above of "he" and "she" in relation to who was giving to whom were only possible through the use of such nominals together with an understanding of the signs and the spatial orientation of the characters.

Mrs. Weasel has now rotated the tipi one-eighth of a circle to the right in order to be able to show the action clearly and perform it easily in the signing space in front of her body. The woman's place is retained slightly to the right of front ⊔ ·⊓ and the young man's space shifts to accommodate a diagonal line of action as the sister feeds her brother (Fig. 6.4).

This clockwise (sunwise) rotation of the tipi continues another one-eighth of a circle in the next scenario as Mrs. Weasel sets up a clear spatial opposition between male and female siblings in the space in front of her. This second rotation of the story space means that Mrs. Weasel now has the tipi doorway behind her as she looks at the brother and sister: it is as if she were looking through the tipi doorway and so the left side of the tipi is now the left side of Mrs. Weasel's signing space and the right side of the tipi to her right (Fig. 6.5).

For the first time, Mrs. Weasel uses the conventional PST sign for WOMAN: an iconic representation of hair coiled at the side of the head. (She uses only the right hand here, but both hands can be used.) This sign does not, as W. P. Clark (1885:171) suggested, simply refer to long hair; the latter would not have distinguished a man from a woman in most Native American societies. She then continues the action of the right hand moving it from Ⓒ (beside the head) out into ⊓ (the space diagonally in front of her) where the woman's space has already been established. En route she changes her handshape from ⩐ to ⌒ ħ so that upon arrival her hand is in the correct shape to make the sign for SITTING THERE. She then uses her left hand in a bilaterally symmetrical utterance that places the young man sitting opposite his sister, in a space ⊔ that is left-forward-diagonal of Mrs. Weasel and in clear view for the audience.

Both hands then gesture simultaneously to indicate that the brother and sister are looking toward one another, followed immediately by the sign that acts as a general negation marker. This is accompanied by a spoken compound word that means "they did not look at each other" *akic'ic'itapisi* (*ak'ita* 'to look' + *c'ic'i* 'each other' + *pi* [plural] + *si* [negative]). The whole phrase serves to emphasize that out of respect they were not looking directly at one another. This is an important feature of social interaction today also, particularly between members of the opposite sex, between younger persons and older ones to whom respect should be shown, and between persons not well acquainted. As mentioned earlier, it is a feature that creates misunderstanding in the school situation, where the non-Indian teacher, uninformed by such norms, embarrasses children with the demand "Look me straight in the eye." For the teacher this action means openness and honesty of communication; for the Indian child it means a profound disrespect for the teacher (cf. Philips 1983). The only exception to this, I learned, may occur in the cozy realm of bedtime storytelling when a grandmother may insist that all young eyes are looking directly into hers. During the storytelling young voices are expected to join in at frequent intervals with *Hą* 'yes'. This indexes the fact that they are following her story. When the *hą*'s eventually cease then grandma knows the children have fallen asleep.[10]

The PST sign that accompanies this spoken compound word for "not looking at each other" is also a compound. It is made up of the verb TO LOOK plus the negation sign, but the root has been spatially inflected to include the reciprocal notion of EACH OTHER in a way that cannot be represented in word glosses. The left-right spatial symmetry previously established as the location of the brother and sister in the signing space in front of Mrs. Weasel is retained, and both hands stay out there as they take on the handshape and movement characteristic of the sign TO LOOK. What has changed to create this spatial inflection is the location of the sign (it is normally performed in front of the signer's own eyes) and the orientation of the hands; instead of pointing forward, the two extended fingers of each hand point toward each other to create the reciprocal EACH OTHER. The negation sign that follows is also inflected by being performed with both hands (normally only one is used) and by both hands remaining out in this same space rather than returning to their usual sign space nearer the torso.

Having set up this opposition on her left and right sides, Mrs. Weasel continues to use the spatial symmetry by again moving both hands simultaneously to indicate that brother and sister were eating in their respective places. The sign for EAT is repeated to indicate the continua-

Photo 6.7. Using only the right hand, Rose Weasel makes the sign WOMAN. Having reached a location near to the side of the head, the fingers are about to fold.

Photo 6.8. Rotating the circle of the tipi once more, the storyteller now has the characters in symmetrical opposition as she signs NOT LOOKING AT EACH OTHER.

Photo 6.9. The symmetrical opposition continues with each hand located in the assigned space for the brother and sister. This spatial inflection of the verb TO EAT translates as THEY WERE BOTH EATING.

Photo 6.10. The uninflected form of the verb TO EAT is performed in a location near to and addressing the mouth.

tive and again this mirrors the elongated vowel and the continuative *ka* in the word *wota:kapic'* 'to be eating'.

These last two utterances give examples at one level of what is meant by simultaneity of performance in a sign language, a feature that contrasts with the linear nature of a spoken language utterance. To speak the words "then both of them were eating" separates in time, albeit briefly, the notions of "both" (i.e., the two of them) and the act of eating. As Langer (1942:80) put it, we cannot talk in simultaneous bunches of names. In a sign language, however, we can. The notions of "both" and "eating" are presented through the identical and simultaneous action of both hands performing the sign EAT, as in the previous sentence the concepts "look" and "each other" are simultaneously encoded in the sign glossed as LOOK AT EACH OTHER. In addition, the "over there" of their spatial location is represented only by the location of the signs, not in words. This symmetrical opposition of right and left hands in ⟨ and ⟩ spaces adds a third simultaneity by restating the male-female, brother-sister opposition in the context of the socially structured living space of the tipi. This simultaneity of performance of parts of signs is a fundamental feature that distinguishes signed languages from spoken ones. This is one major reason why word glosses, which of necessity follow the linear convention of written speech, fail as a method for recording signs (Farnell 1984, 1989).

Mrs. Weasel continues the story with the following words:

8. Ka
   ne wíyą ne eciya
   "Hį misų
   kic'(i)ųk'ų c'eyaka."

8. From over there
   this woman said
   "Ah my brother
   we should have someone
   staying with us."

9. "Wíyą wążiħ oyane c'eyaka."

9. "You should look for a
   woman."

10. "Hą mit'ąken ec'amųk.

    Tók'en emayakiya ne
    ec'amųkta."

10. "Yes my sister I will do it.

    What you have told me I will do
    it."

11. "Wążiħ owanek oyate t'ok'ą
    mnįk," eya.

11. "I will search for one. I will go
    to another tribe," he said.

12. Ec'en oyate t'ok'ą c'a ekta
    ic'.

12. So he went elsewhere to another
    group of people.

13. Żéc'i íka.

    Wįk'oske wąži
    (wana że awįtk'oka hénąk'aś)
    ak'ip'iyeya.

13. Then he was there.

    A young woman
    (now she must have been a
    crazy one)
    he matched up with straight
    away.

14. "Hą
    ne oc'inec'e," eciya.

    "Hą
    waųkic'iyaka waśtec'."

14. "Yes
    I found you because I looked for
    you," he said to her.

    "Yes
    it is really good that we saw
    each other."

15. "C'imnuzįkte no," eciya.

    "Hą
    hįknac'iyįk," eya.

15. "Marry me!" he said to her.

    "Yes
    I will take you for a husband,"
    she said.

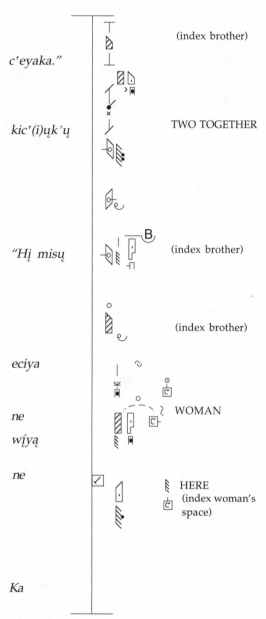

c'eyaka."   (index brother)

kic'(i)ųk'ų   TWO TOGETHER

"Hį misų   (index brother)

(index brother)

eciya

ne   WOMAN

wíyą

ne   HERE
            (index woman's
            space)

Ka

8. *Ka,   ne wíyą   ne   eciya,   "Hį misų,*
   Over there, this woman this said to him ah my brother,
   From over there, this woman said, "Ah my brother,

   kic'(i)ųk'ų c'eyaka."
   together with us be/stay should
   we should have someone staying with us."

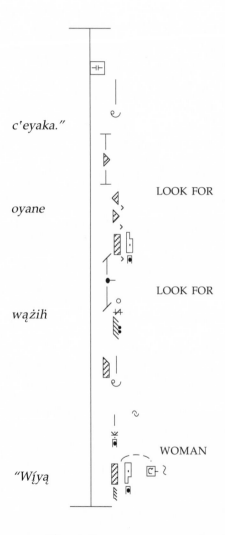

9. *"Wįyą   wąžiħ oyane   c'eyaka."*
   Woman   one   you search/look for   should
   "You should look for a woman."

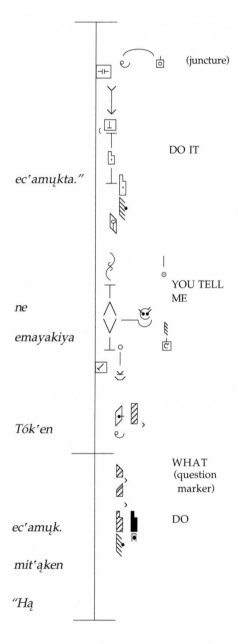

(juncture)

DO IT

ec'amų̓kta."

YOU TELL
ME

ne

emayakiya

Tók'en

WHAT
(question
marker)

ec'amų̓k.

DO

mit'ą̓ken

"Hą̓

10. *"Hą̓ mit'ą̓ken   ec'amų̓k.   Tók'en emayakiya   ne   ec'amų̓kta."*
    Yes my sister   I will do it.   What   you tell me   this   I will do it
    "Yes my sister I will do it. What you have told me I will do it."

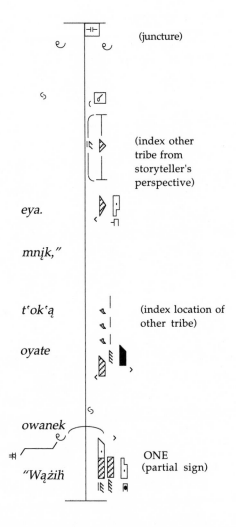

11. *"Wążiħ owanek   oyate   t'ok'ą   mnįk,"   eya.*
    One   I search for   people   elsewhere I will go say
    "I will search for one. I will go to another tribe," he said.

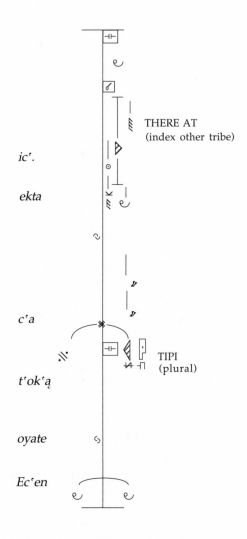

12. *Ec'en oyate   t'ok'ą   c'a   ekta   ic'.*
    So   tribe/people elsewhere thus   there at was at
    So he went elsewhere to another group of people.

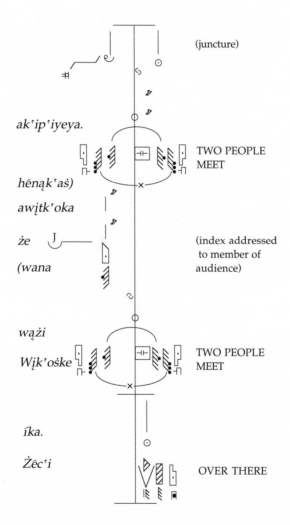

13. *Żéc'i íka.   Wįk'ośke   wąži (wana   że   awįtk'oka hénąk'aś)*
    Then there at. Young woman one (now that crazy one   must be)
    Then he was there. A young woman (now she must have been a crazy one)

    ak'ip'iyeya.
    met/matched up with right away
    he matched up with straight away.

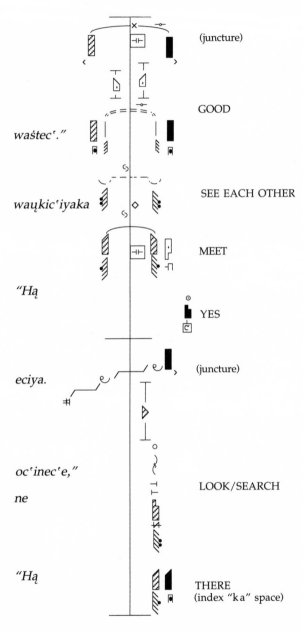

waśtec'."

waųkic'iyaka

"Hą

eciya.

oc'inec'e,"

ne

"Hą

(juncture)

GOOD

SEE EACH OTHER

MEET

YES

(juncture)

LOOK/SEARCH

THERE
(index "k a" space)

14. *"Hą, ne oc'inec'e,"*   *eciya.*   *"Hą, waųkic'iyaka*   *waśtec*
Yes   this   I looked for you   he said to her.   Yes   we saw each other   good
"Yes, I found you because I looked for you," he said to her. "Yes, it is really
good that we saw each other."

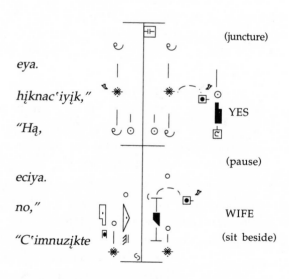

15. *"C'imnuzįkte no," eciya.*
    Marry me   !   he says to her
    "Marry me!" he said to her.

    "Hą hįknac'iyįk,"   *eya.*
    Yes   I will take you for a husband   say
    "Yes, I will take you for a husband," she said.

The location of the sister in the ⌐ space and the young man in the
◌ space remains constant until the scene changes. In sentence 8, Mrs.
Weasel again uses the PST sign for WOMAN and points to the sister's
location ⌐ to make it clear through both words and signs who is talking. She again becomes the agent of action by directly quoting the sister's
speech, and she addresses the brother via a gesture and by directing her
gaze over to the ◌ space. Her two extended index fingers make the PST
sign for TOGETHER, thereby complementing and adding emphasis to
the words "someone staying with us" without repeating the exact semantic content of the words.

In sentence 9, Mrs. Weasel continues in the role of sister and tells
her brother that he should go and look for a wife. Her gestures move
over to the space away from the brother, over to her right side as the
space in which he should look, probably because this ▷ side is empty,
in the sense that Mrs. Weasel has taken over the role of the sister, speaking and moving in the first person, and the ◁ space is still occupied by
the brother as addressee. To locate the action on the right side balances
the use of the space. The handshape and movement for the standard
PST sign TO LOOK FOR/HUNT is used at this point, although the orientation of the hand is nonstandard (fingers are 𝄃 [pointing up] rather
than ⌐ [forward]). The action nevertheless succeeds in alluding to the
sign, and her hands fold gracefully as they relax into the pause that marks
the end of the phrase.

The reply of the brother is given in a moment of stillness, which
adds dramatic effect, and Mrs. Weasel again takes on the role of the
actor, this time as the brother when he says, "Yes my sister."

A variation of the standard PST question marker occurs next and
precedes the spoken term *tók'en* 'what/how'. Here again Mrs. Weasel
merely alludes to a standard PST sign rather than performing it fully.
(She maintains the previous handshape ⌐ instead of changing to ⌣
but uses the side-to-side movement and orientation of the hand of the
standard question marker, again changing just one element from the
standard sign.) In spoken Nakota, there is an enclitic question marker
he that occurs at the end of a sentence, somewhat like a spoken question
mark, but this finds no representation in the sign language. A question
in signs will instead always begin with the question marker. This parallels the placing of *t-* question words in Nakota, which correspond to *wh-*

words in English questions (i.e., "who," "what," "when," etc.). This generic question sign can refer to any type of question, with context determining more exact meaning, but there are also distinct signs for WHICH ONE and HOW MANY.

Following this is the sign YOU TELL ME, which is a verb that also has a spatial inflection, this time to incorporate pronouns. The direction of movement is inflected, that is, the direction of the movement differs according to the previously established location in space of subject and object of the sentence. In this case the sign moves from YOU toward ME, from the space of the sister toward Mrs. Weasel, who is now taking on the role of the brother. If the sentence was I TELL YOU, the direction of movement would be reversed, going from speaker toward addressee. In this case Mrs. Weasel utilizes the ⌊ᵈ space previously set up for the sister as the location of YOU and moves the hand in toward herself as ME, the brother who is speaking. This is followed by one variation of the PST sign for the verb TO DO: a straight line forward from the chest with a pointing index finger which serves to emphasize his sense of agency in the world, moving from "I" forward into the world, as he says, "I will do it." The simultaneous use of both words and signs adds emphasis to his intention to carry out his sister's request.

A puzzling use of the space occurs next (sentence 11) when the space previously designated by the sister as the area of search ▷ appears to have shifted over to Mrs. Weasel's left side now ⌊ₙ . This is solved when one realizes that because Mrs. Weasel is still taking the role of the brother, she has done an imaginary 180-degree turn in the space and the location of the "search" space is forward-left-diagonal from the brother's perspective when his sister was talking.

The scene reverts back to its previous perspective as the brother leaves and goes over to another tribe ▷ . In sentence 12, as she says "elsewhere to another group of people" in words, Mrs. Weasel uses the plural of the sign for TIPI to add the visual image of a group of tipis—a village—to the semantic content of the utterance. (The plural of the PST sign for TIPI interlocks the fingers of both hands, fingers upright ⌊ whereas the single form uses only the two index fingers crossed ⌊ ⌊ to indicate one tipi.) This plural sign is very similar to the sign for TOWN, discussed in Chapter 3. The two signs differ only in the orientation of the hand. The fingers are interlocked and held upright ⊠ or ⊠ to

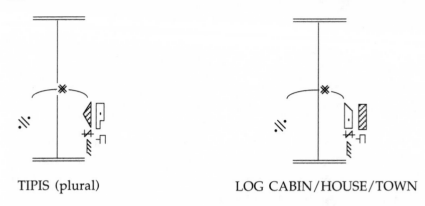

TIPIS (plural)   LOG CABIN/HOUSE/TOWN

Figure 6.6. A minimal pair of PST signs that differ only in the spatial orientation of
the hands.

represent many tipis, whereas when held facing forward the interlocked
fingers represent the interlaced logs at the corners of a log cabin. These
two signs thus represent a minimal pair linguistically, differentiated only
by the orientation of the hand, the other features of handshape, movement, and location being identical (see Fig. 6.6).

This simple shift of spatial orientation from vertical to horizontal
succinctly captures a cruel irony when one considers the replacement of
circular tipi villages by square log cabins and the encroaching towns of
the settlers a hundred years ago. Lakota religious leader Black Elk complained of the change as follows:

> You realize that in the sacred hoop we will multiply. You will
> notice that everything the Indian does is in a circle. Everything that
> they do is the power from the sacred hoop, but you see today that
> this house is not in a circle. It is square. It is not the way we should
> live. The Great Spirit assigned us a certain religion and etc. The
> power won't work in anything but circles. Everything now is too
> square. We get even tents that are square and live in them.
> (DeMallie 1984:290)

At the end of sentence 12 a further gesture into the ⌐⌐ space confirms
the words that follow in sentence 13 by indicating that the brother has
already arrived and is staying there (*íka - i* 'at a place' + *ka* 'continuative'). Later in sentence 13 two index fingers become representative of

the brother and the woman he now meets, and as an aside to her audience (on her left on this occasion) Mrs. Weasel tells us this woman must have been "a crazy one." (It seemed to me that this characterization of the young woman prefigured the terrible events later in the story when this woman destroys her husband's property, kills her child, and blames everything on the sister. However, I learned that such an interpretation was quite erroneous: "crazy" in this context refers to the kind of woman who easily takes up with a man she does not know.) The two index fingers remain touching to tell us the young man and the girl met and "matched up" right away. As the young man tells his new sweetheart that this happened because he was looking for her, Mrs. Weasel again takes the role of actor and adds PST signs for YOU and LOOKING/ SEARCHING, taking the spatial perspective of the brother. Her hands pause in her lap for a moment as she reverses roles to answer as the woman. With a slightly higher tone of voice, she acknowledges his statement by saying simply "Yes" as she nods her head. The woman continues with "it is really good that we saw each other," and Mrs. Weasel again uses the two index fingers touching to indicate the two of them before changing both her hands into handshapes for the PST sign TO LOOK/SEE. These are again placed with fingers pointing at each other and create a spatial inflection of the verb meaning the reciprocal WE SAW EACH OTHER. In this case, however, the hands are held close together in the signing space just in front of Mrs. Weasel's torso, thereby representing the closeness of the sweethearts' positions, in contrast to the distance between brother and sister discussed earlier.

In sentence 15, the young man says "Marry me!" to the girl, and this is accompanied in Mrs. Weasel's storytelling by the PST sign for WIFE, which also means SIT BESIDE ME. Mrs. Weasel repeats this sign and reverses roles again as the girl replies, "Yes, I will marry you."

The two paragraphs just analyzed represent only a fraction of a long, fascinating, and complex story that unfortunately cannot be included in its entirety here. The point has been to provide sufficient exegesis to illustrate the rich semantic content and complex organization of the signing space and the many ways in which signs and words complement each other. More specifically, it has shown just how much of the story itself is encoded in signs, the words having created only a bare skeleton in places.

Photos 6.11 and 6.12. The PST handshape with contrasting orientation used in the minimal pair TIPIS and HOUSE/LOG CABIN.

THE IDEA OF CIRCLE IN PLAINS SIGN TALK

The three ways in which the idea of circle has been utilized can now be summarized. This is followed by an examination of the PST signing space and a summary of several features of PST grammar that have arisen both in this narrative and in the Inktomi myth discussed previously.

The Circle as Narrative Content

Within the boundaries of the general signing space, Mrs. Weasel created a performance space for her story that was organized around the notion of the circle. Mrs. Weasel utilized this form as a powerful polysemic symbol in the actual content of the story, to represent the camp circle, tipi, and kinship relations, but potentially invoking all that these might stand for, as suggested by the earlier discussion.

Earthboy in the telling of the Inktomi myth also introduced a circle into the content of the story, as an appropriate shape for the council between animals and birds—a face-to-face forum for discussion among equals.

The Circle as a Form for the Organization of the Narrative Structure

In both stories, the circle provided a structure for the spatial organization of characters and events internal to the story, thereby merging form and content. In Mrs. Weasel's story, referential gestures were directed to specific locations in the circle that were thereafter designated as representing individual characters. Likewise, in Earthboy's narrative, referential gestures around the council circle were used to refer collectively to participants in the discussion.

The Circle as Grammatical Structure

In addition to the performance space of any particular story, there is a circular space internal to the grammar of PST itself. In this space, spatial inflections create appropriate verb forms and the locations of characters in the space provide a structure for pronominal and demonstrative reference. This spatial grammar of PST is not tied to any particular performance or story but is a property of the structure of the language itself.

THE PST SIGNING SPACE

As these narratives illustrate, people who are skilled in any action sign system—be it a dance idiom, a martial art, a sign language or ceremonial system of some kind—have clear conceptions about the organization of the space around them in that context and its appropriate uses. These conceptions may coincide to a greater or lesser extent with spoken language concepts and cultural norms about everyday uses of the body and space.

PST, as one such action sign system, uses only a portion of the total space around the body. While this can be shown pictorially as in Figure 6.7, it is better represented with spatial symbols so that the third dimension can be represented, as shown in Figure 6.8. The total PST signing space can thus be seen to use just over a quarter of the potential space around the body. This is the raw material, as it were, for the specification of grammatical relations by spatial means.

Figure 6.7. PST sign space represented pictorially.

This signing space, however, is not used equally. Signs rarely extend to the periphery of the kinesphere[11] and are usually concentrated in a central area in front of the chest. In a storytelling context today, a group of people may be sitting around a table in the dining area or on couches and easy chairs in a sitting room. Depending somewhat upon the size of the audience, signs may be slightly larger, extending farther into the signing space than in a conversational context. Signs will only sometimes reach the periphery of the signing space, however, as when the speaker reaches down to refer to the feet or upward to indicate high up in a tree. A hundred years ago a typical storytelling context might have been sitting on buffalo robes around the fire inside a cozy tipi on cold winter evenings. In this case the ground itself provided the lower limits of the signing space.

Contemporary signed performances accompanied by music at public events such as powwows and various high school events use the full extent of the signing space, with signs often reaching to the periphery of the kinesphere in order to be clearly visible to an audience that may be quite a distance away. This can range from a few yards in a school gymnasium, to a proscenium stage and auditorium, to fifty yards across a powwow circle. This use of signing space is probably similar to that of former times when signing was frequently used in public oratory, in the meetings of strangers, and among the scouts who talked across distances out on the Plains.

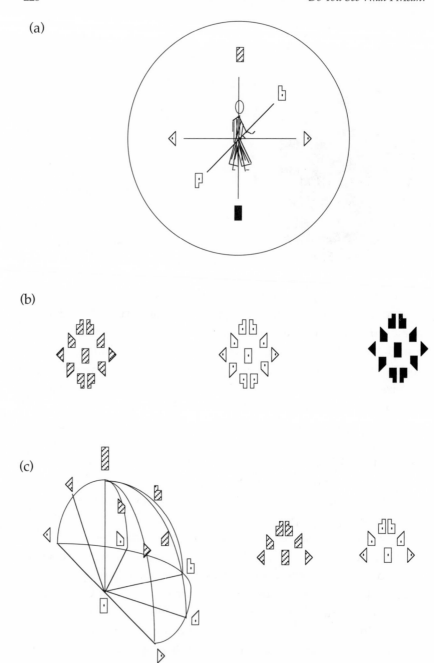

Figure 6.8. The signing space of Plains Sign Talk: (a) the whole kinesphere or three-dimensional space around the body in which all movement takes place; (b) the total set of Labanotation symbols that define spatial direction and level; (c) the PST signing space uses approximately a quarter of the potential space around the whole body.

VISUAL PERCEPTION AND THE PST SIGNING SPACE

That there are significant differences between ways of using our visual perception can be shown by comparing some of the differences between ASL and PST. For example, ASL research involving the physiology of visual perception has indicated that an area of sharp focus and clarity exists at the center of our visual field, and around this is an area of peripheral vision where sharpness and clarity decline. In ASL conversations, the short distance between two participants creates a small area of focus around the neck and the face, and the importance of eye contact in ASL increases this concentration upon a central area. In ASL, therefore, the majority of signs are located in this area of focus. In addition, most of the signs in this area are one-handed. Farther away, in the area of peripheral vision, we are told that ASL compensates for less visual clarity by adding more visual information: two hands are used instead of one, often carrying out the same actions (Baker and Cokely 1980:81). ASL researchers have assumed a universality because of this physiological base, but PST offers a contradictory case.

In Plains Indian cultures generally, as I mentioned above, it is still the case that it is not at all polite to make and maintain eye contact, and therefore the area of visual focus for conversations proposed by ASL researchers does not exist for PST users. The smallest area of the PST space in use is much larger than that for ASL, because participants will deliberately glance down or slightly to the side, using peripheral vision to its full capacity rather than focal vision. Where focal vision is used, it is directed lower than the face of the signer, so that eye contact is unnecessary. In contrast to ASL, facial expression is not a grammatical component of PST and is rarely used.

On two different occasions, it was explained to me exactly how the "Indian way" of looking is different. In the context of hunting game, for example, I was told that an Indian hunter, unlike a non-Indian, does not pinpoint or focus his eyes upon a spot in the forest or across a hillside and then trace a line of search back and forth until something is spotted. Instead he will use peripheral vision to gaze at a large area and wait for signs of movement anywhere in that extended field of vision. The same use of peripheral vision as a diffused but all-encompassing way of looking was also described in the context of seeing for artistic purposes such as drawing and painting.

Thus the ASL assumptions based upon physiological universals need to be restated. While it is certainly the case that the physiology of visual perception gives us a universal in terms of the capacities for focal and peripheral vision, it is not the case that different cultures will utilize these possibilities in the same way. There is a parallel here to Berlin and Kay's (1969) work on color classification. The physiological constraints on color perception in no way determine the classifications and semantic values attached to colors in different cultures. As Sahlins (1975:165) points out, such physiological constraints are important only insofar as they are meaningful. The perception of color affects and in turn is affected by the categories and classifications accorded by different cultures. In the same way the physiology of vision places restraints on and therefore affects, but in no way determines, the structure of ASL or PST. Cultural conventions about conversational norms, such as the values attached to eye contact, may outweigh any physiological constraints. In this case the negative value attached to eye contact by PST users, along with other cultural contexts that encourage the use of peripheral vision, has created a wider conversational space for PST than that of ASL. That peripheral vision can certainly be trained to a high degree of accuracy is very familiar to basketball players, for example, or dancers who have to use peripheral vision to "sense" where other people are onstage while moving very fast themselves.

INTERNAL AND EXTERNAL SPACES

A useful distinction can be made between the structured semantic spaces within which events take place and the use of space that is internal to an action sign system itself. For example, the performance space in which an audience, dancers, and theater exist is separate from the space internal to a particular piece of choreography. That is, the space in which the performance takes place is separate from the patterns of spatial pathways and movements of dancers' limbs that make up a dance itself. The internal form space of a particular dance can thus be recreated in a different external theater space. Likewise, a place of worship, such as a Roman Catholic church, is a space external to the ritual space of the Post-Tridentine Mass itself, hence a Mass can be performed in a hospital or on a battlefield if required (see Williams 1980a). For PST, the kitchen, living room, or community hall, in which a story may be told, are spaces external to the structured semantic space within any particular story. The remainder of the chapter summarizes features of the space internal to PST grammar and some relationships between words and signs.

THE SPACE INTERNAL TO PST GRAMMAR: PRESENT AND NONPRESENT REFERENCE

First- and second-person indexical references are accomplished in PST through pointing gestures to self (index finger directed at chest or nose) and addressee. If a third person referred to in the discourse is present, then a direct pointing gesture can also be made (with an index finger or with the lips). If, however, nonpresent referents are introduced into the discourse, as in the narratives above, then a nominal (e.g., WOMAN, YOUNG MAN, FROG) will be introduced and a point in space set up to represent the person or object. Pointing to that specific location later in the discourse will clearly refer back to that nominal even after many intervening signs. Bellugi and Klima (1982:301) describe this same kind of spatial indexing for ASL (see also Wilbur 1979; Paddon 1979, 1980; Kegl 1977; Hoffmeister 1978), and PST would appear to utilize exactly the same strategies.

West also noted this feature in his morphological description of PST: "One of the most distinctive and important features of sign language involves its technique of assigning a previously executed sign to some point in space and using that point as a referent for subsequent signs, when it is desired to refer to the previous sign" (1960:1, 68). PST has therefore developed grammatical characteristics similar to those found in a "primary" sign language such as ASL.[12]

SPATIAL INFLECTIONS OF VERBS

Discourse roles in PST are indicated not just by pointing but also by changes in movement that create an inflectional system for verbs that I have called spatial inflections. A verb like TELL *ekiya* or GIVE *k'u* is obligatorily marked for person and number when the nominals identified with the verb have been given spatial locations. These locations dictate the verb's path. Figure 6.9 shows the path of movement when TELL is indexed for first- and second-person, and for third-person reference, as in I TELL YOU, YOU TELL ME, I TOLD THEM. When the first- and second-person inflections are combined, they produce another form of the same PST verb, but one that when translated into spoken Nakota would fit more closely to a different verb, *wóknaka* 'to discuss/ to tell a story'. Earthboy's narrative about Inktomi uses this inflection of the sign to indicate discussion around the council circle (Buechel's Lakota dictionary lists the noun form of this verb, *owoglaka*, to mean "a place of council, a council, consultation").

Third-person verb forms are unmarked just as they are in spoken Nakota. A nominal or a referential gesture to a previously established (anaphoric) location—e.g., SHE (referential index) or FROG (nominal)— provides the third-person subject, but the verb form itself is uninflected and is performed by the signer as agent of the action, using what would otherwise be a first-person form. The only exception to this seems to be the reciprocal forms as in SEE EACH OTHER, LOOK AT EACH OTHER.

An interesting example from Earthboy's Inktomi narrative occurs in inflections of a sign for both KILL and BEAT IN COMPETITION. Figure 6.10 shows first- and second-person inflections directed away and toward the signer. Another inflection of the same verb utilizes both hands in a side-to-side movement and means TO ARGUE. This illustrates how a classification of signs according to spoken language meanings inadvertently masks these kinds of inflections that are variations of the *same* PST sign.

RELATIONSHIPS BETWEEN WORDS AND SIGNS

Words and Signs Simultaneously

Sometimes words and signs that are performed together have identical meanings. This often adds emphasis to a course of action (e.g., "I will do it"/I WILL DO IT). Sometimes it clarifies which persons are acting and which are being acted upon in the absence of third-person pronouns or when direct rather than reported speech is the preferred narrative style.

Complementary Semantic Content

Often signs will complement words by expanding upon the semantic content, as in "people/tribe in another place"/TIPI VILLAGE, and "someone staying with us"/TOGETHER.

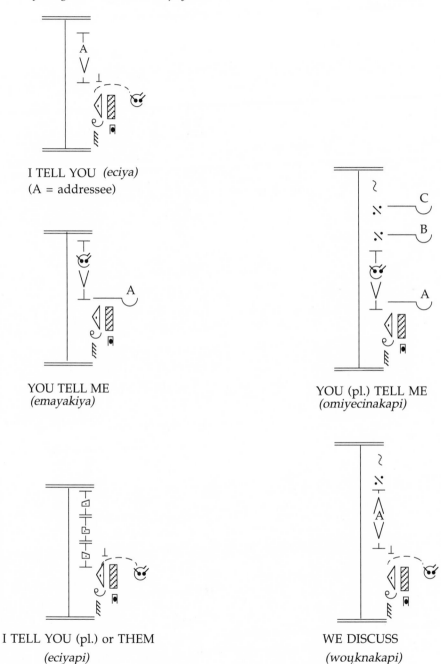

I TELL YOU *(eciya)*
(A = addressee)

YOU TELL ME
(emayakiya)

YOU (pl.) TELL ME
(omiyecinakapi)

I TELL YOU (pl.) or THEM
(eciyapi)

WE DISCUSS
(wouknakapi)

Figure 6.9. Spatial inflections of PST verb: TO TELL/DISCUSS (*ekiya*).

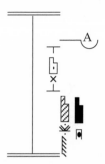

I KILL/BEAT YOU IN COMPETITION *(wakt'a)*

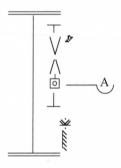

YOU KILL/BEAT ME *(mayaktena)*

THEY ARE ARGUING *(ak'inicapika)*

Figure 6.10. Spatial inflections of PST verb: TO KILL/BEAT (IN COMPETITION)/ ARGUE.

Additional Meanings

At other times information will be encoded in signs that is not represented in spoken meaning, as in "this woman"/KEPT HER BELONGINGS OVER ON THIS SIDE OF THE TIPI; "they landed"/ONE BY ONE; "the others"/SITTING AROUND THIS CIRCLE; "here"/IN THE CENTER OF THIS CIRCLE; "one by one"/COMING FROM ALL DIRECTIONS; "there"/IN THE NORTH. This is apart from the semantic content added by the overall organization of actions of characters as illustrated above.

In the Inktomi narrative, as in all of Earthboy's stories, there is a close correspondence between words and signs such that the full narrative load is carried by both media simultaneously. This does not, however, mean that the full semantic load can be realized without both media. Earthboy often pointed out during our transcription and translation work how interdependent they were:

J.E. See, you know what I think myself—in order to know the sign language you've just about got to know the [Nakota] language itself. It'd be a lot easier for a person to learn the [Nakota] language, then you could watch the hands and you'd know it. But a person who doesn't understand this sign language looking at this tape, well, he won't know what it's all about—he has to know the meaning of those words [signs]. Sometimes one [spoken] word is used several different ways and the sign language is used just one way—so you just about have to know the Assiniboine language or maybe the Sioux to know what's going on there. But a Crow can watch it, maybe a Cheyenne who knows the sign language—he'll get the drift of what's going on.

B.F. So the words add to the meaning, it's not just the signs on its own?

J.E. Yeah. But they would really understand what was being said, because that's how, a long time ago, they converse. Like, well, after they made a treaty, well those warriors got together and that's how they talked. They couldn't understand each other [spoken language] but a Blackfeet would be talking his language and making the sign language and an Assiniboine would be talking his own language and still he'd be making the sign language and they'd both understand what was being said. [13]

As Earthboy states here, PST signs can often be polysemic and interpreted several different ways according to context, when the spoken language makes finer distinctions. An example of this from his Inktomi narrative is the sign performed with the spoken word *uknuśtapikte* 'we will decide/agree' (root - *yuśta* 'to settle', Inktomi sentence 40). This sign can mean FINISHED or THE END, as well as TO SETTLE (an argument), whereas the spoken term refers specifically to settling a question.

Alternatively a PST sign can involve finer distinctions than those that are encoded in the spoken word. An example of this is found in the use of the verb *u* 'to be/existing' in the Inktomi narrative. The spoken word is the same whether applied to animals, humans, or birds, but PST distinguishes between these in the following way:

Animal

A handshape ⋔ that represents any animal (*wamąkaśka*) is located in the low horizontal level of the signing space, palm facing ▮ (down). The minor side-to-side movement is articulated from the wrist using one of the three degrees of freedom[14] that the wrist possesses (a lateral ⅄ ⅄ motion, called adduction and abduction in anatomical terminology).

Human

This handshape ⋔ with index finger extended upward, is located in the middle level ⨀ of the signing space. The movement of the hand is again articulated from the wrist but this time uses a second degree of freedom in the wrist, the one that allows rotation of the wrist around its longitudinal axis (lateral and medial rotation). This action makes the palm facing alter from ⨀ to ◁. A small pathway through space is also created, as the lower arm is included in the side-to-side movement.

Winged Creatures

This is the same handshape and movement of the human variation but is performed in the upper level ▨ of the signing space, around eye level.

The major distinguishing feature of these three signs, then, is the level at which they are performed: low level for animal, middle level for human, and high level for flying creatures. The similarity in handshape and movement for birds and humans reflects a taxonomic division of animated beings into "four-leggeds" and "two-leggeds" that places humans and birds in the same major category (cf. Black Elk's Lakota narrative "The Great Race" [DeMallie 1984:309]). It is the addition of the sign for FLYING together with the spatial level at which the sign is performed that distinguishes birds from humans. It is only because of these three distinctions made in PST, but not in spoken Nakota, that we know Inktomi has been given a human or humanlike form in this narrative.

Word Order and Sign Order

Word order and sign order are sometimes the same, as in the use of the negative marker (e.g., LOOK AT EACH OTHER + NEG.) and in SAW EACH OTHER + GOOD. Enclitics other than the negative marker *śi*, however—such as the plural ending *pi*, the potential/hypothetical action marker *kta*, or command forms—do not appear as added elements in signed sentences. A question marker appears at the beginning of signed sentences, which is the same order as spoken question forms (such as "who," "what," "which") but in contrast to the question marker enclitic *he*, which ends spoken sentences. Representation of commands in PST is sometimes included through an increase in the speed and energy of the action together with a marked stop to the path of the movement, but not consistently, which leads me to exclude it as a grammatical feature. The plural enclitic *pi* is not represented in PST, but plural can be indicated in several ways: by a repetition of the single sign, by a different sign altogether, by an alteration of some aspect of the singular sign, and by the use of number (see Fig. 6.11).

Also omitted from signed discourse are some spoken language features that refer to narrative time passing such as "when" and "then." As previously mentioned, PST, like spoken Nakota, is a language that does not mark verbs for tense, and so nominals such as TODAY, YESTERDAY, NEXT MONTH, and SOON provide time references together with a past time marker that can mean A LONG TIME AGO, A SHORT TIME AGO, or simply IN TIME PAST depending on the length of the movement path (see Fig. 5.9).

Repetition of a Sign

Repetition of movement in a PST sign can indicate continuative action and often parallels the use of an elongated vowel in spoken Nakota. Examples are *wok'u:ka* 'feeding him'; *wota:kapic'* 'eating'; *yąka:ka* 'sitting there'; *eya:kaya* 'saying'. Repetition of a sign can also be used to indicate an increase in intensity as in the Inktomi narrative when the sign TO SAY is repeated for *pąka* 'shout/holler' and for *hotų* 'animal cry' (the frog's croak).

SYMMETRY AND SIMULTANEITY

The three-dimensional nature of the signing space allows parts of PST signs to be performed simultaneously, in contrast to the linear expression of spoken language signs. This simultaneity can be utilized effectively in storytelling to create relationships among characters that are not always apparent from the spoken narrative. This was illustrated in the use of a right-left symmetry in Mrs. Weasel's story that highlighted a semantic opposition between male and female, brother and sister in the socially constructed living space.

AGENCY AND THE USE OF SPACE

The following range of possibilities are open to a sign talker for organizing the use of space. These represent five different perspectives on the action.

Constant Frame of Reference: Cardinal Directions

In the constant frame of reference or "cross of axes," an external frame like the four cardinal directions provides the organizing principle for referential gestures. This frame of reference is very obvious in the Nakota Territory narrative and route directions in Chapter 3, but it is also at work in both of the narratives discussed in this chapter. Mrs. Weasel, for example, orientated the door of the tipi toward geographical south. Earthboy was facing east and so used his right (south) side to indicate the animals from the hot country, as well as the direction of heat from the sun, and his left (north) side to refer to the animals from the cold country.

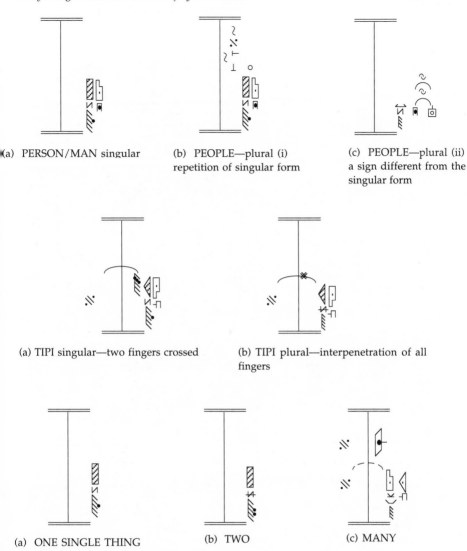

(a) PERSON/MAN singular

(b) PEOPLE—plural (i)
repetition of singular form

(c) PEOPLE—plural (ii)
a sign different from the
singular form

(a) TIPI singular—two fingers crossed

(b) TIPI plural—interpenetration of all
fingers

(a) ONE SINGLE THING

(counting in series begins with
the little finger, however)

(b) TWO

(c) MANY

Figure 6.11. Some ways to form the plural in Plains Sign Talk.

Photo 6.13. Rose Weasel's father-in-law, Old Horn Weasel, was also a skilled sign talker and is shown here at Fort Belknap Agency celebrations in the summer of 1909. Photo by Sumner W. Mattesson, courtesy Milwaukee Public Museum.

Constant Frame of Reference: Local Features

This perspective is also based on a constant cross of axes but is organized around local geographical or architectural features, such that referential gestures indicate a person who lives "over there" in the direction indicated by the sign talker, be it several miles away or next door. The same frame of reference operates when the sign talker is pointing to an object located "over there" inside a room, in the sense that where "there" is, in reference to a particular object, remains a constant regardless of where the sign talker happens to be standing or facing.

Body Frame of Reference: Agent of Verbs

This perspective involves the sign talker taking an agentive perspective on action. Any action (verb) in a narrative (story or general conversation) is described in signs as if the sign talker is doing the action herself or it is being done to her, even if in speech she is using the third person. The body of the sign talker becomes the frame of reference for action. For example, when Mrs. Weasel is describing the action TO COOK OVER A FIRE, she performs the action as if doing it herself, even though she is talking about the sister in the third person.

Body Frame of Reference: Agent of Action

The sign talker takes on the full role of one or several agents in turn, including their speech, often in the first person but also as reported speech. In this case the zero point of the deictic space/time of third person is shifted to coincide with that of the storyteller. An example of this occurs when Mrs. Weasel takes on the role of the sister when she says, "You should look for a woman," and of the brother when he says, "I will do it."

Observer's Perspective

When characters are assigned locations in the signing space and verbs are spatially inflected to convey interaction between third persons, the sign talker is not taking on the role of either or any of them. For example, when, as storyteller, Mrs. Weasel places the brother and his wife-to-be opposite each other in the signing space in front of her, she uses the sign for TO LOOK/SEE with both hands and inflects it to indicate that they saw each other.

Chapter 7

In western societies . . . spoken language generally tends to be associated with 'real' knowledge, where body languages are not often, if ever, associated with 'real' knowledge. In the minds of many, there is an unfortunate equation between linguistic signs and thought and action signs and non-thought.

DRID WILLIAMS 1980B, PT. 2:109.

THE PRIMACY OF MOVEMENT IN ASSINIBOINE CULTURE

The use of PST in storytelling and the other contexts examined so far has suggested a definition of language among Plains peoples that differs substantially from that held by the European and Euro-American philosophical and linguistic traditions. The fact that structured bodily action—language using a visual-kinesthetic medium rather than the oral-aural medium of spoken language—should be included as language in the full sense of the word in turn leads to the proposition that conceptions of relations between mind and body, along with associated dualisms such as thought and action, reason and feeling, mind and matter, might also be fundamentally different.

These are deeply rooted metaphysical and epistemological questions of considerable complexity that I can only begin to shed light on here, but it can be said that in Western thought such dualisms have laid a foundation for an epistemology in which mind and reason, and therefore knowing and knowledge itself, are removed from the body and its movement. In contrast to this, an Assiniboine philosophy of being-in-the-world makes body movement foundational. Evidence from pictographs, indigenous classifications of sign morphology, mythology, spoken and signed language use, and concepts of persons, will be used to illustrate how this is achieved. Assiniboine theories of social and personal action appear to be centered in a form of meaningful social life in which body movement is intrinsic as a way of knowing. This not only makes a sign language possible but highly probable.

THE PRIMACY OF MOVEMENT

The representations of PST signs made by Plains Indians themselves, as they are found on petroglyphs and winter counts, contrast markedly with the kinds of pictorial records and diagrams made by non-Indian observers (Farnell 1984, 1989). They therefore provide important evidence relating to indigenous conceptions about movement and the sign language. These are few in number but sufficient to illustrate the point. Figure 7.1 shows that graphic representations of PST signs by Plains Indians appear as rather abstract designs that contrast with the surrounding iconic representations of persons and objects.[1] This is because what is recorded is the *path of movement* of a sign, not the body parts that produce that movement. This contrasts sharply with the kinds of records produced by non-Indian investigators such as Mallery (1880a, 1880b), Tomkins (1926), and Hadley (1893), who diagram the body itself in the form of hands and torso and who attempt to show the movement with arrows and lines attached to the body parts (see Fig. 7.2).

This difference is not without import, because it highlights a fundamental difference in cultural conceptions about the identity of movement, and provides a very clear example of a rather interesting yet serious stumbling block with regard to Euro-American ways of seeing or not seeing human body movement, which is worth exploring.[2] The graphic representation of PST signs by Native Americans themselves as movement patterns in space supports the argument that the predominant Euro-American view of movement as a series of body positions, rather than a dynamic medium, is both culture-specific and problematic (Farnell 1989).

Ironically, it was the iconic or "pantomimic" form of many PST signs which led to the system being labeled a "primitive language" by nineteenth-century investigators. As it turns out, it was the non-Indian view that presented a static iconic graphic representation, in contrast to the less obviously iconic form of the movement path chosen as a graphic representation by Native Americans. Munn has observed that the pictorial properties of Walbiri (Australian) graphic representations are also of the kind that are often overlooked by Western observers, since the elements are for the most part simple forms of the kind misleadingly labeled "geometric" or "abstract" (1973:4).[3]

Figure 7.1. Graphic depictions of Plains Sign Talk by American Indians. Top part of illustration from Tomkins 1926:85. Used with permission.

(a)

| Jour
Tag | Day | Lever du soleil
Sonnenaufgang | Sunrise | Échanger
Tauschen | Trade |

(b)

SAME   MAKES   MAN HIS   LIFE WALK   THE-STRAIGHT-ROAD.

THE-WORD OF-GOD IS SURE, MAKING WISE THE SIMPLE.

(c)

Figure 7.2. Graphic depictions of Plains Sign Talk by non-Indian observers: (a) Tomkins 1926; (b) Hadley 1893; (c) Mallery 1880b. Hadley and Mallery illustrations courtesy of National Anthropological Archives, Smithsonian Institution, Washington, D.C.

Apart from this evidence from pictographs, my suspicion that move- ment held a primary position in indigenous classifications was confirmed in no uncertain terms when I had occasion to check my Labanotation transcriptions with Earthboy. Fortunately I recorded these sessions on videotape, and upon review they proved to be most instructive. At the time of the interviews, I was in the process of working toward a kinemic level of transcription wherein only differences that altered the meaning of a sign were included in my transcriptions. I began with handshapes and concluded that there were twenty-three distinct handshapes in PST. I then proceeded to check my analysis with Earthboy. My agenda for the work session therefore was clear—to check the handshapes—and it was only later when viewing the videotape that I realized Earthboy had, with some consistency, been working from a different perspective altogether, one that I had ignored at the time. He listened and watched my explana- tions of a particular handshape and made a comment or two either agree- ing or disagreeing, but in many cases he then proceeded to supplement the example given, not with signs that had similar handshapes but with signs that used the same movement pattern or path. Obviously, accord- ing to his classification system, it was the movement path of a sign that was its most important feature and movement that linked signs together as being similar or different in their morphology.

Ironically, one of the reasons I chose the Laban script over other systems, such as that developed by Stokoe (1960) and adapted by Kendon (1989), was its greater capacity for recording movement pattern and changing relationships. To have caught myself in the act of momentarily ignoring the very reason for this decision was a most humbling experi- ence. Fortunately, Earthboy was not persuaded that my way of classify- ing was better than his own. Even with a writing system capable of a sophisticated transcription of movement, I had fallen into a trap set by the metaphysics of my own cultural background and had begun by fo- cusing upon what appeared to be the most tangible part of a sign—the hand in a particular shape—rather than the seemingly less tangible movement. These two sources of evidence for the primacy of movement in indigenous classifications led me to look deeper for possible philo- sophical underpinnings as to why this should be the case.

Tákuśkąśką 'THAT WHICH MOVES'

Although Malinowski wished us to see mythology as "charters for so-cial action," the cultural development of a mythological view of the world is, of course, itself created out of meaningful social practices. Mythol-ogy offers evidence that links the primacy of movement found in Assiniboine classifications of signs with a particular metaphysics: move-ment conceived of as an intangible yet powerful principle called *tákuśkąśką* 'that which moves'. Oral tradition and historical evidence suggest that long ago (prior to 1640) the Assiniboine and Sioux peoples were undivided, and so it is with good reason, although also with due caution, that I have consulted Lakota mythology for further evidence of possible older Nakota conceptions.

Fortunately Lakota mythology was well documented at the turn of the century by learned Oglala holy men such as George Sword, in the work of Dr. James R. Walker. Walker, a physician at Pine Ridge, worked with anthropologist Clark Wissler, and his letters to Wissler describe his great concern and struggle to understand accurately the meanings of terms given to him by the Oglala holy men regarding mythical beings and religious conceptions (see Walker 1983).

My particular interest here is with the concept of *śką*, for which Walker had difficulty finding a translation. In a letter to Wissler he states that *śką* was the shaman's term for *tákuśkąśką* and that according to the best information he had, it meant "the sky, and was also a spirit that was everywhere and that gave life and motion to everything that lives or moves" (Walker to Wissler 1915, quoted in Jahner 1983:9).

Interpreters had designated *tákuśkąśką* as "What moves-moves" or "That which gives motion to everything that moves" and Walker felt this indicated a "vague or nebulous idea of force or energy" (Jahner 1983:9) that nevertheless had to do with the heart of the material he had collected about the creation of the world. Jahner also gives translations of *tákuśkąśką* as "Something-in-movement" and "That-which-moves" (1983:28, 32).

In one of the myths related to Walker by George Sword, "When the people laughed at the Moon," Inktomi created all kinds of problems between spiritual beings, which Walker, recalling the Greek pantheon, calls "the Gods" (i.e., *wi* 'sun', *hąwi* 'moon', *t'ate* 'the winds') and *wazi* 'the chief of the people who dwell under the world', his wife, *kążka*, and daughter, *ite*, wife of *t'ate*. When *hąwi* 'moon' is shamed and hides her face, it is *šką* to whom she appeals, and *šką* who subsequently questions all the participants and hands out punishments that decide the order of things in the universe from then on.

In the myth, *šką*'s decree gives rise to the existence of a third time in addition to the two times already existing, day and night, ruled by Sun. Sun's wife Moon is now to journey far apart from him, covering her face when she is nearest to him and uncovering it when farthest away. She will govern a time that is longer than day or night; the time taken from when she is farthest to nearest is to be called a moon (month). A further narrative in which *t'ate* sends his four sons to the edges of the world creates the four directions and a fourth time, the year, from winter to winter. "You and your sons will govern the fourth time and then your sons will be messengers of the Gods," says *šką*. So the ordering of time, and therein also space (the four directions, the circle of the earth), are expressed in Lakota mythology in ways entirely consistent with Nakota conceptions I have discussed previously.

The contemporary Assiniboine corpus of oral narrative does not contain myths that refer to *šką* in this manner, but the word remains in the vocabulary and has retained much of the same semantic content, so that one can reasonably hypothesize that such was once the case. Today the word *šką* refers to anything moving or moving about or to a movement. In PST the sign is made with a trembling motion of both spread hands. It can also mean trembling or shaking: an earthquake, for example, is *mąk'oc'e škąšką*. To be startled is *škąmahįkna*, and my video camera was referred to as *tákuškąšką*. Motion that has no visible cause is *šką*.

If the concepts Walker worked so hard to elaborate from the Lakota myth are correct, then *šką* is a theoretical construct that places this force-for-movement at the center of an epistemology as well as an ontology. That is, analogous to this causal power for motion in the natural and superhuman order of things may be a conception of movement of the body as a causal power for a way of knowing in the world.

It is striking that in a language that does not articulate terms for abstract concepts such as time and space the term *šką* gives linguistic form to this concept of force-for-movement. *Šką* appears not only as a theoretical concept that like the concept of gravity cannot in itself be seen, but, according to the myth, is a causal power above all others.

Lexical items that refer to actions of the human body itself do not involve the word *śką,* which is appropriate given that human action is perceived of as agent-centered and not movement that appears to have no cause (an appropriate exception being a man's erection). In fact, the relationship is more complex than this. By analogy, the conception of *śką* as a causal power could be a theoretical impetus to the development of notions of personal agency that include body movement as being central to an epistemology, that is, to a way of knowing. Such a conception of agency-in-action that includes the body would seem coterminous with the central importance of dancing in both traditional and contemporary religious expression and with the use of, and classificatory primacy given to, patterns of movement in the sign language. If body movement is thus a legitimate way of knowing, then a sign language is not only possible but probable.

As I have mentioned above, religious practice is fundamentally concerned with gaining "power," as well as making supplications and giving thanks. Gaining power means gaining a stronger sense of personal agency, the ability to achieve both in the community and spiritually, but it is also a notion deeply tied to a random "good luck" from uncontrollable spiritual forces.

Physical being is deeply involved in the attainment of power. Embodied prayer, for example, is found in the form of bodily suffering from the hot steam of the sweat lodge during spiritual and bodily cleansing, and during fasting and periods of isolation away from the comforts of human companionship. Such suffering is perhaps felt most intensely by those who participate in the four days of fasting, dancing, and enduring the heat of the sun during the annual sun dance ceremony. Although deeply misunderstood by non-Indians and frequently labeled torture in the historical record by distressed and horrified white observers, the physical suffering endured in the sun dance ceremony is also an important avenue for seeking and gaining power. To view the involvement as only a physical one would be to misinterpret profoundly, because it involves the whole person in the sense of testing fortitude, concentration, commitment, and belief at the same time that it forces reflection upon the individual's past life and present circumstances. Here too, as encoded in both spoken and signed languages, thinking and feeling are inseparable. For those returning to traditional religious practices at Fort Belknap today, the rationale is clear. The only thing a person truly owns is his or her body, and therefore to make a gift that is a truly meaningful sacrifice in the effort to obtain superhuman help and personal power, it is to the body one must turn. The more pitiful one appears and the more suffering one endures, the greater will be the potential assistance from the grandfather spirits and the creator. There is thus a very real sense in which the act of dancing in the sun dance *is* prayer and not an accompaniment to (spoken) prayer.

MIND IS A VERB

Additional evidence for an action-centered epistemology in Assiniboine culture comes from the use of spoken Nakota and the use of the body in PST as they encode metaphors about thinking and feeling in ways substantially different from Euro-American conceptions. ASL will again provide a useful contrasting case.

In ASL, signs that refer in any way to thought, mind, and intelligence are located around the head, whereas signs concerning emotions and feelings are centered around the heart and chest. The locations of ASL signs reflect popular conceptions about the spatial and bodily locations of these attributes of persons in American society generally (Fig. 7.3). The *valeur,* in the Saussurian sense (referring to unequal weighting or valency according to semantic saliency), attached to these body parts in many Western cultures is clearly demonstrated by ASL, but such location is by no means universal. Figure 7.4 shows how, in contrast to ASL, PST signs translated by Tomkins in 1926 to mean KNOW and THINK are located around the heart, and DOUBT in a literal translation is portrayed as being of TWO HEARTS. Figure 7.5 also illustrates a similar contrast between ASL and PST in relation to remembering.

Tomkins, an amateur collector of signs whose work was designed for an audience of Boy Scouts, was not interested in relations to Native American spoken languages, so his lexicon of signs, like those of more learned and extensive collectors such as Scott (1912–1934), W. P. Clark (1885), and Mallery (1880a, 1880b, [1881] 1972), overlooks problems of translation. Those problems exist at two junctures: between English

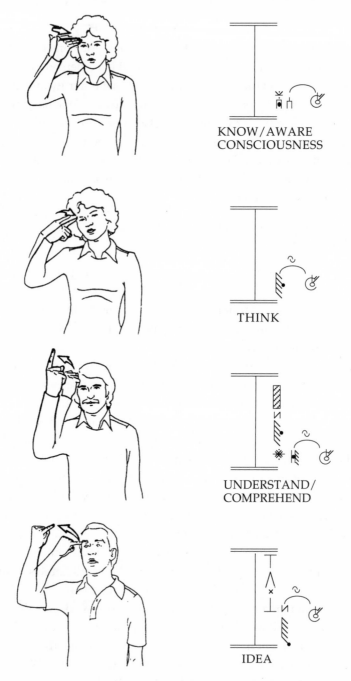

Figure 7.3. Location of "mind" in American Sign Language (ASL). Illustrations from Humphries, Padden, and O'Rourke 1980. Used with permission.

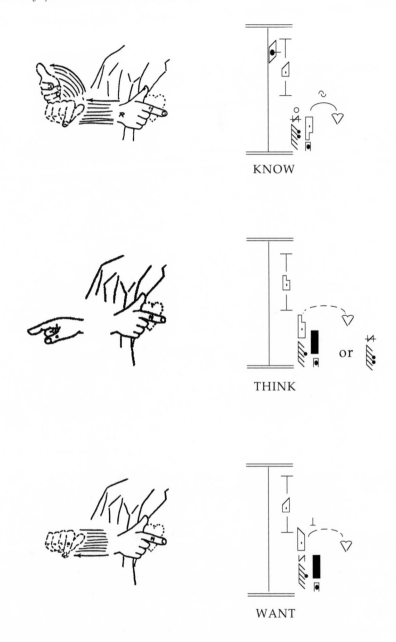

KNOW

THINK

WANT

Figure 7.4. Conceptions of "mind" in Plains Sign Talk. Tomkins illustrates the PST sign WANT but labels it "think." He may have been mistaken because of spoken language similarities between *wac'i* 'think' and *wac'ika* 'I want' in Lakota and Nakota. Among Nakota speakers the sign moves ⌐ not ◁ . Used with permission.

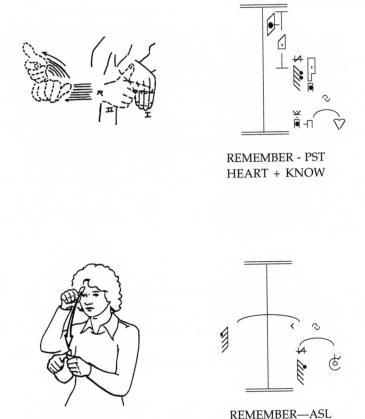

REMEMBER - PST
HEART + KNOW

REMEMBER—ASL

Figure 7.5. Remembering in PST and ASL. From Tomkins 1926 and Humphries, Padden, and O'Rourke 1980, respectively. Used with permission.

and indigenous spoken languages, and between spoken language units and body language units. These disjunctures only become apparent when the signed lexicon is engaged as language-in-use; only then is a "critical lack of fit" (Ardener [1971] 1989:7) between two worldviews apprehended.

For example, when I asked how to say that someone has a good mind in Nakota, I was taught the phrase *t'awac'į waśte*. When I asked how to say this in signs, I was taught to move a pointed index finger from the heart side of the chest away from the body, with the finger pointing straight forward, followed by the sign for GOOD (Fig. 7.6).

Two things are important about this: first, in contrast to Euro-American conceptions, there is no reference to the head as a place where mind is located; and, second, emphasis in this sign is upon the movement of the hand, not upon a place as a location for mind. Later I learned that to say "she thinks clearly" one would use the same word *wac'į* in the phrase *tayą t'awac'į* and the sign was almost the same.

Consistent with the lack of any clear distinction between verbs and nouns noted earlier, "mind" in Nakota acts more like a verb than a noun, an action than an object. *Wac'į* 'to think' seems to be a verb about thinking but one with a very wide semantic range. According to Lakota scholars, it can be used in the sense of "intention," "willpower," or "one's will" and "unbounding consciousness."[4] Deloria (ca. 1940) defines the term for Lakota speakers as both a noun, meaning "mind" and "reason," and as a prefix added to active verbs that indicates "a willingness, desire, will or disposition to do, an intention or plan." In Nakota, *t'awac'į mneha*, for example, means "strong-willed" and *t'awac'įknuni* means "undecided." *Wac'į* is one of four Nakota verbs relating to thinking and one in which remembering seems to be involved; for example: *t'awac'į* 'to be thinking of somebody, remembering'; *amawac'ani he?* 'were you thinking about me?'; *wac'įt'a* 'stupid or forgetful'.

The phrase *t'awac'į wašte* seems to indicate a general disposition— "it means they really like what you're doing" and "a good person in every way" were other meanings given to me. The Lakota also use the phrase to mean "a generous person" (Raymond Bucko, S.J., personal communication, 1988; see also Buechel [1970] 1983). In other words, as the sign language emphasizes, mind is not a place, it is a disposition toward others: a capacity of a whole person, not a place in the head separate from a body.

Notions of personhood involve a complex combination of a strong sense of agency (emphasizing personal autonomy in decision making, for example) without resort to individualism because of the emphasis placed upon kin relationships. People are defined and define themselves fundamentally in terms of social relationships,[5] and so it is not surprising that the sign moves from the heart toward the social space of relationship, linking the space between speaker and addressee.[6]

The possessional prefix *t'a* is involved in this social view of mind. It is a prefix denoting separable possession unlike those prefixes used with

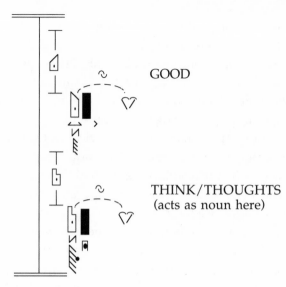

GOOD

THINK/THOUGHTS
(acts as noun here)

(a) *Tʿawacʿį waśte*
She/he has a good mind

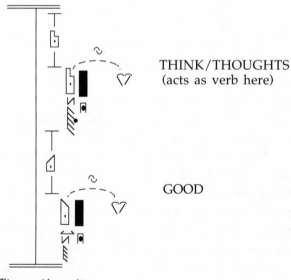

THINK/THOUGHTS
(acts as verb here)

GOOD

(b) *Tʿawacʿį waśte*
She/he thinks clearly

kinship terms, for example, which denote inseparable possession. Your mother or grandfather are always and inseparably yours, whereas your thinking and thoughts (*mit'awac'i̧*), while certainly yours, are separable from you in the sense that they can be shared. (Note that *t'a* also appears as a prefix denoting animal body parts as distinct from those of humans, e.g., *nige* 'stomach', *t'anige* 'paunch of an animal/tripe'.)

The *t'a* that appears as a suffix in *wac'i̧t'a* is interesting because it is a verb meaning "to die" but one that encodes the notion of a continuum between life and death rather than an absolute line. For example, *t'asakt'a* 'to faint/to be horrified, frightened to death', and *wac'i̧t'a* 'stupid/forgetful' (also Lakota *t'át'a* 'feebleminded' [DeMallie, personal communication, 1989]). This implies that the conception involves duration: the longer one is *t'a*, the more absolute it becomes until irreversible, at which point one's *nagi* 'spirit/soul/shadow' will leave the body *t'ac'a̧* behind.

Two other verbs that deal with thinking were described by consultants: *wókc'a* 'to think/to think about' and *iyukc'a* 'to think about it/to think over'. *Taya̧ iyukc'api* means "to be thinking straight," "to be agreed." *Wokc'a* is used in the sense of "to have an opinion." To ask *nukc'a he?* is to ask "what is your opinion?" or "what do you think?" The prefix *i* of *iyukc'a* seems to add an object, as in the first-person form, *imnukc'a* 'that's the way I think about it'. *Iyukc'a* also relates to potential action in a way similar to English, as in "I'm thinking of going to town" (*t'iota ekta mni̧kte imnukc'a*). In PST, the sign that accompanies or is translated as *imnukc'a* is similar to that described above for *wac'i̧*, but instead of moving straight forward it takes a path to the diagonal. This may be a parallel to the *i* prefix, the diagonal moving toward a potential object (i.e., thinking about something, or in relation to something).

Figure 7.6 (*opposite page*). Assiniboine embodiment of "mind." The sign glossed as THINK/THOUGHTS is a polysemic one that, like its spoken equivalent, can act as a noun or a verb. Note that the two signs GOOD and THINK/THOUGHTS merely change their order in these two sentences. In (a) THINK/THOUGHTS acts as a noun qualified by the adjective that follows it. In (b) it acts as a verb and ends the sentence. The order of signs indicates a shift of grammatical function that is unmarked in speech.

The PST sign that often accompanies *wokc'a* is an allomorph of the sign LOOK FOR performed in a lower area of the signing space and coming forward from the chest rather than from the eyes. By so doing it provides an active metaphor (thinking is looking from the heart), one that is again focused outward. Despite a superficial similarity to metaphors used by English speakers, there are substantial differences. Although among English speakers seeing is a powerful metaphor involving mind, it is one that is applied not so much to the process of thinking as to an end product called understanding. To see is to perceive something, to hit upon the object; hence understanding is popularly conceived of as an uncovering, a single mental event, something that occurs at an instant of time, as for example in the phrases "Ah, I see what you mean" and "Now I get the picture" (see Lakoff and Johnson 1980). Likewise, the "conduit metaphor" discussed by Reddy (1979) emphasizes how English speakers conceive of thoughts and ideas as "things" and use numerous metaphors of getting, giving, putting, packing, and inserting ideas as objects of exchange in communication. In contrast, where PST uses a visual metaphor in the variant of the verb TO LOOK (from the heart), it is one that emphasizes an active searching, a process of thinking rather than a product.

Herzfeld (1987:39) has drawn attention to the powerful role of the literate tradition here in shaping epistemologies that give rise to such objectifications in metaphor: "Power is control of discourse; and the act of writing, itself at once an index and a metonym of the power of the literate over the rest of the world, reorganizes experience to suit the whims of the powerful." The great literate/oral divide (that still defines the use of the term "a civilization") has meant that the analysis of culture has been exclusively calibrated to a model of literacy (see Ong 1982:12–13).[7]

The effects of literacy notwithstanding, in a Cartesian framework understanding is viewed as the product of an inwardly focused individual intellect: one looks inward, not out toward the space of relationship. In contrast, for the Assiniboine, again we find that thinking is conceived of, not as an inwardly focused process going on privately inside the head, but as an outwardly focused looking or searching. This is entirely consistent with religious metaphors in which gaining supernatural aid, spoken of in terms of achieving "power," while certainly a highly personal endeavor, involves events such as a "vision quest," a period of fasting and isolation for a person in search of spiritual assistance that will come in visual form, while the seeker is either awake or dreaming. Also, the long process of gaining wisdom through knowledge of "Indian ways" is often spoken of in active terms of following "a [red] road."

This metaphorical location around the heart of what in English we divide into two attributes of persons—thinking and feeling—suggests vast cultural differences in conceptions about knowing and feeling. The combined location supported by spoken and signed languages alike suggests a fundamental lack of separation in Assiniboine epistemology: to know is "to know in one's heart," that is, passionately and with deep conviction. But this is a personal knowledge, obtained through both personal effort and supernatural assistance that makes no claims to objectivity or universal truth such that it should be imposed on anyone else. This attitude to knowledge applies to the education of the young also, in that children at home are often not taught explicitly until they come to ask for assistance, that is, when they desire to know and are ready to engage in the effort necessary to learn.

This deep involvement of feeling in thinking is expressed in other forms of the verb *wac'i*. The sign that Tomkins glossed as DOUBT, which involves two actions of the hand over the heart, is glossed in Nakota as *wacinupa*, not "two hearts" but "two minds," performed over the heart.

Feelings are involved also in the use of *wac'ik'o*, for example, which means "quick-tempered" or "a person who gets mad easily," who "easily takes offense" and is "quick to anger." *Wac'isica* is a "quick-tempered person," *wac'iya* means "to depend on." Other terms for feelings often include the word and sign for "heart" (*c'ate*), as in the term *c'atesica* 'heart bad', meaning either sorrow or a person who is mean, selfish, or ornery, context determining which one is meant. In PST these can be distinguished by using HEART + DOWN for the former and HEART + BAD for the latter. Similarly, *c'atewaste* 'heart + good' in PST and Nakota means "feeling good" but also "good- or kind-hearted" in the English sense of the term. Other signs center around the heart and involve other qualities of persons, including BRAVE (HEART + STRONG) and its negative, REMEMBER (HEART + KNOW/HEART + HOLD) and its negative, and STUPID (KNOW + NOTHING). A sign used frequently by people who know some signs but not the sign language proper means

SMART/WISE and is located at the head, but this is a metaphor that comes from the sign for WOLF or COYOTE, a symbol of craftiness, and represents the wolf's ears, not a locating of mental ability in the head.

Other signs referring to these kinds of semantic domains that are centered around the head include ANGRY (*sikna*), CRAZY (*witk'o*), and SACRED/MYSTERIOUS/HOLY (*wak'ą*). An interesting feature of the last two is that they are a minimal pair, both performed just above the head by making small horizontal circles (Fig. 7.7). The difference between them is the direction of rotation of those circles. In *wak'ą* (SACRED/MYSTERIOUS/HOLY) the hand makes clockwise circles, consistent with the direction of the sun and therefore more accurately described as sunwise. This is the direction in which dancers progress around a dance arbor. Observers and participants alike in the sun dance lodge must always proceed sunwise around the center pole. The ritual actions an individual must make with the pipe prior to smoking, and the passing of the pipe among participants in ceremonies, are all done in a sunwise direction, as is the passing out of food at gatherings of all kinds.

In contrast, when signing *witk'o* (CRAZY), the hand makes anticlockwise circles. This is consistent with the way the fool dancers (*witk'oka wac'ipi*), sometimes called *heyok'a*, do everything backward. At the former Assiniboine fool dances, and at current sun dances if they are present—as happened in 1989 and 1990—fool dancers travel the "wrong" way, going around the sun dance lodge anti-sunwise.[8] The two directions of motion encoded in the two signs thus create what seems to be a classic structural opposition between order and disorder and all that is implied by the polysemic notions of SACRED and CRAZY. When I checked this interpretation, however, one consultant was of the opinion that the sign could be performed circling in either direction and meant either sacred or crazy. This apparent contradiction does not alter the consistent difference I had noticed in performance but instead reflects the belief that sacred and crazy are not so much oppositions as different aspects of *wak'ą*, the mysterious and holy but also the uncontrollable.

In contrast to these Assiniboine and PST conceptions about thinking and feeling, the Western positivist drive toward rationality has led to a situation in which feelings and emotion are deemed contaminants of objective thought and real knowledge. Thought and feeling, coterminous with mind and body respectively, have been increasingly

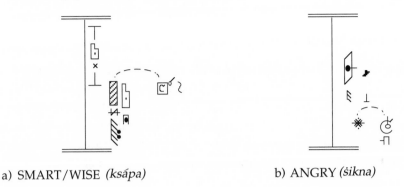

a) SMART/WISE *(ksápa)*   b) ANGRY *(śikna)*

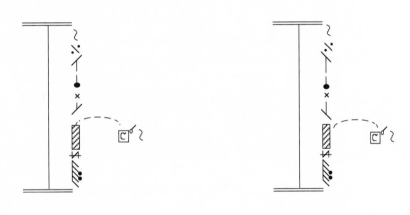

c) SACRED/MYSTERIOUS/HOLY *(wak'ą)*   d) CRAZY *(witk'o)*

Figure 7.7. Some PST signs located at the head: (a) is a metaphor that uses the sign WOLF; (c) and (d) form a minimal pair that contrast only in the direction of the movement path; (c) takes a sunwise (clockwise) circular path ⌐ while (d) takes an anti-sunwise circular path ⌐ .

separated from each other in the search for ever more pure forms of objectivity. It is only during the last thirty years that post-positivist conceptions of objectivity began to emerge (see Varela 1984; Gouldner 1970; Kuhn 1962; Langer 1942; Polanyi 1958; Pocock 1973). This has relevance when accounting for the absence of the body from social theory (see Turner 1984; Varela 1994).

VERBS OF MOVEMENT

Confirmation of my interpretation of *šką* and the primacy of movement comes independently from an article by Jahner (1980) who states, "The starting point for studying the [Lakota] world-view has to be the idea that movement itself is the primal image for life." Jahner considers this an idea not unique to the Lakota but common to many Siouan-speaking groups. A clear articulation of the general outlines of the concept is found, for example, among the Omaha:

> An invisible and continuous life was believed to permeate all things seen and unseen. This life manifests itself in two ways. First by causing to move—all motions, all actions of mind and body are because of this invisible life; second, by causing permanency of structure and form, as in the rock, the physical lakes, the animals, and man. This invisible life was also conceived of as being similar to the willpower of which man is conscious within himself—a power by which things are brought to pass. (Fletcher and La Flesche [1911] 1972:134, quoted in Jahner 1980:131)

This causal power to move that *is* life involves all motion, "all actions of mind and body." There is no presence here of a deterministic Newtonian world with its billiard ball model of causality in a mechanical world, nor a Cartesian separation of the equally mechanical but sensate physical, material body from a nonmaterial mind. Here life as motion unites mind and body in action. The analogy I proposed above between the theory of a causal power to move and a causal power of persons that involves agency (see Harré 1984)—or as phrased here, "the willpower of which man is conscious within himself"—is independently confirmed in this statement by Fletcher and La Flesche.

Jahner also draws attention to the belief that permanency of structure is brought about by the same power that manifests itself as movement: form is completed movement, or movement at rest. Stone is movement held in abeyance, and so, as Deloria noted in an interview (1937–1938:28–31), persons could receive messages from stones if they "moved with" the stones—that is, if they arranged their actions according to culturally defined moral standards. This conception is again found in a statement by an unnamed Omaha chief to Fletcher:

Everything as it moves, now and then, here and there, makes stops. The bird as it flies stops in one place to make its nest, and in another to rest in its flight. A man when he goes forth stops when he wills. So the god [*wakonda*] has stopped. The moon, the stars, the winds he has been with. The trees, the animals, are all where he has stopped, and the Indian thinks of these places and sends his prayers there to reach the place where the god has stopped and win help and a blessing. (Fletcher 1884:276, quoted in DeMallie and Lavenda 1977:160)

DeMallie and Lavenda note that the precision and clarity of this statement of the Omaha conception of *wakonda* (cf. *wak'ą*) is marred only by the English interpreter who could not resist the temptation to simplify the native conception by anthropomorphizing it. Fletcher also reports a further use of the Omaha *wakonda* in the word *wakondagi*, one of the uses of which is to describe the first manifestation of a new ability in a child, an indication of an individual and independent power within the child to act (1912:106–107, quoted in DeMallie and Lavenda 1977:166). This would seem to tie in with the concept of *śką* (one of the *wak'ą* beings) as a causal power to move and the causal power of persons.

Prereservation social organization, as noted earlier, for the Assiniboine as for the Lakota, was visualized as a series of nested circles: the cosmos, the world, the camp circle, and the tipi. At each level, prescribed patterns of movement created order, sunwise movement representing order, anti-sunwise movement disorder and unnatural behavior. At each level of social organization, a person could think of her or his personal identity as intimately related to a particular place, a specific point in the various circles of social organization that created the social person and defined the self, but no individual's place was ever static. Movement among the various circles of being came about for reasons of prestige and power, and was inescapable because of the progression of time. Spatial imagery was and is used to articulate the notion of time passing, realized through movement in space. Life is viewed as movement around a circle of four stages, from birth to youth to maturity to old age. For every death, people say, there is a birth, and so the circle of life continues. While overt structures of social and political organization have altered dramatically, much of the symbolism remains, backed up by features of a language that encodes place (movement at rest) and movement between places in specific ways.

The Nakota language describes point-to-point locomotion precisely, by specifying the onset, process, and completion of motion and by foregrounding social relations, because travel toward and away from places of belonging is marked. PST can accommodate this precision of the spoken language among Assiniboine sign talkers, but PST grammar does not coincide with the spoken language structure.

Nakota verbs of motion, like English "come" and "go," refer to direction toward the speaker or away from the speaker, making them deictic. In PST there are two basic forms that encode these two directions. COME is performed with an upright index finger that is placed away from the body in preparation for movement toward the signer's torso during the sign. GO is performed with a handshape that changes from folded to extended and directs movement away from the body of the signer.

In spoken Nakota, however, while *ya* 'to go' and *u* 'to come' are general in reference, one does not usually designate only a basic direction like this. In addition to direction, verbs mark different stages of completion in the process of motion: intention to come, departing, on the way, and arriving. These in turn differ according to whether the "coming" or "going" refers to coming or going home to where the person in transit belongs, or coming or going to a place away from home. The English question "Are you coming?" must be specified as one of the following in Nakota: "Will you be coming home?" "Will you be coming here (not home)?" "Will you leave to come home?" "Will you leave to come here (not home)?" "Are you on your way coming home?" "Are you on your way coming here (not home)?, "Will you arrive home?" "Will you arrive here (not home)?"

This involves the speaker/signer in a deictic space of some complexity. The choice of verb depends upon where the speaker happens to be at the time. Buechel (1939:166) represents these verbs graphically for Lakota in the following diagrams, which I have adapted for Nakota.

In Figures 7.8–7.10, A is the person spoken of who is leaving his home at the Agency, visiting his neighbor B at Lodgepole, then returning to his home. S is the speaker, anybody who is talking about the locomotion of A. The speaker must select different verbs according to whether he is in A's home, at B's home, or somewhere else altogether. The following sentences reflect choices he might make.

1. The speaker, S, is in A's home at the Agency (Fig. 7.8).

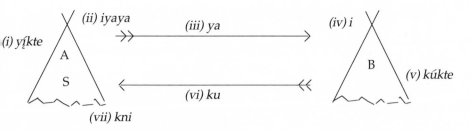

Figure 7.8. S is in A's home, speaking of A.

a. If A is going away from S, toward Lodgepole, S would say of A:
i. *Hayakec wase wakpa ékta yįkte.* Tomorrow he will go to Lodgepole.
ii. *Wase wakpa iyaya he?* Did he set out for Lodgepole?
iii. *Wase wakpa ekta ya he?* Is he on his way to Lodgepole?
iv. *Wase wakpa ekta i.* He is at/has gone to/has been at Lodgepole.

b. If A is coming toward S, from Lodgepole, S would say of A:
v. *Hayakec, t'ipi ekta kúkte.* Tomorrow he will be on his way home.
vi. *Wanuḣ ak'e kúpic'.* Maybe they are coming back again/are on their way home.
vii. *Wanuḣ knípi c'a.* Maybe they came back home (arrived home).

2. The speaker, S, is at B's home, in Lodgepole (Fig. 7.9).

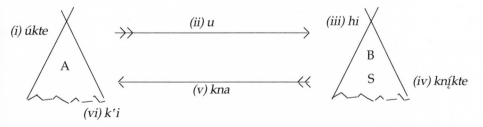

Figure 7.9. S is in B's home, speaking of A.

a. If A is coming toward S, toward Lodgepole, S would say of A:
i. *Mit'ąkona įś úkte néįś.* My friend will be coming.
ii. *Mit'ąkona u.* My friend is on his way coming here.
iii. *Nitąkona hi.* Your friend has arrived/is here.

b. If A is going home, away from S, away from Lodgepole, S would say of A:

iv. *Yamnic'a śten* **kn̓kte**. In three days' time he will go home.

v. *Wana t'íta* **kna**. Now he is on his way home.

vi. *Wana t'íta* **k'i** *żec'a*. Now he has arrived home.

3. The speaker, S, is somewhere else, neither in Lodgepole nor at A's home (Fig. 7.10).

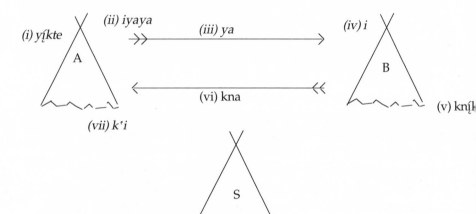

Figure 7.10. S is elsewhere, speaking of A.

a. If A is traveling from his own home to B's home in Lodgepole:
i–iv. S would use the same terms as in 1a.

b. If A is traveling from B's home in Lodgepole back to his own home:
v–vii. S would use the same terms as in 2b.

That is, comparison of the third option with the former two shows that it combines both, in that the terms of the "going" set—traveling away from home and arriving away from home, speaker located at that home—are used for the outgoing journey and the "going home" set—traveling toward home and arriving home, speaker not located at that home—for the returning journey.

The significance of these distinctions lies in the way that they structure many kinds of discourse. Direction and location index the place where one belongs, which leaves the choice of verb open as a discourse strategy for locating persons in their appropriate social space. It can be manipulated to include or exclude persons from belonging. For example, one of the nicknames I acquired in the context of one family for a short time was *t'ehą́kniś* 'she didn't come back for a long time', acquired because I had gone to Fort Peck for a week without letting them know I was going. The name both scolded and teased me, but at the same time was a compliment because they used *kni* 'coming back home/returning to one's place', a verb that included me as someone who could and should feel at home with them. Properly speaking, they should have used the *k'i* form to say I had returned to my home, a place away from the speaker's location.

Locations of belonging also imply specific kinds of responsibility because of the way kinship roles structure responsibility and obligations. An interesting manipulation of this in signs is found in Figure 7.11, which shows the response of an elderly woman sign talker who was asked to sign "You will go to buy food" (*wóyute op'et'ų nį́kte*). As the notation illustrates, she translated this into signs that gloss as EAT + MEAT + OTHER SIMILAR THINGS + TIPI (DWELLING PLACE) + COME/BRING. So, while the words say "go" to buy food, taking her away from her deictic center, she has reversed this to say in signs that she will bring food back home, using the sign COME/BRING. Given her felt responsibility to feed her family at home, she has encoded in the translation into signs what is important to her about going to buy food: bringing it back.

In PST the overall pattern of this locomotive semantic is followed, but the constant frame of reference in relation to the cardinal directions and actual positioning of places relative to the speaker determines the placing of gestures within this schema. So for example, in Figure 7.12 the speaker says and signs, "I will go to town from here," using the *ya* + *kte* form of "going." He uses the sign GO and directs the movement path of the sign toward north, the direction in which town lies from his house. In Figure 7.13 the same sign talker says, "I'm on my way back home [from Lodgepole]," again using the GO sign directed northward, the difference being that he is now talking of the direction of his home viewed from Lodgepole, the place he was coming back from in the elicited sentences, and thus the place he had located himself deictically from

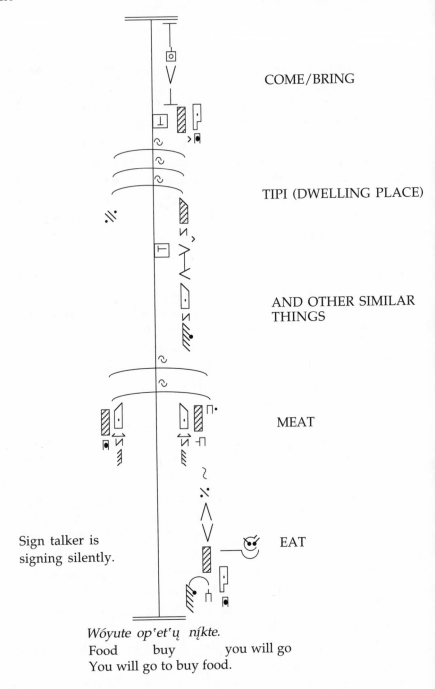

COME/BRING

TIPI (DWELLING PLACE)

AND OTHER SIMILAR
THINGS

MEAT

EAT

Sign talker is
signing silently.

Wóyute op'et'ų nį́kte.
Food   buy   you will go
You will go to buy food.

Figure 7.11. Verbs of coming and going in Nakota and Plains Sign Talk.

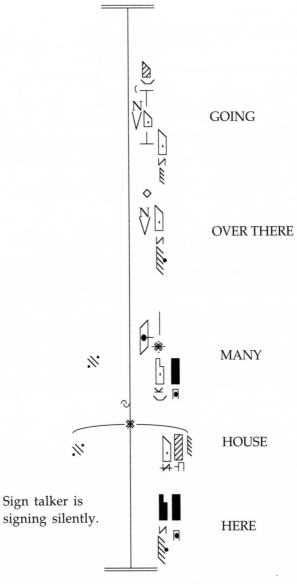

GOING

OVER THERE

MANY

HOUSE

Sign talker is
signing silently.

HERE

Netahą   t'iota kák'i   mnįkte.
From here town   over there I will go
I will go to town from here.

Figure 7.12. Verbs of coming and going in Nakota and Plains Sign Talk.

which to speak/sign. The difference between potential going, departing, and being on the way is not made explicit in signs, but context and the addition of time markers such as "today" or "tomorrow" remove ambiguity.

Similarly, Figure 7.14 uses the *i* verb, which means to arrive at or to have been at a place away from home. In signs the pointed upright index is used and placed at the edge of the signing space, again in the geographical direction of the place mentioned, which in this case was southeast and 凸 forward-right-diagonal of the signer's location. Although the handshape is the same as the sign for COME, there is no movement toward the signer; the place one has arrived *at* is what is marked here. The COME handshape marks that this place one is at is not one's own because it is suggestive of a readiness to return.

This sign COME/BRING belongs to a semantic grouping that does not coincide exactly with spoken language structure but has its own logic, based upon amount and type of movement. Others in the set share the same basic handshape of the upright index finger and include the signs for PERSON/MAN, ONE/NOW, TO BE/STAY/LIVE (HUMAN), TO BE AT, TO COME/BRING, and TO ARRIVE, each one distinguished by a movement path, a location, or the use of the second hand (Fig. 7.15). There is a movement continuum involved in these signs—from stillness, through slight movement, to obvious movement path—that is iconic of the degree of movement in their semantic content, beginning with the held positions of PERSON/MAN, ONE/NOW, and TO BE AT. The sign that appeared in translation of the word *ųpi* 'they live/are/stay' discussed in the "Inktomi and the Frog" narrative (Chapter 6) uses this same handshape with only small movements from side to side to indicate human *be*-ing (in the sense of the verbs "to be," "to exist"), a place of being, where one stays. At the opposite end of the continuum the signs COME/BRING and ARRIVE use a clear, straight path of movement to designate locomotion. In this way the signs form a semantic grouping that has its own logic and is not a part of spoken language structure (Fig. 7.15). It is precisely this kind of semantic content that has led some investigators to suggest that parts of signs in a sign language act more like morphemes than phonemes (West 1960; Klima and Bellugi 1979).

In PST there are three basic signs that indicate COMING, GOING,

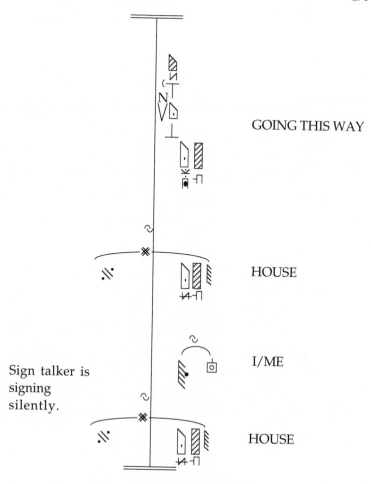

GOING THIS WAY

HOUSE

I/ME

Sign talker is
signing
silently.

HOUSE

Wat'i   że   żec'i   waknac'.
Home   that that way I am on my way back.
I am on my way back home.

Figure 7.13. Verbs of coming and going in Nakota and Plains Sign Talk.

and ARRIVAL. Thereafter it is placing in space that creates the finer distinctions that correspond to the variety of spoken Nakota verbs. The sign ARRIVAL combines the COME handshape with movement toward the other (usually left) hand that acts as a barrier to further movement, thus conveying the notion of cessation. Alternatively, ARRIVAL can be indicated by creating a curved path of movement in space with the lower

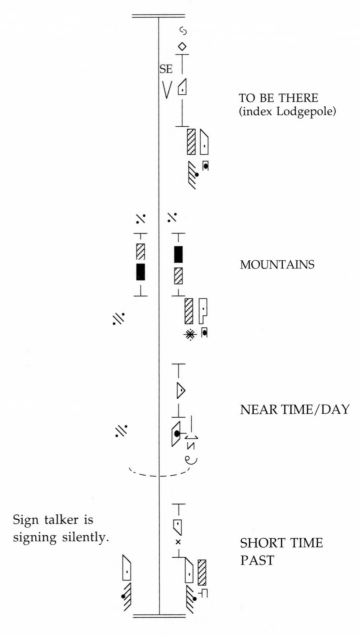

TO BE THERE
(index Lodgepole)

MOUNTAINS

NEAR TIME/DAY

Sign talker is
signing silently.

SHORT TIME
PAST

Ḣtánihą   íyaḣe   ekta waicʼ.
Yesterday mountains there I was at.
Yesterday I was out to Lodgepole.

Figure 7.14. Verbs of coming and going in Nakota and Plains Sign Talk.

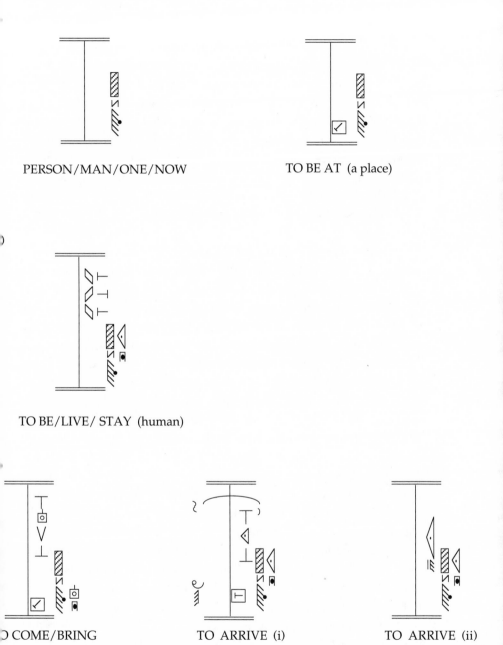

Figure 7.15. A semantic grouping using one handshape: (a) signs using the still handshape; (b) signs with minor movement; (c) signs with a clear movement path.

arm moving the hand from upright to side left, the path of movement coming to a definite end point instead of involving the other hand. This is a different shape of pathway than the straight path created by bringing the hand directly toward the torso or toward the other hand. Either of these allomorphs would indicate arrival "here" at the place of the signer, or "there" at some previously designated place corresponding to either *hi, kni,* or *i* in spoken form. Further information could be provided to designate whether this is an arrival home or not, as for example when the sign for HOUSE/HOME is placed in the space at the end of the movement path to designate ARRIVAL HOME (*kni*), or the name of person or place signed prior to ARRIVAL, thus indicating arrival there.

Another way of signing ARRIVAL THERE (*i*) is to use the two-handed sign that designates ARRIVAL and place it in an appropriate location in the signing space so that it coincides with the actual geographical direction of the place arrived at. The sign can be placed away from the signer's torso anywhere in the signing space to correspond to a specific location. For example, Figure 7.16 shows how a sign talker who was facing north moved both hands to perform ARRIVE next to her right shoulder. This accurately located Lodgepole, the place of arrival, southeast of her. Figure 7.16 also shows how speech and signs complement each other at the semantic level. The spoken verb used in this utterance is *i* 'to be at' and because of the lack of verb tense in Nakota it can mean either past action ("was at") or present ongoing action ("is at"). The addition of the word *wana* ("now") together with the signed inflection of TO ARRIVE AT places the action in the present. Note also how the PST sign for the community of Lodgepole again utilizes the visual imagery encoded in the Nakota name for this place. In Nakota, Lodgepole is called *Wase Wakpa* or "Red Paint Creek," so named because of the red earth powder found in the area and used to make face paint. The sign is made by rubbing the fingers of one hand (right hand in this case) against the cheek, thereby indexing this function.

Geographical factors can also outweigh the speaker's deictic center when signing COMING BACK HOME. Figure 7.17 illustrates how the sign talker, situated at the Agency, has used the northwesterly direction of movement from Lodgepole to the Agency to sign NOW HE IS ON HIS WAY HOME (*ku*) rather than directing the sign COME toward her

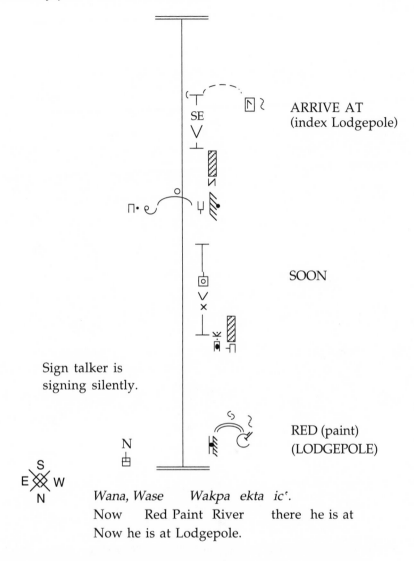

ARRIVE AT
(index Lodgepole)

SOON

Sign talker is
signing silently.

RED (paint)
(LODGEPOLE)

Wana, Wase   Wakpa ekta ic'.
Now   Red Paint   River   there he is at
Now he is at Lodgepole.

Figure 7.16. Deictic location of PST verb: TO ARRIVE. The spoken verb in this elicited phrase is *i* 'to be at', whereas the signed version uses TO ARRIVE AT. Perhaps the use of *wana* 'now' in speech at the start of the phrase has led the sign talker to provide a more continuous sense of the action. The signed version translates more accurately as "Soon she will arrive at Lodgepole." The Nakota name for the place called Lodgepole means "Red Paint River/Creek" and refers to the availability of the red earth powder used to make face paint. The PST sign utilizes this etymology.

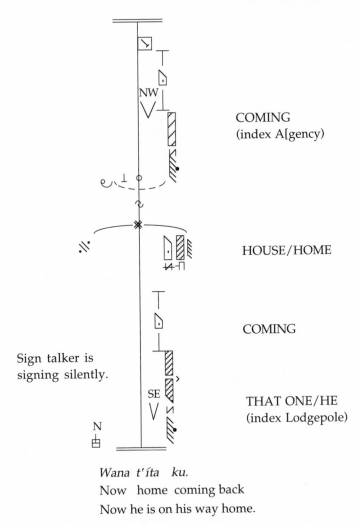

COMING
(index A[gency])

HOUSE/HOME

COMING

Sign talker is
signing silently.

THAT ONE/HE
(index Lodgepole)

Wana t'íta   ku.
Now   home coming back
Now he is on his way home.

Figure 7.17. COMING HOME: geographical factors override actor's deictic center.

own torso. In another example (Fig. 7.18), the signer uses the COMING
sign but directs it away from herself, using the second hand as a moving
target until HOME is set up in the signing space when the two hands
come together to indicate ARRIVAL. This coincides with *k'i* 'arrival at
home but away from the speaker'.

The location of the speaker/signer at neither destination can also be
represented in signs. Figure 7.19 illustrates a translation of the sentence

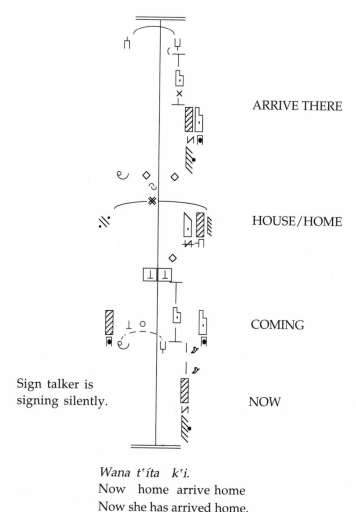

ARRIVE THERE

HOUSE/HOME

COMING

Sign talker is
signing silently.

NOW

Wana t'íta k'i.
Now   home   arrive home
Now she has arrived home.

Figure 7.18. Deictic use of PST verbs: TO BE COMING, TO ARRIVE.

"Now she is going home" (*kníkte*), in which the third person is set up in the 🄳 space and GOING HOME takes a straight path sideways across the signing space, moving neither toward nor away from the signer's deictic center.

Nakota grammar also lends support to the thesis in another way. The causes of action are encoded linguistically in ways that make them very explicit. Nakota verbs that refer to instrumental action make use of

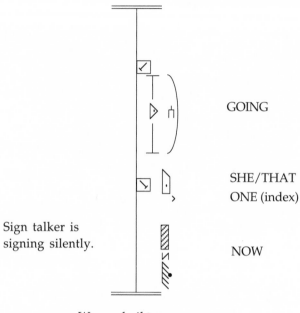

GOING

SHE/THAT
ONE (index)

Sign talker is
signing silently.

NOW

Wana   kn̨ikte.
Now   will be going home
Now she will be going home.

Figure 7.19. GOING: third-person reference without geographical location. The third person is set up in the ⟍ space, and movement goes across the signing space, neither toward nor away from the signer's deictic center.

prefixes that encode action according to the part of the body used or the type of body motion that accomplishes the action. For example, the prefix *ya* indicates action using the mouth as in *yatka* 'to drink' and *yawaśte* 'to speak well of someone'. In the latter example the instrumental prefix turns the stative verb *waśte* 'to be good' into an active transitive form. Other instrumentals are (*na*) by foot; (*yu*) by manipulation with the hands, by pulling or holding; (*pa*) by pushing or pressing; (*ka*) by striking with a tool; (*wa*) by cutting, by using a cutting edge; and (*wo*) by piercing, or by using a point (see Boas and Deloria 1941:45; Taylor and Rood 1972, Lesson 18.4). While it is beyond the scope of the present work to explore this further, Nakota verb forms are very specific about action and causes, which is entirely consistent with the linguistic representation of actions *with* action itself, as encoded into conventional gestures and a sign language.

ACTION IN SOCIAL PRACTICES: GREETINGS AND THE BODY

In Assiniboine culture, the metaphorical location of thinking away from the head discussed above does not leave the head devoid of semantic value. On the contrary, the head is a highly salient body part. Lakota and Kiowa pictographic records, for example, consistently show the personal names of individuals as iconic representations of animals or birds arising from the head, as illustrated in Figure 7.20.[9] In addition, signs relating to senses such as hearing, listening, seeing, looking, tasting, eating, drinking, and smell are located around the face and head near their respective organs, as might be expected.

In PST, however, the most prominent use of the head is as a locus for tribal names and greetings. Signs for many tribal names are performed near, or touching, parts of the face and other areas of the head. Examples include BLOOD (a division of the Blackfeet confederacy)—circular action of fist on the cheek (sign also means BLOOD and RED); SIOUX, ASSINIBOINE—flat hand drawn across the throat, meaning "cut throats"; NEZ PERCE—"pierced noses"; CREE—finger down side of face; FLATHEAD—iconic of flattened head; and KIOWA—hair cut at one side (see Fig. 7.21).

In prereservation days, these tribal signs were of the utmost importance for identifying strangers as friends or foes. When scouts or warriors were out alone on the prairie and met a stranger, the first communication would be in signs across the distance between them. Walker describes in some detail what might occur when scouts were ahead of, or spread out far to either side of, a moving column of people and equipment as a band were moving camp:

If at any time a scout discovered signs of persons he first examined them to learn whether they were made recently or not. If he saw someone he would, while screening himself closely, observe such a one and if he concluded that it was a friend he would show himself and raise his right hand high above his head with the palm forward and then wave it from side to side, which in the sign language of the Plains meant that he wished to speak to the one signaled. If the one signaled was friendly, he extended his right arm in front and made a downward hooking motion with his

FIG. 71—Winter
1835–36 — Big-
face killed.

FIG. 115—Summer 1854—
Black-horse killed.

FIG. 118—Winter   1855–56 — Big-head
kills an Ä'lähó.

FIG. 148—Winter
1870–71 — Set-
ängya's bones
brought home;
drunken fight;
negroes killed.

FIG. 73—Winter
1836–37—K'iñä-
hiate killed.

FIG. 87—Winter
1842–43—Crow-
neck died.

FIG. 124 — Winter
1858-59—Gúi-k'áte
killed.

Figure 7.20. The head as semantic domain for naming practices on the Plains—
pictographic representations of personal names. Examples reprinted from Mooney
[1898] 1979. Used with permission.

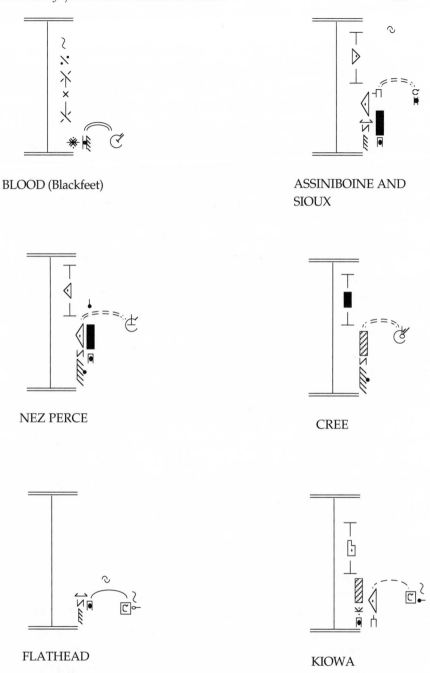

BLOOD (Blackfeet)

ASSINIBOINE AND SIOUX

NEZ PERCE

CREE

FLATHEAD

KIOWA

Figure 7.21. The head as semantic domain for naming practices on the Plains—some tribal names in Plains Sign Talk.

extended index finger, moving the whole hand. Then they approached each other and conversed, after which the scout returned to the marshals and reported what he had learned. If there was a friendly camp on its way for a [buffalo] chase, a meeting was arranged and an agreement made either to chase together or to hunt in different territories.

If the scout was in doubt about the one observed, whether he was a friend or an enemy, he would watch him long and closely, and if he could not satisfy himself in this way, he would then show himself and signal as given above. If the one signaled was in doubts about the friendliness of the one signaling he would either not answer the signal or would raise his extended right arm to about halfway between horizontal and perpendicular and wave his right hand from side to side, which in the sign language of the Plains meant "Who are you and what do you want?" The scout would then draw his right hand across his throat from left to right, then raise his closed fist in front of his face and bring it suddenly towards his face, extending his fingers while doing so, as if throwing something into his face. This in the sign language of the Plains meant that he was an Oglala Dakota. He would then make the sign that the other had made, which would mean "Who are you and what are you doing?"

If the one signaled was friendly to the scout he would give the sign for his tribe and they approached and conversed. If he was an enemy he would refuse to answer and the two would warily watch each other, each trying to learn as much of the other as possible, and, if the opportunity offered, to take the other's horse or his scalp. (Walker 1982:84–85)

The signs described in this passage are from the standard PST lexicon. The first "wave" is not a greeting but a method of drawing someone's attention. It is frequently used today by many, regardless of their knowledge of sign language. It is used across distances instead of a shout to attract attention or, smaller in size, across a room for the same purpose. The reply described by Walker is the sign YES. The next sign is the standard question marker, the meaning of which would be extended in this context to "Who are you," the correct response in this language game being one's tribal sign. The particular tribal sign described here is a combined one. The first part—the hand drawn across the throat—identifies the person as a Sioux or Assiniboine. The second part of the sign, iconic of throwing something into the face, refers to one of the divisions of the Lakota Sioux, the Oglala, whose name means "to scatter one's own." One interpretation of this refers to an argument between two chiefs during which ashes or dirt were thrown into the face of one by the other. His followers were ever after nicknamed "those who had dirt or ashes thrown in their faces." Regardless of historical fact, it is this interpretation that became encoded in the sign language (cf. W. P. Clark 1885:272; Scott 1934).

Today it is still the case that "you address yourself where you're from, not your name," and occasionally signs still serve exactly the same function between strangers. For example, a few years ago when Earthboy was visiting the Browning Museum of the Plains Indian on the Blackfeet Reservation, west of Fort Belknap, the following incident occurred:

See, at this building like this there was a line going here,

they were eating, and I was across here.

So this guy was — he kept looking at me. So finally I asked him in

sign language, I said "What are you?"

Oh he said, ... "I'm a crow," ..... he said, so from there we

started talking. Like ...."maybe you're hungry," ....I said.

He said "Yes," he said, and he asked me different questions see.

In time these people here they were watching what we were

doing see. I could just as well have walked over there and asked
him those questions, but you know, I was across the room you

know making signs. It kind of seemed — I don't know how I'd put
it, but it's more like a show we put on you know, which we didn't
intend to. They were all watching us, they didn't know what we
were saying — maybe some of them did, but I don't know.

Cryptic comment upon the contrast between Indian and non-
Indian ways of greeting is contained in the following description:

J.E.: Long time ago, when two strangers met, like men, they won't
run up there, smile and grab each other or nothin'. They just stand
there and look at each other you know. Finally one of them would
ask you, he'd ask "Where did you come from, he'd say.

Well, if he was from up west, he'd ask of me

"What kind of person are you ?" he'd say.

If he said . . . . "I'm Blood," . . . . . . then he'll know, see, what he's

talking about, then he'll ask him his name or something, or if he's
looking for somebody.

B.F. So it's more important to stand and look first . . .

J.E. Yeh. Or maybe if he's lookin' for somebody, maybe he'll
go up to somebody and ask him in sign language "Do you know

such and such a person?" See, that's how they got
started, but otherwise if he's just standin' around waiting to

get wacha-call-it [acquainted],
then they'd just look at each other for a while see, kinda "size

each other up" you'd say: see what he would say, or what kinda
Indian he was.

B.F. Any rules about who would speak first, you know if it was
. . . ?

J.E. No, not really. [pause] Well, usually the host does. Sometimes
he would do the asking questions first.

Because English has gradually replaced PST as the *lingua franca*,
such incidents are increasingly rare. As Lois Red Elk recalled;

My mom was visiting my Uncle Gerald and we happened to
be walking in the house the same time as his company. And my
mom turned around and she saw that they were strangers, but
they also wanted to identify themselves to each other, and the
old man happened to be from the Nez Perce tribe and he just
looked right at my uncle and he made the sign you know,
"nose pierced." And my uncle, ... acknowledged, and he

went like this . . . ."cut head" which is a particular

band of Yankton Sioux, and it was just astounding that those two
had that form of communication, and they knew what they were
doing, and they acknowledged each other but it was just like
something out of the past - you don't see that hardly anymore.

The face, although an important component in these conventions for identifying and greeting strangers, plays an entirely different role from that expected by Euro-Americans. Facial expressions in the sense of smiles or grimaces, often assumed to be universally understood, simply play no part here. Instead, action signs using the hands around the face convey appropriate information for participants to know how to proceed in this language game of "greetings." A smile even today is not a necessary part of greeting; in the past it may have been viewed as somewhat bizarre behavior in this context.

As with color categories (Berlin and Kay 1969; Sahlins 1976), so with physiological universals regarding facial expression: while there are many facial expressions that look the same across cultural boundaries, it cannot be assumed that they mean the same things. All peoples in the world may "smile." What is of anthropological interest is again the lack of fit in terms of what such an apparently familiar action sign may mean and how and when it is used, none of which can be assumed. Within American culture, for example, one can smile out of embarrassment, at a momentary loss for words, when putting on a "brave face," and so on, as well as out of happiness or pleasure. Perceived intentions and context of use have to determine what is meant (see La Barre 1947; Hall 1966).[10] The stereotypical stoic and straight-faced Indian, so beloved by Hollywood, is one found only in the company of strangers, and is not "sullen" and "unfriendly" (formerly interpreted as "hostile" and "warlike") as such behavior would be for a Euro-American. The Native American is instead assuming the polite and appropriate countenance of those newly met.

Misunderstanding goes both ways, of course. Many Native Americans view the greetings of the "white man" as simply ridiculous. As indicated by the cryptic comment quoted above, all that shaking of hands and hugging and smiling is viewed as entirely improper and a display of the insincerity they have learned to expect from non-Indian Americans. One often hears sarcastic comments and jokes made about "white people" and what appears to be their constant smiling (cf. Basso 1979).

Prior to the early 1800s, the offering of a hand to shake was equally strange as a form of greeting on the Plains, as illustrated by the following report about the introduction of Nakesinia (Red Calf), a Crow chief, to French fur trader La Rocque:

> When we offered to shake hands with this great man, he did not
> understand the intention, and stood motionless until he was
> informed that shaking hands was the sign of friendship among
> white men: then he stretched forth both his hands to receive ours.
> (McKensie 1804–1806, quoted in Wood and Thiessen 1985:245)

The shaking of hands has long since been adopted as a form of greeting between both strangers and acquaintances. Some young people and AIM (American Indian Movement) members have also adopted the kinds of complex variations also seen among African-American youths and college fraternity members that mark a person as an insider. There is, however, a distinct quality of handshake among Assiniboine and Sioux women that is a relaxed gentle touch of the fingers only, not the whole hand. This serves to transmit important information about ethnic identity for the participants. The gentle touch, not a shake, confirms that the person engaged in the act is Indian (if this is not obvious from appearance) and if not, then at least it is someone who is familiar with Indian ways. For Euro-Americans, this lack of pressure in the hand and contact of mostly fingers, rather than whole palm, seems rather cool and distant. They expect this action to contain an expression of emotion: for them the firmer the grip and the wider the smile, the greater the investment of "friendliness," a quality deemed essential to successful social interaction.

Ardener (1989:166–173) has drawn attention to similar important differences between the Ibo "handshake" and the English one, a difference that is backed by spoken language distinctions. The Ibo taxonomy of the body is divided differently, and the Ibo "hand" or *aka* extends all the way up to the upper arm. A reasonable handshake involves a grasping of the lower arm rather than only the hand as defined by the English taxonomy. To offer only a hand, as an English person would, is perceived as a rather unenthusiastic greeting. The Nakota taxonomy does not coincide with that of English either. Whereas "arm" in English usually includes the hand, in Nakota "arm" extends from shoulder to wrist only; the hand is a different body part.

It becomes clear how, in these kinds of cross-cultural comparisons of action signs, word glosses such as "handshake" often cover up distinct action signs and their meanings in unfortunate ways. As we have

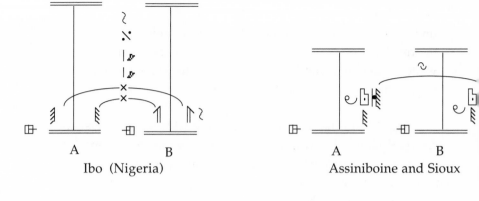

A   B   A   B

Ibo (Nigeria)   Assiniboine and Sioux

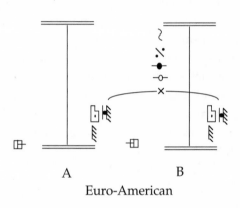

A   B

Euro-American

Figure 7.22. Three distinct action signs glossed as "a handshake."

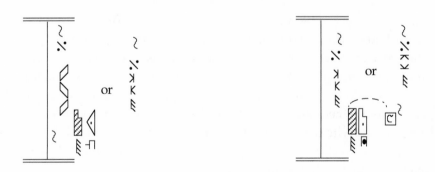

or   or

Assiniboine (Plains) "Attention."   Euro-American wave of greeting/dep

Figure 7.23. Two distinct action signs glossed as "wave."

seen, for many Assiniboine and Sioux women (at least in Montana), a handshake involves neither the hand (as bounded by the English term) nor a shaking action.

Handshakes and the like belong to an area of human social life that is commonly taken to be the most observable, the kind of behavior that can be relatively objectively described. As Ardener ([1971] 1989:172) reminds us, however, action and thought even in this apparently simple zone are inextricably linked and mediated by language. In both Nakota and English, as with Ibo and English, there are apparently inter-translatable terms for the gesture of shaking hands, but they cannot be said to refer to the same action sign across cultures (see Fig. 7.22). For the Native American woman offering relaxed fingers, a hearty grip is a gesture with a different meaning, a gesture that is not only a greeting but also an indicator of ethnic identity and ethnic awareness. To paraphrase Ardener, the instance may appear to be socially trivial, but the relationships between Native Americans and non-Indians have no more characteristic a framework than this.

The word "wave" used by Walker in the description given above presents further problems of the same kind because it does not describe the same action sign for Nakota speakers and sign talkers as it does for English speakers. For the English speaker, "wave" is normally a gesture of greeting or departure, one that has several allomorphs, including waving the hand from side to side or up and down from the wrist. A larger gesture of "waving the *arms* around" may be used to attract attention. In contrast, *wówipi* in Nakota, which is translated as "they wave" (*wówiye* 'flag/cloth for prayer offering'), refers to neither the same physical action nor the semantic content of the sign Walker mentions. The action sign Walker glosses as "wave" means instead "come here" or "hey there," and is accomplished with a rotation of the wrist that makes the hand turn around its axis $\\}$ rather than bend ⋎ or Κ. The transcription in Figure 7.23 describes the two distinct action signs involved, a greeting in one body language and a call for attention in the other, which if glossed as "wave" are conflated.

Likewise, the spoken Nakota term *yuġata* can be translated into English as "to stretch the hand out," but the action sign is specific to raising the hand up as in prayer, or to vote or swear in court, with the palm facing forward. Any stretching of the hand will not count. (In

Lakota, with a different instrumental prefix *yuġata* becomes *naġata* meaning "kick"—as when a newborn baby kicks and stretches or a turtle does with its legs [Deloria, ca. 1940]). Although the action itself is recognizable *as* an action sign to an English speaker, appropriate to the context of a courtroom, the English language does not have a word gloss for this action. Nakota does, but what is meant by the word gloss *yuġata* is defined by its use in Nakota body language and that cannot be assumed to be the same as an English speaker's (cf. Williams 1982 and 1988 with regard to similar problems with word glosses such as "to kneel" and "to bow").

Before leaving the subject of greetings it is appropriate to mention the distinct lack of such socially prescribed utterances on a day-to-day basis at Fort Belknap. The absence of prescribed greeting formulas achieves other performative ends. Relatives and friends who see each other frequently will often enter each other's houses and sit down without any exchange of words or acknowledgment of any kind. There is no lexicon of terms in either PST or Nakota for everyday greetings and partings such as "Good morning," "Hello," or "Goodbye." And only in bureaucratic contexts, as for example at the tribal building or the hospital, or to non-Indians, will such terms in English perhaps be used. This practice has the effect of extending domestic living space beyond the walls of individual houses out into the community, as it were. Just as Euro-Americans do not normally greet family members when passing from room to room within a house, at Fort Belknap people pass from house to house without greeting. To enter and quietly sit, or help oneself to coffee, is to mark oneself as an insider, a relative, in a world where there are for the most part relatives or strangers. To draw attention to oneself is not necessary or appropriate. When words are exchanged, they will be of conversational content, often humorous, rather than conventional greeting formulas. Often conversations will simply start up as if the person just arrived had been there all the time.

There are therefore certain kinds of disjuncture that are often felt between Native Americans and Euro-Americans in greeting situations because of different expectations. The more expected an action or utterance is, the less marked for meaning it becomes, whereas the less probable an utterance or action, the more meaning it will have in that context. So for a Euro-American socially prescribed utterances such as "Hi, how's it goin'?" or "How are you today?" and the expected responses such as "Fine, an' you?" are unmarked because expected. A marked utterance in this context would be the unexpected; for example, silence and a straight face would gain far more meaning precisely because it would violate expectations. For an Assiniboine person these expectations are reversed: the unmarked because expected utterance is the act of entering without speech intruding upon those present, a physical presentation of self into the social or conversational space that means familiarity and belonging. The marked because unexpected utterance in this context would be some kind of greeting formula. It is more polite *not* to say anything and not have people notice you than to draw attention to yourself. To do so marks you as an outsider. Such contrasts between silence and speech create misunderstandings on both sides of the Native American/Euro-American divide because attention becomes focused on the meaning of the unexpected as violations of norms.

Chapter 8

. . . tell me, do you see these stories when I tell them
or do you just write them down?

ZUNI STORYTELLER TO DENNIS TEDLOCK (1983)

[It is] essential for people who work in the social sciences to be alive to
philosophical problems. That is, I don't think you can do social science
effectively without being clued in to philosophical debates, because at
the heart of the social sciences are major difficulties in characterizing
what human beings are like and what human agency is. Such
questions are in some part philosophical, and to be alert to what
philosophers are writing about those issues seems to me important.

ANTHONY GIDDENS (1987)

CONCLUSIONS

In Chapters 1 and 2, I illustrated how Victorian presuppositions about the "natural" and "primitive" nature of the body and movement led to a view of manual gesture and sign languages as evidence of a more primitive form of communication in a presumed evolution from manual gesture to speech to writing as a progression toward higher forms of knowledge.[1] The more removed from the body and context, the more worthy of being called civilized, because knowledge is to be concentrated in the mind and merely carried around by a (highly controlled) body. Such presuppositions provided a powerful rationale for a colonialism that included not only political and economic hegemony but power over spoken language, daily practices, comportment, and especially dancing in the case of Native American cultures.[2]

That such basic epistemological presuppositions are involved in anthropological theorizing seems self-evident. Their import, however, has been insufficiently recognized. The legacies of Plato and Descartes have left largely unexamined and unchallenged assumptions about relationships between body and mind, thinking and feeling, knowledge and experience, subjective and objective. Yet such basic presuppositions are crucially important, since it is they that ultimately determine the theories and the very perception of the problems at issue. This is emerging as a fruitful area for anthropology and philosophy to meet as work on indigenous theories of meaning about such presumed categories as emotion, knowledge, passion, person, self, and history challenges the Western philosophical tradition.[3] At the same time, developments in philosophy have led to the recognition that matters once seen as inevitably epistemological in character rest upon shifting social arrangements of forms of life rather than on some unquestioned basis of transcendental knowledge. In particular, the work of Wittgenstein, Austin, Ryle, Harré, Taylor, and Johnson provides theoretical impetus to develop anthropological thinking about the nature of language and agency and the role of the body in language practices.

The process of shifting my professional persona from that of dancer and dance educator to anthropologist has made me acutely aware that it is precisely such epistemological presuppositions that have led to the absence of the body in social theory. I suggested earlier that this may be why many anthropologists do not appear to *see* movement empirically. Where they do, it is viewed as behavior, not action, and so many find it hard to imagine how movement might "mean" at all, far less contribute anything to our understanding of persons, social structure, and cultural practices. In the interests of articulating a post-Cartesian discourse that may better serve interpretations of indigenous theories of meaning, I have tried to show how gesture and spatial orientation can be viewed as integral to discursive practices.

Once one has in mind the idea that speech and signs integrate to form language, then the hitherto unemphasized fact that people spoke and signed at the same time takes on a strong evidential quality. Within the new theoretical framework presented here, certain phenomena with which everyone was capable of becoming acquainted, but which had scarcely been noticed as significant, become potent items of evidence for an anthropology of human movement. For example, another anthropologist had recommended that I work with Mrs. Weasel because when she told stories she "waved her hands around a lot." This is not, then, theory as thought with no appeal to experience, but rather demonstrates the power of hypotheses to provide themselves with evidence culled from experience. As Harré puts it, "Theory becomes a device for focusing our attention. Theory precedes fact, not because *necesse* determines *esse* as Koyne would have it, but because a theory determines where, in the multiplicity of natural phenomena, we should seek for its evidence" (Harré 1986a:83).

Although I have necessarily concentrated upon an exegesis of Assiniboine uses of manual and vocal gesture, the theoretical implication is that such fundamental links between visible body action and speech may apply to all language communities if we know where to look. And knowing where to look means employing theoretical perspectives that facilitate a radically different conception of language, the body, and human agency. In turn, knowing where to look requires methods that teach one *how* to look. The Laban script has played an important role here as a "mode of registration" (Ardener 1978:104), that is, as a means to apperceive and conceive of movement without the necessity of translating into spoken language terms.

Particular cultural expression of links between visible body action and speech will be dependent upon the kinds of features I have examined above: spatial orientation and deictic classifications, cultural construction of persons and their attributes, indigenous theories of causation and movement, and metaphorical uses of spatial terminology as well as the values attached to different modes of communication. There are sure to be more.

A strong case for a similar theoretical position relating manual gesture to speech has been made by McNeill in his article "So You Think Gestures Are Nonverbal?" (1985; see also 1992). McNeill bases his argument on the very close temporal, semantic, pragmatic, pathological, and developmental parallels between speech and manual gestures among English-speaking American subjects. While my work agrees with that of McNeill in many respects, a major point of departure stems from the location of his work in cognitive psychology. He suggests that manual gestures share a "computational stage" with speech that makes them both part of the same "psychological structure." McNeill thus subscribes to an internalization fallacy. According to the "hidden processors" view, rules operate "in" individual psyches, guiding hidden impersonal generative processes that are presumed to take place there. Harré refutes the possibility of such hidden processes, recognizing that the powers to produce speech-informed action cannot reside in any asocial organization of the material substance. "It is not because of what they are made of that the hidden generative processors or mechanisms of the psychoanalytic tradition, cognitive psychology and Chomskian linguistics cannot possess the power to produce speech-informed action. It is because they are conceived to operate *individualistically*" (see discussion in Warner 1990:138).

The post-Cartesian discourse I have attempted to achieve here depends upon a relocation of agency away from a material metaphysics in which hidden entities and internal mental processes are presumed to provide a causal mechanism (that in the end should be capable of complete physical realization). Agency resides, rather, in what Harré has called "personal powers," wherein the powers productive of human action are ascribed not to processors but to persons. This means that it is to the social entity, the person, that such powers belong, and so the rules governing speech-informed actions are socially located, in the expectations that persons make of themselves and one another as they interact (Warner 1990).[4]

The articulation of mind as a social formation (Harré 1986a, 1987), a theory that builds upon the work of Mead (1933), Vygotsky (1962), and Wittgenstein (1980), has presented an alternative system of conceptual controls to those of Cartesianist legacy. At the same time it has provided the kind of discourse in which I have found it possible to articulate a social construction of the moving body—or rather the whole person—in action, thereby including actors as movers into the definition of language and social action. If mind is socially constructed, then it is so in conjunction with physical being. Social actors are not only embodied but they consistently and systematically use bodily movement according to cultural schemes *in* discursive practices, and not simply in addition to them.

DEIXIS AND THE MOVING BODY

Given the intricate connection between vocal and manual gesture in the Assiniboine case, I explored the consequences of shifting to an action-centered theory of deixis, bringing the body—acts of pointing—back into the notion of deixis rather than accepting the reductionism implicit in the metaphorical usage of the term "pointing" in talk about indexicality. What I mean by the embodiment of deixis is a recognition that the zero point of the deictical space is not merely the "here and now" of a speaker but is the body itself. Time and space are measured—that is, given psychological and social value—from the "here and now" of the body of the actor—or rather, from the embodied person as mover—in spaces not only physical but simultaneously moral and social. In this deictic space, at the level of organizational principles both syntactic and semantic, I have shown that there can be important connections between the media of movement and sound. Close attention to the intricate structure of storytelling performances, for example, revealed exactly how it is that action and speech together create a richly evocative performance genre in which both media share a commitment to the creation of meaning, and the whole becomes astonishingly more than the sum of its parts. Nakota sign talkers do not hear one language and see another; both media are integrated to present a unity of meaning. To talk of this in terms of using two languages at the same time would be to violate this essential unity.

An examination of the use of demonstratives and naming practices in Nakota and PST allowed us to enter into a languaging practice committed to the use of visual imagery encoded in both speech and action. This is an imagery deeply connected to time and space as season and landscape, mediated through personal as well as cultural histories, diminished through experiences of prejudice but expanded through cultural pride and quiet resistance.

The necessity of understanding both media to make sense out of route directions illustrated a simple isomorphism between saying "over there" and doing ⸾⁀⁔. Both types of utterances report upon a relationship between the location "there" and the "here and now" of the person making the utterance, a relationship that is created with some purpose in mind (and body). Deictic words can be used with or instead of deictic actions. They are not two distinct conceptions. Speech is not necessarily a symbolic transformation of an action; the reverse can equally be the case.

Perhaps a reorientation can allow us to think of knowledge in a wider sense, so that knowledge of spatio-temporal organization does not only consist of saying "here" and "there," but is necessarily part of any actual performance of getting from here to there. The fact that we do not pay particular attention to such action is best thought of in terms of being out-of-focal-awareness through habit (Polanyi 1958) rather than as the product of the "unconscious" or some kind of special "practical consciousness" or "bodily intention." Habit precludes the necessity to focus our attention on saying the words "here" and "there" also, but intentionality of action and meaning is present in both cases, in the doing and saying. A person who is walking and argues that walking doesn't mean anything falls into the behaviorist trap of separating the gross physical movement from a conception of action. A person walks across the road to pick up the mail perhaps, or to arrive at the store, and in so doing uses Ryle's "knowing how," knowledge that is not normally put into words.

I am not, of course, suggesting that it is always possible to translate movement into words or vice versa; the two media have their own unique properties for making meanings that are quite different. The movement content of a modern dance work, for example, while certainly not tacit knowledge, does not translate into words (but that should not be taken to mean that the meaning cannot be talked about, even if there is no narrative involved). It would be equally impossible to try to dance the conclusions of this book or to translate them into a poem. These are different ways of making meaning along two axes that each provide a continuum: one that ranges through propositional and nonpropositional aspects, the other through "knowing that" and "knowing how" (Ryle 1949). The two axes are shared by both media.

An unfortunate corollary of the tendency to think of language as a product of a language machine in the head producing and storing knowledge, rather than as discursive practices, is a view of physical action itself not as embodied knowledge but as simply raw experience, a realm that is outside linguistic or cultural conceptions or merely "prelinguistic" in a developmental sense.

Child development studies, for example, increasingly draw attention to the importance of bodily movement and spatial awareness in the development of concepts, yet there is an implicit assumption that once a child has learned a word with which to label a "concept," perceived to be in the head, the learned action itself is not part of any knowledge system, "cognitive processes" and "concept formation" being the focus of educational attention.[5] Both the exploratory sounds and movements of a developing child are labeled "prelinguistic," but it is only the sounds that are thought to develop significance. If cognitive development precedes language acquisition, as Bowerman (1980) argues, this is surely in large part a classification and categorization of self and not-self, space, action, objects, and interrelationships between them, the significance of which is socially constructed. The discourse of cognitive development studies, however, consistently disembodies such categorization by viewing the successful actions of a child as evidence of something else—a developed "concept"—rather than knowledge in and of itself.

Manual gestures in particular are still often actively discouraged in Anglo-Saxon and Euro-American cultures during the learning process as undesirable markers, either of an inability to express oneself with words or of lower-class origins. Williams reminds us that actions too develop into culturally specific body languages or action sign systems:

> Human knowledge of the world comes to us through many channels and many mediums. Our first topographic knowledge of our many personalized worlds consists of a kind of spatial exploration of our own bodies and its limitations, then our immediate environment and its limitations. Gradually we are introduced into the vernaculars of everyday body languages and their conventions. We learn to define ourselves and others as much through the syntactical structures and "grammars" of events as we do through speech, beginning with "standing," "walking," "sitting," "crawling" and all the rest. At the same time we learn these and a mind-boggling variety of other actions, locations and spatial referents, we learn the *local system of relevances* that are typical of our language and cultural setting: we learn the orientational metaphors that organize whole systems of actions with respect to one another—and most of these have to do with spatial orientation. We learn the obligations, freedoms, choices and constraints that constitute our moral and semantic spaces. (1982:175)

That such knowledge is of fundamental importance to our sense of being-in-the-world has been well illustrated by Giddens' discussion of the effects of imprisonment and torture, during which radically altered routines and moral degradation seriously undermine "ontological security" (1984:62–64). Less serious alterations and their effects we are used to calling "culture shock." The serious role that such disruption of established bodily practices plays in the disorientation of children from Native American and other "ethnic" backgrounds in the educational process has not been investigated, however. Problems are assumed to be primarily those associated with spoken language learning.

All human actions (aside from symptomatic physiological reflexes such as coughing, scratching, or sneezing) are part of complex socially constructed ways of using the body, regardless of how mundane or everyday they seem to be. This was Mauss' point ([1935] 1973). A division of actions into "instrumental" and "symbolic" is therefore unhelpful. Actions are often considered to be symbols only if they become figurative and enter performance or ritual contexts; other actions are discounted as merely instrumental. However, such categories are as artificial and limiting as dividing spoken discourses into the everyday or propositional (instrumental) and the poetic (symbolic). These are differences of degree and function, rather than of kind (see Jakobson 1960; Friedrich 1986).

Caution is required therefore in order to avoid a residual dualism in the use of Langer's phrase "the symbolic transformation of experience" as a way of talking about art (Langer 1942) and language. While art as understood in the Western world certainly aims to transform the everyday, experience is not a "raw" precultural or acultural possibility, because what counts as an experience is of necessity mediated through a form of life, through cultural classifications and categories of the body and space that occur in conjunction with, and not separate from, spoken language formulations. Wittgenstein's ([1953] 1958) detailed attention to the problem of pain draws attention to problems associated with this subjective/objective, inside/outside dualism.

The desire to transcend this kind of dualistic thinking about body and mind has led some investigators to embrace a phenomenological perspective, a subjective and individualistic stance that fails because it ends up privileging the body through exactly the kind of alinguistic and acultural "experience" discussed here (e.g., Merleau-Ponty 1962, 1963; Sheets-Johnstone 1981; Jackson 1989). Such approaches fail in their attempts to transcend dualistic thinking because they posit a "bodily intention" or bodily experience that remains just as removed from "mind," "rationality," "knowledge," "language," and all the rest as was the Cartesianism they are attempting to transcend.[6]

Rather than posit some kind of universal bodily experience that all humans share by virtue of their common physiology—a biological determinism in disguise that separates the body from language and culture—this study has suggested a different kind of universal that provides a theoretical space to link language and the body. This involves a simple reformulation centered on the notion of deixis, so that what is universal in language is no longer expressed as the presence of pronouns, demonstratives, and the like in all languages of the world, but an awareness of self as a physical being, a body in space and time that through kinesthetic experience in a cultural and linguistic context, involving interaction with other selves, utilizes the process of deixis to create and attach an enormous variety of meanings to space and time. This makes of deixis not simply a variety of devices for organizing spoken discourse about physical spaces and time, but a fundamental means for the creation of social spaces for action that includes the body.

And what of the stories? I have admittedly been engrossed here as much with certain problems posed by my own culture as those posed by understanding Assiniboine forms of life and storytelling practices. New notions of objectivity demand such reflexive depth, however, and if we have much to learn from the painstaking dissection of storytelling performances, we can also learn from their powers of synthesis and artistic merit. I cannot claim, for example, to have done justice to the texture or text of the two and one-third stories included here, and they represent only a minute portion of a sizable corpus. As crafted poetic artifacts, they contain much that is still to be explored, in terms of both the formal structure and the figurative devices; and if there are "figures of speech" there are also "figures of action."

In recognizing a story as artistically shaped, one escapes the error of thinking that if we knew only enough about Assiniboine culture we would automatically understand *the* meaning of a story (K. Kroeber 1981). Diversity of interpretation is both possible and desirable, because such narratives are works of art and any exegesis is not a way of attaining a single definitive reading; it is but one way among many to enter into the rich complexity of meanings provided by this particular American Indian oral/gestural tradition. Understanding this tradition involves discovery of indigenous aesthetic principles, however, not subjecting it to the judgments of a single literary canon (see Herzfeld 1987:39). If our limited linguistic and anthropological knowledge compels us to recognize that our analyses are tentative, an analogous inconclusiveness surrounds many texts of artistic merit in our own tradition, and we do well to remind ourselves that "it is our scholarship, not Indian literature, which is 'primitive' or undeveloped" (K. Kroeber 1981:9).

I am not sure what place such stories and PST will retain in Assiniboine communities. Elders who know these stories are precious few, and occasions for the telling diminish as mainstream American television and the VCR increasingly occupy those cultural spaces. There is puzzlement and irony in the historical circumstance. Elders who were beaten as children by teachers and missionaries for displaying any signs of Indian language or customs understandably did not teach their children because they wanted to protect them from being subjected to the same humiliations. They were repeatedly taught to devalue everything remotely Indian in order to "advance" in the modern world, and so a certain pessimism exists on the part of some as to the very possibility of an Indian future (itself expressed in a story about seven trees, seven branches, seven nests, and seven eggs, each of which represents a generation, after which there will be no more Indians as recognizable today). Earthboy, for example, who learned these stories from his Assiniboine mother and Cree father and other old-timers, had not told them for a long time. His children (with the exception of an older daughter raised by grandparents) speak only English. Rose Weasel's daughters and son speak Nakota, but her grandchildren and great-grandchildren do not, and so, despite frequent and loving contact, they are largely cut off from her knowledge and artistry.

Earthboy speaks of a "generation gap" between those who accepted the demise of the old ways as inevitable and the young people today who are interested in vitalization through their linguistic, religious, musical, and dance traditions.

Many elders perceive a cruel irony in the renewed interest in Native American culture by Indian educators, who are attempting to combat its devitalization by claiming a space for "Indian culture" in the curriculum. This irony extends to the interests of anthropologists who in collecting stories, creating dictionaries, and recording the language are, after all, representatives of those who still impose *their* definitions of what is to count as knowledge and language.

One of the criticisms some Native Americans have of the anthropological record is that it constantly tells them that they and their traditions are dying out: "Why does no one talk about the changes in the white man's culture that way?" they say. "You don't live like your grandparents did either!" Their complaint is justified and insightful. Ironically, however, in earlier days the misguided assumption that customs were dying out provided in unexpected ways some distinct advantages for the study of PST. It prompted General Scott, for example, to obtain money from Congress to film a sign-language conference at Browning in 1930, thus providing an early film record of the language in use. Twenty years later, in the 1950s, Kroeber too noted that the Plains sign language was "falling into disuse" and urged Voegelin (at Indiana University) to find a student who could undertake a linguistic study of it "before it was too late." Consequently, La Mont West embarked upon a pioneering study of PST as a language from the point of view of descriptive linguistics. To continue the chronology of events and the rhetoric of demise, in 1984 when I first began to inquire into the possibility of doing fieldwork on PST, the general opinion among Plains scholars was that this long-standing and distinctive language was now dead—a "lost" tradition along with the buffalo-hunting economy and buckskin dress of bygone days. Fortunately I was encouraged (and was stubborn enough) to go and see for myself, the results of which are presented here.

I therefore hesitate to join with my predecessors and continue this rhetoric of demise with regard to PST. Here, as with so many aspects of Native American culture today, the differences between us are not on the surface in the material trappings of blue jeans, pickup trucks, and television sets, or in the occupations of rancher, schoolteacher, firefighter, and student. They reside instead in a certain philosophy of knowing and being that does not separate mind from body in definitions of what counts as knowledge and language. This is an epistemology manifested in social action as strategies for relating to self, others, and landscape in ways that I have tried to articulate here. I like to imagine that PST will continue to play a role in the expression of such a philosophy.

APPENDIX A
PHONETIC KEY

The orthographic symbols of special significance for Nakota are as follows:

p˙ t˙ k˙ are aspirated voiceless stops as in *p*enny, *t*ell, *c*atch, or *k*ettle. This aspiration is phonemic in Nakota.

p t k are unaspirated voiceless stops as in *sp*end, *st*op and *s*cream. In English these do not appear in the same environments as aspirated stops and are not phonemic. To an English speaker's ear they often sound more like *b, d*, and *g*, but they are not voiced like the latter.

ˀ are glottal stops like the gap in English oh-oh (for example, in Nakota *t'a*).

c˙ voiceless palatal affricate, as *ch* in *ch*urch.

ġ voiced velar fricative as *g* in Spanish pa*g*ar.

ħ voiceless velar fricative as *ch* in German a*ch*.

ż voiced palato-alveolar fricative as *s* in plea*s*ure.

ś voiceless palato-alveolar fricative as *sh* in *sh*op.

ą į ų are nasalized vowels as in s*ang*, *in*k, or s*ung*.

— represents an elongated vowel held for dramatic effect; it is not a phonemic component. Before Nakota *ka*, however, an elongated vowel marked with : appears to act as a continuative marker.

Stress is on the second syllable of a word unless otherwise marked.

Passages set in poetic lines have a slight pause between lines, and a space between lines indicates a longer pause.

Words in upper case letters indicate a translation of a PST sign, e.g., HERE.

APPENDIX B
KINETIC KEY

The script that has been used to write the movement texts in this book and in the companion CD-ROM, *Wiyuta: Assiniboine Storytelling with Signs,* is called Labanotation. In recognition of the fact that writing movement is not a familiar concept to most readers, I explain here some of the basic principles of the Laban script and also provide a key to the graphic signs.

LABANOTATION: A SCRIPT FOR WRITING HUMAN ACTIONS[1]

Different disciplines in Western academic contexts measure and record human movement in very different ways. There is, for example, a fundamental distinction between the methods used in biology and physiology and those employed in the social sciences and humanities. Investigations of the biological/physiological kind are usually concerned with metric measurement and involve such notions as angles of displacement, muscle force, velocity, and principles of mechanics. Such methods are generally adopted in kinesiological and biomechanical contexts and, in contrast to social scientific and humanistic investigations of human movement, make no attempt to deal with meaning. Consistent with a dualistic division of persons they divide a natural entity (the human organism) from a cultural entity (the body).

In contrast, a movement script must be capable of writing all anatomically possible bodily action in ways that will preserve the identity of the movement, make possible accurate reproduction of it, and maintain its semantic content. This entails a concern with recording *action*

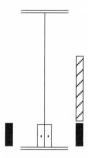

Figure B.1. A transcription of the action "I raise my right arm" using the Laban script.

rather than gross physical movement. The difference is captured in the well-known philosophical example of the difference between "the arm goes up" (a description of a gross physical movement) and "I raise my arm" (a description of an action). As Best puts it, "One cannot specify an action, as opposed to a purely physical movement, without taking into account what the agent intended," that is, there are reasons for, and purposes to, actions (Best 1974:193). Equally important is seeing actions in context; "most of what we may want to know about a person's intentional action cannot be understood by a narrow concentration upon his physical movement but by . . . standing back from it and seeing it in context" (Best 1978:78). Harré and Secord present the difference as follows:

> What we see in social reality is not, for example, an arm moving upwards, but a man trying to attract attention, a man greeting a friend and so on. When we see an action of a certain sort we thus connect what we see with a conceptual context utterly different from that involved in seeing movements, and this context determines the form of explanation that is appropriate. (1972:38)

In this regard, it is important to note that Labanotation is always written from the actor's perspective rather than the observer's and so has a built-in assumption of agency. Figure B.1 records the action "I (the person acting) raise my arm" rather than the gross physical movement engendered by the phrase "the arm goes up." To an ethnographer, however, this description remains inadequate until some context is provided in

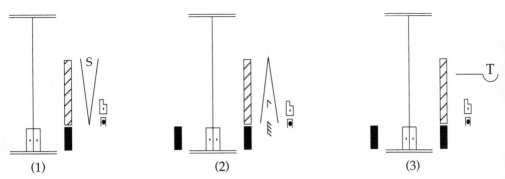

Figure B.2. Labanotation transcriptions of three actions that look the same.

which to understand this raising of the arm as an action with a reason or purpose. The description can then be amended accordingly. For example, three occasions of raising the arm might look identical but could be any one of the following three actions:

1. I am reaching up toward the subway strap in order to grasp it and maintain my balance.

2. I am stretching my hand up away from my shoulder because I am stiff from typing at the computer all morning.

3. I am raising my hand to ask permission from the teacher to leave the room.

The differences between these three actions that are identical in appearance are clearly distinguished in the Labanotation description of them. Even without any previous knowledge of the Laban script, the reader should be able to discern similarities and differences in the collection of graphic signs that constitute the three written actions in Figure B.2. Notice that the differences lie in the signs $\vee$, $\wedge$, and $\frown\smile$, each of which denotes a certain kind of relationship: $\vee$ denotes action toward something, $\wedge$ denotes action away from something, and $\frown\smile$ denotes an action that addresses something or someone. In all three actions the actor moves the right arm from ▮ (hanging "place low" by the side of the body) lifting it toward ▨ ("place high" above the shoulder). In addition, however, in Figure B.2 (1) the actor moves her arm toward S (the subway strap); in action (2) she moves her right hand ⸙ away from the

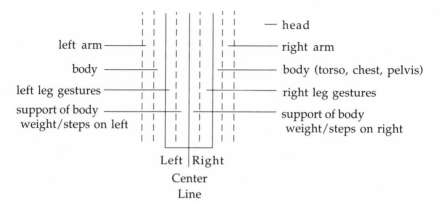

Figure B.3. The basic Labanotation staff provides syntactic order for the symbols of the script.

right shoulder ↖ ; and in action (3) she addresses T (the teacher). What the script records is neither talk *about* the body (the objectivist perspective) nor talk *of* the body (the subjectivist/phenomenological experience of moving) but rather "talk" *from* the body—the enactment of the body in the agentive production of meaning.

The placement of the graphic signs in relation to the vertical lines of the basic "staff" determine that the arm is moving, and not some other body part. The central vertical line divides the right side of the body from the left, and each "column," moving outward from the center line, is reserved for a body part, as illustrated in Figure B.3.

A movement notation has to solve several problems, including how to represent all the parts and surfaces of the body with two-dimensional graphic signs and how to organize the writing of those signs when some or all of those body parts are moving simultaneously and/or sequentially in three dimensions of space. And all of this movement necessarily takes place through time and occurs most often in relation to other persons who are also moving. The task is complex but not insurmountable.

Body

Figure B.4 illustrates how Labanotation solves the problem of representing the joints, limbs, and surfaces of the body. The graphic signs are arbitrary but iconically motivated. They thus offer an aid to memory

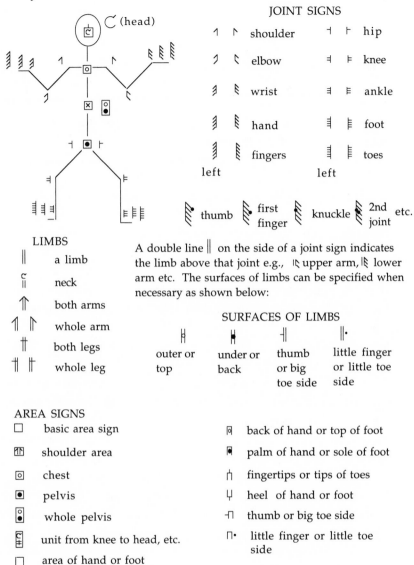

JOINT SIGNS

⅂	�	shoulder	⊣	⊦	hip
		elbow			knee
		wrist			ankle
		hand			foot
		fingers			toes
	left			left	

thumb   first finger   knuckle   2nd joint   etc.

LIMBS

‖ a limb

neck

both arms

whole arm

both legs

whole leg

A double line ‖ on the side of a joint sign indicates the limb above that joint e.g., upper arm, lower arm etc. The surfaces of limbs can be specified when necessary as shown below:

SURFACES OF LIMBS

outer or top   under or back   thumb or big toe side   little finger or little toe side

AREA SIGNS

☐ basic area sign

shoulder area

chest

pelvis

whole pelvis

unit from knee to head, etc.

⊓ area of hand or foot

back of hand or top of foot

palm of hand or sole of foot

fingertips or tips of toes

heel of hand or foot

thumb or big toe side

little finger or little toe side

Sides of an area can be specified using a set of minor directional pins ↓ low, ⊥ middle, ↑ high—e.g., ⓞ upper front side of chest, ⊙ lower left back diagonal side of pelvis, ⓒ front middle area of head, i.e., face. Signs for parts of the face are also built out of these units, e.g., eyes, ⊂ right ear, mouth.

Figure B.4. Labanotation: graphic signs for body parts and surfaces.

but the number of signs required is greatly reduced in comparison to a system that attempts a pictographic representation of the body. Such specification also provides a system of finite differentiation between body parts. Taxonomies of the body differ considerably across languages and cultures, of course, and the flexibility of description possible with the Laban script allows the ethnographer to take this factor into account (see Farnell 1994; Williams and Farnell 1990).

Space

The medium in which the parts of the body move must also be made finite in some way. Problems have frequently arisen with attempts to use conventional numerical measurement to solve this problem because a baseline or point is needed *from* which to measure. Laban developed a different approach. Using a Euclidean view of space, he conceived of the body as being surrounded by a sphere of space, as if it were inside a balloon. This spherical space is divided along three dimensions by three axes perpendicular to each other (up/down, right/left, and front/back), with the body at the center. Each of these major directions and interme-diate divisions is assigned a graphic sign, as illustrated in Figure B.5. The script uses this simple set theory rather than mensuration. Each graphic sign that refers to spatial direction is built out of the basic rect-angle ☐ . A change of shape denotes the front ⌐/back ⌐ , and left ◁ / right ▷ dimensions and a change of shading (high), (middle), or ▮ (low) accommodates the up/down dimension. Again the graphic signs are iconically motivated to assist reading.

This same scheme provides a framework for indicating the direc-tion of pathways for the whole body (called track data, as when a per-son moves from one place to another). Locating a smaller imaginary cross of axes at each joint specifies the direction of individual limbs and smaller body parts. The relationship that obtains between the distal (far) end of a limb and the proximal (nearest the torso) end determines spa-tial direction. For example, the direction of the arm in Figure B.1 is judged by the spatial relationship between the hand (distal end) and the shoul-der (proximal end). The hand moves directly above the shoulder, and so direction for the arm action is stated as "moving to place high" using the graphic sign . Before being lifted, the arm was hanging down be-side the torso with the hand directly below the shoulder. This position

Spatial direction is indicated by both the shape and the shading of the graphic sign. Direction of a body part is calculated by comparing the location of the "free" (distal) end of a body part in relation to its "fixed" (proximal) end. For example, if the arm is stretched out in front of the body at shoulder height, the hand (free end) is forward of, and level with, the shoulder (fixed end), so would be designated as being ⸢ forward middle. If the hand was lower than the shoulder it would be ■ forward low.

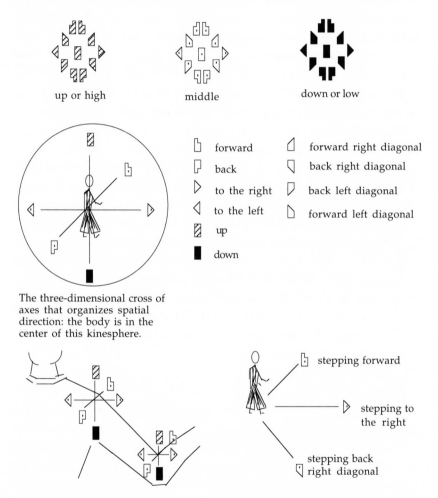

up or high   middle   down or low

The three-dimensional cross of axes that organizes spatial direction: the body is in the center of this kinesphere.

⸢ forward   ⟁ forward right diagonal
⸥ back   ⟁ back right diagonal
▷ to the right   ⟁ back left diagonal
◁ to the left   ⟁ forward left diagonal
▨ up
■ down

⸢ stepping forward

▷ stepping to the right

⟁ stepping back right diagonal

Gestural data: a smaller cross of axes is imagined at the center of each joint so that direction for each part of a limb can be specified.

Track data: direction symbols for moving the whole body from one place to another. These would be placed in the central support column on the staff (see Fig. B.3).

Figure B.5. Labanotation: graphic signs for specifying spatial direction.

for the arm is a "default" position (assumed unless stated otherwise) and is described as ▉ , having moved to, or being in, "place low."

As with taxonomies of the body, there are cultural and linguistic variations to spatial orientation, as well as to the semantic values attached to spatial directions.[2] That such features can also become components of movement texts was shown in Earthboy's story about Nakota territory in Chapter 3. At the start of the text is a spatial orientation key w⊕e = e⊗w , which tells the reader that the Assiniboine conception of the cardinal directions is in operation throughout the movement score; much as the key of C# minor might operate at the start of a musical score. The key is built upon the Labanotation symbol for a "constant cross of axes," ⊕, which means that direction is determined from features that are "constant" in the environment. In this example it was the cardinal directions, but it could be other geographical features, the walls of a room, the sides of a village plaza, or the location of the musicians— any externally located features that a person uses to judge direction. A constant frame of reference contrasts with a body frame of reference, ⟡, in which the body of the actor determines direction (e.g., the actor's conception would be that the hand goes forward from my body, rather than toward the east, or toward the right side of the ceremonial plaza, or toward the singers). Labanotation provides a series of "systems of reference" keys like this that enable these kinds of important conceptual distinctions in spatial orientation to be made clear in the text (see Hutchinson 1977; Williams and Farnell 1990).

Time

Scripts of all kinds deal with time by assigning a direction for reading, an axis for the sequential flow of sound or action. Readers of languages written with the Roman alphabet read from left to right; readers of Arabic, from right to left; and readers of Chinese, from top to bottom. Labanotation reads from bottom to top. This was not an arbitrary choice for Laban; he originally devised a script that also read from left to right, but he changed it in order to accommodate the flow of time when many parts of the body are moving simultaneously. The horizontal axis provides for actions that occur simultaneously, and actions that occur sequentially are shown in vertical succession. Reading vertically, the left/right symmetry of the body from the actor/reader's perspective is mirrored in the script, and the flow of time moves upward as one reads. When the timing of actions is controlled by music or other rhythmic divisions, the time axis of the staff can be divided into beats and bars in a manner similar to musical notation. Spatial direction signs normally lengthen vertically to indicate the time taken for performance, but they can also be given a standard length in action sign systems where absolute timing is not important (e.g., sign languages). In writing Plains Sign Talk I have used a standard length of symbol unless timing makes a difference in meaning.

Additional Dynamics

Actions also involve degrees of muscular tension or strength so that dynamics such as acceleration and deceleration, the impetus or initial point for the action, accents, relaxation, vibration, and phrasing may be added to the description.[3]

Relationships

Relationships between body parts and those between the person acting and objects or other people are important components of social action and can be described with the kinds of relationship signs mentioned above (see Figure B.6).

These parameters of the body, space, time, dynamics, and relationships, and the graphic signs that specify them, provide a means by which to record "talk" *from* the body—to record the agentic production of meaning using the semiotics of body movement.

WRITING PLAINS SIGN TALK WITH LABANOTATION

The Staff

The standard Labanotation staff shown in Figure B.3 can be altered, if necessary, to accommodate specific needs. My transcriptions of Plains Sign Talk are written on a staff adapted to the specific needs of writing a sign language. The central columns for weight support, leg gestures, and torso have been eliminated because movement of those body parts is not constituent to PST. The center line still divides the right from the left side of the body, and the columns are assigned as shown in Figure B.7.

Relationships:

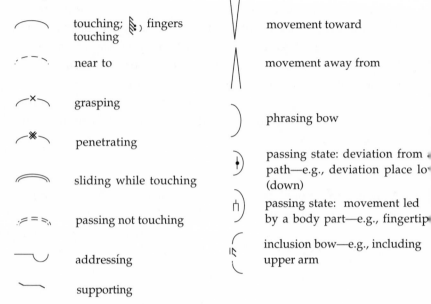

touching; fingers touching	movement toward
near to	movement away from
grasping	phrasing bow
penetrating	passing state: deviation from path—e.g., deviation place low (down)
sliding while touching	passing state: movement led by a body part—e.g., fingertip
passing not touching	inclusion bow—e.g., including upper arm
addressing	
supporting	

Minor direction signs and relationships:

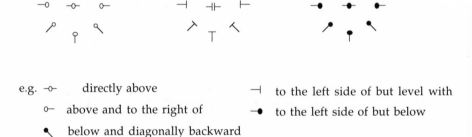

e.g. -o- directly above

    o- above and to the right of

    ⬉ below and diagonally backward

⊣ to the left side of but level with

⬤ to the left side of but below

Figure B.6. Labanotation: graphic signs for relationships and minor directions.

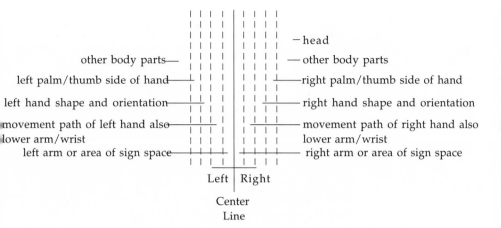

Figure B.7. The Labanotation staff adapted for writing Plains Sign Talk.

A "sign" in PST consists of a *handshape* (or handshapes) that is *oriented* in space and that undergoes *movement* through space, perhaps to a *position* (or location) near to or touching another body part.

Handshapes

While detailed kinological analysis of PST remains to be done, as a starting point I have identified twenty-four handshapes that are constituent to the sign language as used among Assiniboine people today. These have been written using the basic Labanotation symbols for hand ᚼ and fingers ᚼ, fingertips ᚼ and palm ᚼ, with the addition of symbols that identify movement along the longitudinal axis (extension or stretching ⋀, folding ⋋, and contraction ×) and across the lateral axis (widening ⌣ and narrowing ⌣—see Figure B.8). The touching bow ⌢ identifies parts of the hand or fingers that touch. To assist fluency of reading and writing, PST signs are not written with all components explicit. Full structural descriptions of handshapes are shown in Figures B.9, along with the abbreviated versions that are found in the texts.

Orientation of the Hands

Determination of a hand's orientation is established by the relationship between the distal end (fingertips) and the wrist (proximal end). In addition, because the lower arm allows the hand to rotate around its own

Stretching, folding and contraction of body parts:

И   stretching/extending along a longitudinal axis

И   three-dimensional extension

×   contraction (a bending in which the proximal and distal
     ends of a limb stay in line and the middle part—e.g., elbow—
     displaces). Increasing degees of contraction:× × ✳ ✳ ✳
     e.g., a three-dimensional contraction of the hand to six
     degrees makes ✳ a fist

✳   three-dimensional contraction

⋎   folding (a bending that curves a limb with multiple joints).
     Increasing degrees of folding: ⋎ ⋎ ⋎ ⋎ ⋎
     Folding over backward ⋏ side right Κ , etc.

⌣   lateral extension or widening

⌣   stretched as wide as possible

⌢   lateral narrowing—e.g., fingers together

⌢   narrowing as much as possible—e.g., fingers overlapping

Turns:

     [symbol] body part turns to the right (pin indicates
            degree of turn—e.g., a quarter turn to right)

     [symbol] body part turns to the left

Repeat signs:

     ⋋   repeat identical movement on both sides

     ⋋   left/right lateral symmetry—e.g., left hand
          moves to left, right hand to right

     ⋋   repeat from previous "bar" line across staff ——

Other:

♪ light accent	○ hold
♪ strong accent	◇ space hold
≋ shaking	ৎ or ৎ release of a hold or a previous contact
૨ ad lib ⋋ or ⟩ repeat ⟨ ad lib	› same body part as stated previously
℮ relaxed	⊙ back to normal
	⊕ in the shape of

Figure B.8. Labanotation: graphic signs denoting stretching, folding, and contraction of limbs, turns, repeat signs, and others.

axis, a second marker is often needed to determine rotation. The direction in which the palm is facing ◙ or the direction of the thumb side of the hand ⊓ best serves this purpose. Sometimes a more appropriate description might be to specify the degree of rotation 𝑓 in the wrist (see "Turns" in Figure B.8).

As an example, consider the sign glossed as EARTH/COUNTRY, shown in Figure B.10. This PST sign utilizes a handshape in which the hand is "normal" (fingers straight but not stretched) with the fingers together ⏝. The fingers are pointing directly forward (⊟ forward middle), and the palm faces directly upward (⊠ place high). This composite graphic sign gives both the shape and the orientation of the hands.

Movement of the Hands

When making signs, the hands can change shape, make movements in the same place (e.g., turning, shaking), or move to a different location in the signing space. Because the hands are the most salient body parts involved in PST, I have described movement to a different location in terms of movement of the hands through paths in space rather than in terms of movement of the lower and upper arms. In Figure B.10 the reader can see that after the handshape and orientation description, a movement path is designated by the graphic sign for a straight path ⊥ moving directly sideways ▷. The actor first creates the handshape and orientation and then moves both hands along this movement path to the side. Figure B.11 shows additional types of movement paths. The graphic sign ✕ on the left side of the staff indicates a repeat. In a PST text this means that the left hand repeats what the right hand does. The hands make the same shape and the same movement, but there is a lateral symmetry to the movement—i.e., the right hand moves to the right and the left hand to the left. If the left hand also moved to the right side, then the single repeat sign ✕ would have been written instead. Readers familiar with the Laban script will recognize this type of description as a gestural path and distal part description. It should also be noted that the handshape abbreviations act as units, and so the *whole hand* takes these paths that are written in the lower arm/wrist column. If a path sign occurs in the hand column instead, it refers to movement of the specific part of the hand or the finger designated. When actions are too minor to count as a path, the minor direction symbols are used (see Figure B.6).

1.

or =

⊙

relaxed hand, no special shape
⊙ back to normal sign in hand column
cancels previous shape and hand relaxes

2.

=

normal hand, fingers slightly apart

3.

=

extended or flat hand, fingers together

4.

=

hand extended, fingers separated

5.

=

hand (including fingers) wide, fingers separated
with a slight folding of the entire hand

Figure B.9. Handshapes in PST with Labanotation transcriptions and abbreviations.

6.

$$\overset{\times}{\smile} = \overset{\times}{\underset{\text{\tiny lll}}{\smile}}$$

hand (including fingers) wide, fingers separated
whole hand contracts three degrees; clawlike
shape

7.

$$\ast = \underset{\text{\tiny lll}}{\ast}$$

hand and fingers completely contracted into fis

8.

$$\overset{\frown}{\vartriangle} = \underset{\text{\tiny lll}}{\overset{\frown}{\vartriangle}}$$

narrowed hand, fingers closed in and thumb
resting in middle

9.

$$\underset{\text{\tiny lll}}{\overset{\frown}{\text{h}}} = \underset{\text{\tiny lll}}{\overset{\frown}{\cdot}}\,\underset{\text{\tiny lll}}{\overset{\frown}{\ell}}$$

fingertips and thumb tip touching and
pursed to a point

10.

$$\overset{\times}{\boxed{\bullet}} = \underset{\text{\tiny lll}}{\}}\,\underset{\text{\tiny lll}}{\overset{\frown}{\text{lll}}}$$

fingers folded at metacarpal joints (knuckles),
fingers straight and touching, thumb at side
touching index finger

11.

hand folded three degrees (right angle) at
metacarpal joints (knuckles), fingers and
thumb straight and separated

12.

hand folded at metacarpal joints
but narrowed also

13.

fingers only are folded tight, metacarpal
joints remain extended

14.

fingers touching and folded four degrees,
thumb tip touching first finger

15.

thumb extended and curved in opposition
to all other fingers curved equally

16.

fist with thumb extended and separated

17.

fist with index finger extended

18.

fist with index finger extended but crooked (contracted one degree)

19.

fist with index and second fingers extended and touching

20.

fist with index and second fingers extended and separated

21.

fist with thumb and index finger extended and separated

22.

thumb and index finger folded to make a half-circle shape, rest of hand in fist. This shape is used to indicate the sun.

23.

thumb and index finger contract and touch tips to make a circle, rest of hand in fist

24.

thumb and index finger extended with tips touching, rest of hand in fist

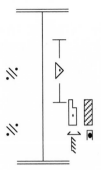

Figure B.10. Labanotation transcription of PST sign EARTH/COUNTRY.

Pathways

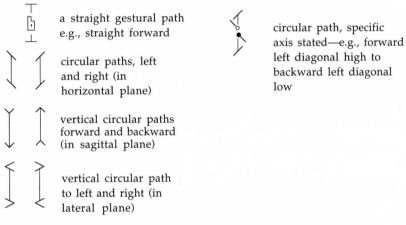

a straight gestural path
e.g., straight forward

circular paths, left
and right (in
horizontal plane)

vertical circular paths
forward and backward
(in sagittal plane)

vertical circular path
to left and right (in
lateral plane)

circular path, specific
axis stated—e.g., forward
left diagonal high to
backward left diagonal
low

Areas of the PST signing space

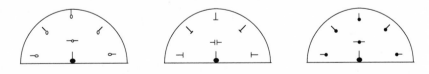

☐ general area sign

e.g., ⊞ center of signing space; ◩ upper right diagonal area of signing space, etc.

Figure B.11. Labanotation: graphic signs for pathways and areas of the PST signing space.

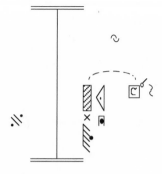

Figure B.12. The PST sign BUFFALO.

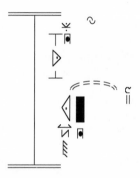

Figure B.13. The PST sign ASSINIBOINE/NAKOTA.

Areas of Signing Space

Unless otherwise written, signs are performed in a central area in front of the chest. There is considerable latitude in placing, however, before the meaning of a sign is altered. This provides a further reason not to describe signs with upper and lower arm movement. When signs depart from the central area, I have indicated this change with minor direction pins placed within area signs. These have been placed in the central column when that positioning is helpful to the reader to indicate when the sign moves out of, or back to , the central area, e.g., ⊟ hand moves to right side of signing space or ⊡ hand moves into upper left diagonal area of signing space (see Figure B.11).

Examples

The PST sign BUFFALO is written as shown in Figure B.12. Both index fingers ⸙ are pointing upward ▨ and are contracted × (bent) a little in an iconic representation of the horns of a buffalo. The palm faces sideways. The hands move near to the sides of the head (general upper diagonal forward area ⌷⁰ "ad lib" placing—i.e., not exact). The left hand is laterally symmetrical to the right hand, and so the repeat sign ⋋˙ can be used.

The PST sign ASSINIBOINE/NAKOTA is written as shown in Figure B.13. An extended (flat) right hand with the fingers together ⸙ and pointing to the left ⟨ with the palm facing down ▮ moves near to the front of the throat ⌇ and slides ⸴⁼⁼⁼⸌ past the throat, moving on a straight path to the right ▷. The right hand folds at the palm ⸗ at the end of this path before this relationship is released ∿.

In the CD-ROM *WIYUTA: Assiniboine Storytelling with Signs,* the Labanotation texts and spoken Nakota transcriptions can be studied in conjunction with the complete videotape recordings of the storytellers' performance. Hutchinson (1977) is the standard "dictionary" of Labanotation symbols and orthographic conventions, and Williams and Farnell (1990) provide a series of lessons with special attention to anthropological contexts.

NOTES

INTRODUCTION

1. The term "action sign" was coined by Williams (1975) to denote a human signifying act that utilizes the medium of body movement. Action signs are meaningful units of movement, culturally and semantically laden, that combine to make larger stretches of meaning in "action sign systems" as various as idioms of dance, the martial arts, ceremonial systems, ritual activities, sign languages, liturgies, and so forth.

2. For example, Mallery 1880a, 1880b, 1881; Clark 1885; Scott 1912–1934; Dodge 1882; Hadley 1893; Seton 1918; Tomkins 1926. In the 1950s two publications by Native American authors appeared: Cody 1952 and Hofsinde 1941. In linguistics, West (1960) analyzed PST from the perspective of descriptive linguistics with encouragement from Voegelin (1958) and Kroeber (1958). See discussions in Kendon 1989, Farnell 1984, and Taylor 1975 for an overview.

3. The places listed are those known to me as having sign talkers. There are likely to be others. I have not attempted a survey such as that carried out by West in 1956 (see West 1960). Knowing of my interest, several people have told me of sign talkers on the southern Plains also.

4. The denials were not attempts to conceal knowledge from me but a function of my use of the term "sign language," which many people interpreted to mean having the ability to use PST fluently enough to communicate across spoken language boundaries and without speech if necessary (like those who use ASL, the sign language of the deaf in America). People at Fort Belknap today remember many Assiniboine and Gros Ventre individuals, men and women, who in previous generations had been fluent, and they compared their own abilities accordingly. Widespread fluency was characterized as being "before the school class" of people were born; that is, before English was forced upon them at the turn of the century. The use of "class" here means generation— another variation of which was "this younger class"—rather than school class-

room or social class, an interesting use of the word in a strongly egalitarian society.

5. See Parks and DeMallie 1989, however, for problems regarding this trilogy of terms.

6. See Birdwhistell 1970 on kinesics and Hall 1966 on proxemics.

7. See, for example, Hymes 1975; Bauman 1977, 1986; Sherzer 1987b; Tedlock 1983; Bauman and Sherzer 1989; Sherzer and Woodbury 1987.

8. There is an enormous literature in the field generally labeled nonverbal communication or nonverbal behavior. Most of this work is based in psychology and is therefore individualistic, often behaviorist, and usually separated from spoken language use. See Scherer and Ekman 1981; Siegman and Feldstein 1978; and Harper, Wiens, and Matarazzo 1978 for examples of landmark publications in the field. McNeill (1985:351) has pointed out that a few psychologists and psychiatrists have considered speech and gesture to be part of the same "psychological structure," but no linguists have held that view.

9. See Silverstein 1976 and Sherzer 1987b for a summary of these developments.

10. Bauman and Sherzer (1989) discuss the way in which attention to language-in-use has permeated the study of language from a wide range of disciplinary vantage points, including anthropology, linguistics, folklore, and sociology. Works I have found most useful on speech act theory and functional grammar include Searle 1969; Austin 1962; and Silverstein 1976. On sociolinguistics and the ethnography of speaking I have learned much from the numerous works of Hymes, particularly 1974, 1975 (see 1981 for bibliography); Bauman and Sherzer 1989; and Gumpertz and Hymes 1964, 1972 (a useful bibliography of fieldwork in this area can be found in Philipsen and Carbaugh 1986). Jakobson (1960), Fernandez (1986), and Friedrich (1986) have been central for their perspectives on poetics. Williams (1981, 1982, 1988, 1991) provides clear statements of a semasiological approach to human movement. Kendon 1982, 1983, 1986, 1989, on sign language and gesture, and Kaeppler 1972, 1985, and 1986 have also been important.

11. "I rightly conclude that my essence consists in this alone: that I am only a thing that thinks. Although perhaps I have a body that is very closely joined to me, nevertheless, because on the one hand I have a clear and distinct idea of myself—insofar that I am a thing that thinks and not an extended thing—and because on the other hand I have a distinct idea of a body—insofar as it is merely an extended thing, and not a thing that thinks—it is therefore certain that I am truly distinct from my body and that I can exist without it" (Descartes 1641:93).

12. Descartes' position was not entirely new; he continued the Platonic disdain for the body in the modern form of a radical individualism. We would be hard pressed to find a clearer charter for the absence of the body in Western social theory, and indeed in Western academic circles generally, than the following excerpt from Plato's dialogue, the *Phaedo:*

All these considerations, said Socrates, must surely prompt serious philosophers to review the position in some such way as this. . . . So long as we keep to the body and our soul is contaminated with this imperfection, there is no chance of our ever attaining satisfactorily to our object, which we assert to be truth. . . . The body fills us with loves and desires and fears and all sorts of nonsense, with the result that we literally never get an opportunity to think at all about anything. . . . That is why, on all these accounts, we have so little time for philosophy. . . . It seems, to judge from the argument, that the wisdom which we desire and upon which we profess to have set our hearts will be attainable only when we are dead. . . . It seems that so long as we are alive, we shall continue closest to knowledge if we avoid as much as we can all contact and association with the body, except when they are absolutely necessary, and instead of allowing ourselves to become infected with its nature, purify ourselves from it until God himself gives us deliverance. (Hamilton and Cairns 1961:49)

13. See, for example, Jackson 1989 and Hanks 1990.

14. Grene (1985) has advanced a similar position to that taken by Varela on the contributions of Merleau-Ponty and suggests that his ideas on perception are now scientifically out of date, having been updated by the perceptual theory of J. J. Gibson.

15. This section and the diagrammatic formulation that follows were worked out in conversation with Varela about his paper. The ideas are a collaborative effort.

16. "Intentions" here means only that the bodily acts are movements intended by the actor; they are a result of agency and not an "unconscious" spilling over of emotional "content," or "true" feelings that contradict spoken discourse, the latter view being typical of a populist approach to nonverbal communication that unfortunately uses the term "body language." The agentic perspective instead places physical actions on a par with the intentions of speakers to create speech acts. This is not to say that the actor-speaker's intentions are necessarily understood correctly by other participants in the course of social interactions. Processes are set in motion by which certain trains of consequences occur, intended and unintended.

17. MacIntyre (1981:108) has drawn attention to the lack of any moral worth to what counts as success in Goffman's schema. Goffman's world is empty of objective standards of achievement, for standards are established only through and in interaction itself: "The goal of the Goffmanesque role-player is effectiveness and success in Goffman's social universe is nothing but what passes for success" in the regard of others, hence the central importance of presentation of self.

18. Following Davies and Harré, I take the position that social structures are coercive to the extent that to be recognizably and acceptably a person we must operate within their terms. But the concept of a person we bring to any

action includes not only that knowledge of external structures and expectations but also the idea that we are responsible for our own "lines" and there are multiple choices available—we are producer, author, and player, and other participants coauthor and coproduce the "drama." We are also the audience with multiple and often contradictory interpretations based on our own emotions, our own reading of the situation, and our own imaginative positioning of ourselves in the situation, each mediated by our own subjective histories. Lived narratives can change direction and meaning to such an extent that the metaphor of a prestructured play begins to lose plausibility as a viable image to explain what it is that we do in interaction with each other (Davies and Harré 1990:52).

19. The use of "rules" here and the idea of rule-following do not mean a conception of language as an internal machine or that the rules exist "in the head" or in "structures of the mind" somewhere prior to speech. Following Wittgenstein, I mean, rather, the social rules and conventions being followed by participants in discourse, formulations that can be discovered through the accounts they are ready to give of what is being done or attempted, and what counts as the right way to do and say things in specific contexts. In other words, "people use rules to assess the correctness of their actions; rules do not use people as the vehicles of their causal efficacy to generate actions" (paraphrase of Wittgenstein in Mühlhäusler and Harré 1990:7).

20. Work on the *semantics* of physiology and biology such as that by Bastien (1985) and Martin (1987) in terms of models of body concepts is, of course, highly relevant, as is much recent work in medical anthropology: the point is that such conceptions and practices are not somehow independent of and prior to human contexts, beliefs, and intentions.

21. See especially Jackson 1983 and Blacking 1977, plus the unfortunate uncritical perpetuation of such Cartesianism in Scheper-Hughes and Lock 1987:29.

22. Weber distinguished between the physical, potentially observable part of action, which he referred to as "behavior" (*Verhalten*), and the ideational, unobservable part, which he referred to as "meaning" (*Sinn*). The combination of the two is action (*Handeln*). Ardener (1973) provides clear discussion and historical background of the use of the term "behavior." Reynolds (1982:331) discusses the reasons for preferring the term "behavior" for animals and "action" for human beings; see also Williams 1982 n. 3, and 1991, Chap. 10.

23. Williams specifies the problem in this way: "How is one to deal, for example, with the movements of, say, a yam farmer in the Cameroon? Yam planting is preeminently 'practical' and 'instrumental,' but what are we to do with the bits of sacred potash or herbs dropped into the mound and/or the ritual which may precede or follow the planting? (See Ardener 1973). To the farmer all these actions may form a structural whole. The actions may not constitute a distinction between 'instrumental' and 'symbolic' actions at all. Yet, how many times are they described in this way, as if the western categorical distinction

were also part of the folk model of the actions? And yet another example: what is one to do with the movements in the Roman Catholic Mass, all of which can be performed by anyone, and all of which (excepting one) are 'instrumental' actions, i.e., taking, distributing, breaking, and pouring. 'Blessing' is the problematical action to the investigator who starts with a dichotomy between instrumental and symbolic or practical and artistic actions, or something of the kind. And how does one explain the so-called 'everyday' movements when they are incorporated into a ritual or a dance?" (1991:242).

24. This is one reason why Williams found certain Saussurian principles helpful when developing a semasiological approach. Unfortunately the notion of *langue* has become synonymous in the minds of some with an abstract objectivist view of language as a system unto itself with an inner logic irreducibly distinct from other social and conceptual systems. While certainly one interpretation of the legacy of Saussurian linguistics, it is not a necessary entailment of the idea.

25. Williams used the term "body language" initially as an alternative to "nonverbal communication," but unfortunately it was popularized in a superficial and misleading book of the same title by Fast (1970) (see Williams 1991:207). This has made other researchers somewhat skeptical about its use, myself (and Williams) included.

26. Several of Kendon's papers (1972, 1980a, 1980b, 1983) give examples of his extensive work on relations between gesture and speech. See also Kendon 1982 for an excellent historical overview of the study of gesture and discussion of the term. His most recent contribution (1989) is an important study of sign languages of Aboriginal Australia. McNeill 1992 also adds to this literature.

27. This interest can be said to go back at least as far as Tylor and his preoccupation with sign languages. The Durkheimian *année sociologique* tradition produced contributions by Mauss ([1950] 1970, [1938] 1985) and Hertz ([1909] 1960) and has been continued in the work of Mary Douglas (1966, 1970). Benthall and Polhemus (1975) and Polhemus (1978) produced motley collections of papers from widely different sources. Oddly, this excluded work referring to the human body *and* its movements. Thus the ethnoscientific approach of Kaeppler and Williams' semasiology was omitted, as was Best 1974. Other collections of essays include Blacking 1977 and Spencer 1985. Fisher and Cleveland 1958 offers an example of the psychological/phenomenological approach and Hinde 1972 an example of the tradition in nonverbal communication outside of sociocultural anthropology. The latter approach carries on "a tradition established by Darwin, arguing that bodily expression is a cross-cultural universal that is transmitted from generation to generation through biological inheritance" (Williams 1991:220). Williams 1991, Chap. 9 provides critical discussions of these various approaches as well as of kinesics and proxemics.

28. From Aihwa Ong, "Facts of Life: Kmer Refugees, Biomedicine, and Culturally Correct Citizenship," n.d. Cited in Martin 1987:xvi.

29. For a detailed discussion of the idea of literacy in relation to movement, see Williams and Farnell 1990; Page 1990; Farnell 1984, and in press.

1. THE NINETEENTH-CENTURY LEGACY

1. See Rodnick 1938:12–14. Compare Cowan 1990 on dance as unsettling of Greek social order.

2. I use the term "gesticulation" following Kendon's usage (1980a) but to indicate a more creative and probably ad hoc use of gesture than might be the case in situations in which spoken languages are understood.

3. See Ardener 1989:159–163 and Williams 1984.

4. See Langer 1942, Chap. 4 for discussion of the difference between discursive and nondiscursive (presentational) forms of knowledge. Although this dichotomy certainly served Langer's important purpose at the time, it is no longer adequate to account for "the symbolic transformation of experience" in all its complexity. For example, a nondiscursive or nonpropositional use of spoken/written language is usually emphasized in poetry, but even the most prosaic everyday use of language, as well as theory construction in science, is full of metaphors and other tropes. More in line with our contemporary understanding are analyses according to the semantico-referential, indexical, and iconic functions of utterances within each semiotic modality rather than classifying according to form type per se as "discursive" or "presentational" (or digital versus analogic, a contemporary metaphor for the same distinction). These three aspects of meaning making can be viewed as resources and opportunities available to agents for ordering cultural practices of diverse kinds. Ryle's distinction between "knowing how" and "knowing that" adds further resources to this open strategy.

The same range of possibilities applies to human movement systems. There are, for example, fully discursive sign languages; dance idioms (e.g., Bharata Natyam and Hawaiian dances) that use propositional knowledge in conjunction with spoken language meaning; less formal gestural practices that vary in their referential, indexical, and iconic content; dance systems that aim to eschew referential meaning altogether (e.g., Cunningham's contributions to American Modern Dance); and aspects of these and other systems such as the martial arts and everyday skills that are part of "knowing how" rather than "knowing that."

2. BIAS AGAINST THE ICONIC

1. *Peirce's Letters*, quoted in Jakobson 1987:442.

2. Jakobson 1987:446. This was Jakobson's opening address to the First International Congress of Semiotics, Milan, June 1974. Critical of the Bally and Sechehaye editing of Saussure's notes as being "so reworked and touched up by the editors that it causes quite a number of errors in the master's teachings"

(1987:445), Jakobson was paraphrasing from Engler's critical edition of Saussure's *Cours de linguistique generale* (1967:47–49).

3. See Verdenius 1972.

4. Although occasionally confusing, given the various semiotic uses of the term "sign" in various theories of signs, in a sign language "signs" are a convenient label for units loosely similar to "words" in spoken languages. I use the term in this way throughout.

5. Tylor is commonly characterized incorrectly as an "armchair anthropologist" along with Frazer and others prior to the establishment of the fieldwork tradition in anthropology. He did, in fact, conduct fieldwork, not among a group of "primitive others" in an exotic colonial setting, the hallmark of modernist anthropology, but in the Berlin Deaf and Dumb Institute. There he collected over five hundred signs and observed and interviewed both deaf and hearing persons about the nature of the language and their methods of teaching. Before this, in 1855, he had at age twenty-three traveled in Mexico with a friend who was an amateur archeologist. As Bohannan notes in the introduction to the abridged version of *Early History*, Tylor published a book about his Mexican experiences in 1861. While this may have been little more than a travel book about Mexico, Bohannan observes, the experience was formative in the development of Tylor's anthropological insights and that "little more" contained the seeds of what was to become modern anthropology.

6. West (1960) mentions the problem of this tendency for consultants to adapt signs in discussing his own attempts to perform them while doing research on dialects of PST in 1956.

7. By "grammatical signs" Tylor here refers to several grammatical devices invented by hearing teachers of the deaf to correspond to spoken language forms. From his fieldwork at the Berlin Deaf and Dumb Institute, Tylor recognized that these were not part of "natural gesture language" and that this kind of grammatical addition was against the principles of Sicard, who had said: "As a foreigner is not fit to teach a Frenchman French, so the speaking man has no business to meddle with the invention of signs, giving them abstract values" (1808:xlv.18).

Several educators of the deaf in America have invented these kinds of variations of ASL in order to try to help deaf children in a literate world. Two manual codes for English are SEE (Signing Exact English) and LOVE (Linguistics Of Visual English). All of these work on a one-sign-equals-one-word/syllable principle and attempt to represent the vocabulary and structure of English. In conversational situations between hearing and deaf persons, the extent that these kinds of devices are used varies according to the knowledge of the hearing person. ASL as used between deaf persons does not normally utilize these kinds of devices. As Tylor commented: "These partly artificial systems are probably very useful in teaching, but they are not the real gesture language, and what is more, the foreign element so laboriously introduced seems to have little power of holding its ground there. So far as I can learn few or none of the factitious grammatical signs will bear even the short journey from the schoolroom to the playground, where there is no longer any verb 'to be,' where the abstract conjunctions are unknown and where position, quality, and action may serve to describe substantive and adjective alike" (1865:18).

8. Silverstein (1976) develops Jakobson's (1965) article and the latter's use of Peirce.

9. Peirce's classification of signs (1932, Vol. 2, Chaps. 2, 3) involves a hierarchy of sixty-six types, but the tripartite division into icon, index, and symbol is the simplest and the basis for the more complicated classification (see Peirce 1956:98–118). Although there are problems of various kinds (see Burks 1949 for critique), the trichotomy has stood the test of time and much critical discussion and remains a useful organizing principle here.

10. See discussion in Ullmann 1962 for further examples.

11. See also Harris 1981.

12. See also La Barre 1947, Pouwer 1973, and Williams 1980b for numerous examples and critical discussion of the "universality" thesis.

13. Letter from Boas to Mallery, June 6, 1887, Mallery Papers, National Anthropological Archives, Smithsonian Institution, Washington, D.C.

14. Differences between Saussure's concerns with sign relations and those of Peirce are discussed in Singer 1984, Chap. 1.

3. GEOGRAPHICAL AND HISTORICAL SPACES

1. George Catlin, a Pennsylvania-born former lawyer and self-taught artist, made a series of journeys into the region between 1830 and 1836 and painted extensively, creating the famous Catlin Indian Gallery to exhibit his work in New York in 1837. The exhibition traveled to London and Paris, and Catlin remained in Europe lecturing and touring for a number of years. He also wrote extensive notes on his travels between 1832 and 1839, which he published in 1841.

Karl Bodmer, a Swiss, accompanied Prince Alexander Philip Maximilian du Wied, a German explorer who traversed the Upper Missouri region from 1832 to 1834 and wrote extensively on his experiences (in Thwaites 1904–1907, Vols. 22–24). Maximilian included notes on the use of the sign language and collected a short vocabulary.

Samuel Seymour was an English-born scenic designer and landscape artist in Philadelphia and New York City, and one of the first artists of any training to venture west of the Mississippi when he accompanied Major Stephen Long's expedition to the Rocky Mountains in 1819 and 1820.

2. Maximilian Wied [1843] 1905:vi.

3. Catlin's self-appointed task of a lifetime was that of "rescuing from oblivion the looks and customs of the vanishing races of native man in America."

"Art may mourn when these people are swept from their earth," he wrote, "and the artists of future ages may look in vain for another race so picturesque in their costumes, their weapons, their colors, their manly games and their chase" ([1844] 1973: vii).

4. See Miller 1986 for a summary of the extensive participation of Assiniboine men acting as middlemen in the fur trade between Hudson's Bay and the Interior.

5. For sources, see *The Handbook of North American Indians*, Vol. 13, *The Plains*, DeMallie, in press.

6. See Sahlins 1985, Fabian 1983, Eggan 1975.

7. Many complexities and difficulties surrounding ethnic identity and economic, political, and religious organization on Indian reservations occur because the reservations are shared by people of different tribes who in many cases were former enemies. Fowler (1987:257) notes that of the thirteen reservations on the northern and central Plains (Montana, Wyoming, and western North and South Dakota), six are occupied by more than one tribe. This does not seem to feature in many ethnographies of the northern and central Plains. See Fowler 1987: 257n. 3 for critique of this neglect.

8. Ewers (1974) has argued convincingly that the Milk and Missouri River valleys were occupied by several groups during the eighteenth and nineteenth centuries. No one group had exclusive control. Oral history locates Assiniboine bands on the Milk, Musselshell, and Missouri Rivers. That part of Assiniboine history which can be reconstructed through non-Indian documents suggests that in the nineteenth century the Assiniboines were located between the Missouri and the Assiniboine Rivers. They traded at the junction of the Missouri and the Yellowstone from 1829 on and wintered mostly north and east of the Milk River. Their population was reportedly reduced to about four hundred tipis by a smallpox epidemic in 1838. Territory to the north was shared with the Cree, with whom they had allied after separating from the Sioux sometime before 1640. They are mentioned as a distinct tribe in the Jesuit Relations for that year (see Thwaites ed. [1610–1791], Vol. 18:230). Exactly what such a mention implies in terms of complete or only partial separation cannot be ascertained. De Smet (1863:1142) tells us the separation was due to a quarrel between two women over the division of buffalo meat. Contemporary storytellers tell of a dispute between two leaders over the division of buffalo meat, but say it was the Sioux who split away from the Assiniboine and not the reverse. See also variants in Clark 1885 and Keating 1824:388–389. A similar story was given to Lowie among the Crow to account for their separation from the Hidatsa, which leads Lowie to dismiss this Assiniboine story as history (1909:7). See Eggan 1975 for a critique of Lowie's intransigence over the lack of historical value in oral traditions. A complete bibliography of sources of Assiniboine history and tribal relationships can be found in *The Handbook of North American Indians*, Vol. 13, *The Plains*, DeMallie, in press. See also Miller 1986.

9. This difference raises interesting questions for future research on how the grammar of PST might differ according to context. For example, it may have been the case that when people talked in intertribal contexts the grammar of PST was simplified, much like a pidgin spoken language. Indeed, this may have been at the heart of its success as a lingua franca. In intratribal contexts, however, the grammatical structure may have been, and may still be, quite different in view of the fact that both words and signs are understood. In the presence of deafness there exists a third possibility: a fully developed propositional syntax similar in kind to that of ASL as used by deaf children of deaf parents (which is different from versions of ASL used by hearing people or those who have learned ASL later in life in educational institutions). The storytelling context itself may impose features of performance not found in everyday conversational contexts and there may be gender differences involved as well as generational differences and influences from the imposition of English. All these interesting questions must await further research, however.

10. Harrington (n.d.) notes that prior to the building of dams and irrigation projects on both the Missouri and the Yellowstone, the Missouri was a most unpredictable river. There were three annual risings, the first and largest in March or April often accompanied by flooding through ice jams. A later swelling came in early June, caused chiefly by the swelling of the Yellowstone River fed by melting snows and called "the wild-rose rise," which Harrington doesn't explain but which is probably a translation of an Indian name. The third annual rise was called "the squash flower rise" and was caused by the headwaters of the Missouri and the Milk Rivers. It often followed immediately after the second rise. The water was usually laden with mud and in former times, Harrington tells us (and see also Lewis and Clark accounts), trees in the stream and driftwood on ever-changing sandbanks indicated violent action from the floodwater. It was an extremely hazardous river to navigate in either canoes or boats of any size, as attested to by the difficulties and loss of steamboats plying their way up to Fort Benton in the mid- to late nineteenth century.

11. According to Harrington, the word "Missouri" is a French loanword altered from Peoria, one of the Algonquian languages, and used to designate western neighbors, who subsequently became known to Europeans as the Missouri Indians. Earliest written records with the name "Missouri" in them date back to 1673 in the records of the Joliet-Marquette expedition. By the eighteenth century, the name "Missouri" had assumed its present spelling in both French and English. Harrington traces evidence that suggests the name can be traced from the Peoria word for their neighbors the *we-mesolita* 'he who has a canoe', and that not only the people but the river itself was labeled after this prominent tribe that inhabited the lower portions of the river. The Hidatsa-Mandan name for the river also referred to canoes. This pattern of a name in English or French arising out of an Algonquian name given to western neighbors repeats itself in the case of the Assiniboine also; see Introduction.

12. The Yellowstone River is also called the Elk River in the Crow spoken language according to Harrington (n.d.).

13. Scott (1912–1934) disputes this, saying that the Indians at Fort Berthold called it Yellowstone because of the attractive yellow quartz pebbles to be found on the riverbed. The yellow rock of the canyon walls exists only along a short stretch of the river and much farther west than the location of Fort Berthold. What this probably indicates is that the name given by the Fort Berthold Indians was translated into English but given a different referent by explorers.

14. See Scott 1912–1934.

15. The original trading post of Fort Belknap was located on the south side of the Milk River, south of what is now the town of Chinook. It was established by Abel Farwell for Durfee and Peck Company and later sold to Colonel J. J. Wheeler, an Indian trader who in turn sold it to J. W. Power. An Indian Agency was established there in July 1873 and Major Fanton was the agent in charge. Tom O'Hanlon operated the trading post at the fort. It became a point for distributing rations to Gros Ventre and Assiniboine bands, and was also an important stopover for freighters and travelers making the long trek between Fort Benton on the Missouri and Fort Union at the junction of the Missouri and the Yellowstone, also an Assiniboine trading post. This Agency was discontinued in 1876 and reestablished under Major Lincoln in 1878. In 1888 the Agency moved to its current site as part of the newly established reservation. An older trading post called Fort Browning was built near present-day Dodson in 1868, but was abandoned in 1872 because of Sioux hostility, which prevented trading by the Assiniboine, Gros Ventres, Metis French/Cree, and French/Chippewa. See Noyes 1917.

16. Noyes 1917 provides details of this and interesting firsthand accounts of the early relations between Indians, "squaw men," and later settlers, as well as the Little Rockies gold rush and the subsequent wrangle for political power and economic development in the region.

17. Cf. Basso's accounts (1984, 1988) of place naming and topography among the Cibecue Apache.

18. See Hallowell's (1955) discussion of the cultural construction of Salteaux spatial orientation, for whom north, south, east, and west represent quite distinct places, in contrast to our use of them as abstract directions linked to the earth's magnetic poles and lines of longitude and latitude. Haugan's (1969) study of Icelandic spatial orientation provides a further example. Icelanders have a dual system of semantics for the four directions: one set of meanings is based on celestial orientations and immediate geographical features, the other on practices developed from overland travel that relate direction to the coastline.

19. Such a perspective is simply a heuristic device here and not an assertion of the ethnographer's omnipotence. See Clifford 1988, Chap. 3, and Stocking 1983 for interesting discussions on the creation of authority through the use of perspectives and viewpoints in ethnographic writing.

20. This is an important feature of the Laban writing system for anthropologists because one is writing quite literally from "the native's point of view" and not confined to an observer's perspective. Reading the text means reading as if one were performing oneself, as we can choose to do when reading a spoken language text written in the first person.

4. MORAL AND ETHICAL SPACES

1. Lowie (1909:42–45) records useful details of some Assiniboine religious practices, and the acquisition of "power." Related concepts in Lakota Sioux beliefs can be found in DeMallie and Lavenda 1977, Walker 1980, and DeMallie 1984.

2. James Owen Dorsey recognized this problem in his "Study of Siouan Cults": "In considering the subject from an Indian's point of view, one must avoid speaking of the supernatural as distinguished from the natural. It is safer to divide phenomena as they appear to the Indian mind into the human and the superhuman, as many, if not most natural phenomena are mysterious to the Indian. Nay even man himself may become mysterious by fasting, prayer and vision" (1894:365).

3. Kendall's article is about Northern Yuman personal names as texts. In it she refers to Boas' use of Plains Indian names as an example of the importance of linguistic investigation for understanding features of Indian life. Boas says, "The translation of Indian names which are popularly known—like Sitting Bull, Afraid-of-his-horse, etc.—indicate that the names possess a deeper significance. The translations are so difficult that a thorough linguistic knowledge is required in order to explain the significance adequately" (1911:58). As Kendall points out, however, despite Boas' intention to illustrate the relevance of linguistics to ethnology, he fosters the impression that the significance of names is to be understood by exploring their grammatical properties, when it is the social and cultural contexts in which personal names are given—the highly situated meanings—that make exegesis as well as translation important. This argument can be widened to include not only personal names but the names of tribes and bands as well as local geographical place names. Names are signs whose meanings cannot be established outside of social interaction.

4. Lowie (1909:67) gives details of this ceremony as the Grass Dance (*peżi-owac'* or *peżi mįknake owac'*) which, he tells us, is a modernized version of the *ak'ic'ita* or soldier organization. Buechel's Lakota dictionary gives *mįknaka* as "to gird around the loins."

5. Lowie's account of this ceremony, written in 1909, perhaps indicates that the sexual taboos were still in effect at that time, but one cannot tell whether Lowie observed a dance himself or is reconstructing the detail from informants' statements about earlier practices (Lowie 1909:67).

6. The classifier WATER has two variations, one of which also means TO DRINK. This precedes signs that indicate the size and type of body of water

referred to: RIVER, DITCH, LAKE/OCEAN, CREEK, RAPIDS. As a classifier for types of drinks, it precedes TEA (DRINK + LEAVES, which in spoken Nakota is also *waȟpe* 'leaves'), COFFEE, SODA/LEMONADE (DRINK + SWEET), BEER (DRINK + BOILING).

7. Mallery 1881, Clark 1885, Hadley 1893, Seton 1918, and Scott 1934 all provide lists of tribal signs and discussions of possible etymologies. There was and is some local variation according to frequency of contact; for example, people at Fort Belknap do not have signs for individual southern tribes such as the Apache or Pueblo Indians, which are grouped together as SOUTHERN PEOPLE.

8. J. Owen Dorsey published a report in 1890 about a forthcoming extensive monograph on Indian personal names that classified according to animals and colors and gave details of references to myths and clan names. Unfortunately the monograph was never completed, but notes toward a manuscript are housed in the National Anthropological Archives in Washington, D.C.

9. Personal naming is an important topic in its own right that I have only begun to touch upon here. It would properly involve not only translation and linguistic investigation but an exegesis of the circumstances in which these personal names are chosen and given, changed, and used. While certainly of interest, this would be a digression from the present task, which is simply to point out certain common threads between naming practices in signs and speech. Interesting work has been done in this area among Native Americans by Kendall (1980) on Yuman names as texts; Fletcher (1899) on a Pawnee ritual concerning changing a man's name; Guemple (1965) on Eskimo name sharing; and see also "Names and Naming" in Hodge 1910. Tooker and Conklin 1984 contains further essays, and Alford 1987 presents a cross-cultural study of naming practices and further bibliographic sources.

10. An interlinear translation of what Rose Weasel said is as follows:

Tók'en néna c'aže k'o snonyapiš,
They didn't know these [English] names

eyaš "waȟpe"
they just said, "when the leaves are out"

"waȟpe p'eġit'o"
"when the grass is yellow"

"wana waȟpįc'aȟ"
"now the buds are coming out"

"c'ap'a wašteše."
"the cherries are ripe."

Tók'en hąwi c'aže k'owa snonyapiš.
They didn't know what the names of the months meant.

"Wana osnisnįk," eyapi.
"Now its getting cold," they said.

"Waniyetu žehą, wana uc'," eyap(i) "osnisni."
Winter is coming now," they said, "its cold."

Eyaš "Waniyetu c'okan," eyapi.
Just "It's the middle of the winter," they said.

"Osnisni c'okan wana sam ųkiyap žetahą wana mnoketu en ųyąpikt," eyapi.
"Now we have passed the middle of winter" from then, "now we will get summer," they said

11. Davies and Harré (1990:46) articulate clearly the way discursive practices create such views of self and others: "Who one is is always a question with a shifting answer depending upon the positions made available within one's own and others' discursive practices and within those practices, the stories through which we make sense of our own and others' lives." I would want to add to this a consideration of the way bodily presentation and actions can equally be part of such positioning.

5. GETTING TO THE POINT

1. Black Elk, the Lakota holy man, also mentions south as "where you always face" (because the trail to the afterworld goes south) in his interviews with author John Neihardt in 1944. See DeMallie 1984:307, 308.

2. This and other statements about the four directions in quotation marks in the text are expressions by consultants and are taken from my field notes for 1987 and 1988. In relation to symbolic associations connected with north, the Oglala Sioux religious man and author Sword told J. R. Walker (1917) that because of an offense against the feminine god (the companion of the south wind), the Great Spirit condemned the north wind to dwell forever with his grandfather Wazi, the wizard. The Assiniboine conception would seem to echo this theme, but I was not given any explicit formulation of this, nor a translation of *wazi* in these terms.

3. "Frame of reference" and "cross of axes" are technical terms in Labanotation. Cross of axes is used to describe three intersecting axes, one in each dimension—up/down, right/left, and front/back—placed, as it were, on the mover's body. Frames of reference vary according to how this cross of axes is utilized. For example, if you were lying on the floor and told to put your arms up, you might choose to lift the arms toward the ceiling and so be working from a standard frame of reference, where going against gravity is up. Or you might stretch them above your head and along the floor, in which case you would be moving from a body frame of reference, where what counts as up is determined by the body itself, not by any outside considerations. Three major systems of orientation articulated so far are (a) standard frame of reference, in which up and down remain constant but front is judged according to the facing of the mover's torso; (b) constant frame of reference, as illustrated by the Assiniboine adherence to the four directions, in which features of an external spatial system or performance space determine how directions are organized; and (c) body frame of reference, described above. There are others, and anthropological research is likely to add to the possibilities. See Durr and Farnell 1981; Williams and Farnell 1990.

4. Other differences that arise are due to translations from Nakota verbs to English tensed verb forms, word order, and the English verb "to be," which is

not represented in Nakota grammar. Labov (1968) has described how "Black English" used in the African American community has been similarly stigmatized, as was nonstandard working-class British English, labeled by Bernstein (1964) as a "restricted code" versus an "elaborated" middle- and upper-class code.

5. Recent studies of problems in Native American education have indicated that there are communication breakdowns in the classroom because of cultural differences not only in the structure of language but also in assumptions about how verbal exchanges should be structured. Cazden and John (1968) suggest that the "styles of learning" through which Indian children are enculturated at home differ markedly from those to which they are introduced in the classroom. Hymes (1971) has pointed out that this may lead to sociolinguistic interference when teacher and student do not recognize these differences. Philips (1983) discusses how the lack of appropriate conditions for speech use from the Indian point of view contribute to the reluctance of Indian children to talk in the classroom. The contribution that a lack of gestural communication might make to this problem has not been investigated.

6. On deixis in general, see Lyons 1977, Vol. 2; Bühler 1934; Benveniste 1971; Collinson 1937; Fillmore 1966, 1970; Frei 1944; Hjelmslev 1937; Jakobson [1957] 1971; Kurylowicz 1972. Detailed studies on spatial orientation and deixis are found in Hanks 1990, Pick and Acredolo 1983, and Jarvella and Klein 1982.

6. STORYTELLING AND THE EMBODIMENT OF SYMBOLIC FORM

1. The word "medicine" as used here in the term "medicine rock," has been a common epithet used by non-Indians since the eighteenth century to refer to anything concerning the "superstitions" of Indians. This rather contemptuous attitude toward traditional medical practices and religious beliefs by those aiming at the assimilation of Native Americans is clearly expressed in a book of regulations issued by the Indian Office in April 1904: "The usual practices of so-called 'Medicine Men' shall be considered 'Indian Offenses' recognizable by the court of Indian offenses, and whenever it shall be proven to the satisfaction of the court that the influence or practice of a so-called 'Medicine Man' resorts to any artifice or device to keep the Indians under his influence, or shall adopt any means to prevent the attendance of children at the Agency schools, or shall use any of the arts of a conjurer to prevent the Indians from abandoning their rites and customs, he shall be judged guilty of an Indian offense" (cited in Rodnick 1938:13). Rodnick tells us that such attitudes were not new but merely a crystallization of ideas long held by the Indian Office, intended to suppress native culture and encourage the adoption of white norms and values. "Indian Offenses" that were banned included the "sun-dance and all other similar dances and so-called religious ceremonies" as well as "plural marriages."

Despite a clear separation of roles, both religious leaders and medical practitioners were labeled in English as "medicine men" and a wide variety of religious objects and substances lumped together with herbal remedies as "medicine." Since distinctions between the sacred and the secular are not a part of Plains Indian epistemologies, religious concepts are necessarily involved in healing procedures in a way that they are not in Euro-American biological concepts of disease and healing. This fact, in conjunction with ethnocentrism and prejudice against non-Christian beliefs, was probably a source of these kinds of misunderstandings. The term "medicine" has remained in popular use among non-Indians but can also be heard as an English translation by Native Americans in the absence of a more suitable term. Today it may be used in a disparaging way by Native Americans uninterested in, or critical of, both traditional practices and those attempting to revive traditional religious events.

2. Tourists tend to be completely unaware of this practice, as illustrated by the comments of one woman who complained about "people who just dump their cigarettes out like that."

3. This and other stories discussed in this book can be examined further using the CD-ROM that accompanies this book.

4. For a similar theme among other Plains tribes, see Wissler and Duvall 1908:19 (Blackfeet); Kroeber 1907–1908:59 (Gros Ventre); Dorsey and Kroeber 1903:16 (Arapaho); Simms 1903:281–324 (Crow); Schoolcraft 1856:39 (Ojibway); Hoffman 1893:134 (Menominee); Jones 1907:365 (Fox). Lowie (1909) cites a version among the Cree reported in Petitot 1886.

5. Old Horse, a Lakota Sioux holy man, told Walker that Inktomi "is a little one. His body is like a fat bug. His legs are like the spider's, but he has hands and feet like a man" and "he can make himself appear like an old man," or a stranger offering to lead a young man to a woman (Walker 1980:128–129). See also Walker 1917:90, Dorsey 1894:471–473, and Deloria 1938:1–46, for other Sioux descriptions. Lowie, who did not have access to these later materials about the Dakota and Lakota, found few elements in the Inktomi tales that are shared by the Assiniboine with their fellow Siouan-language speakers. He concluded that Assiniboine mythology emphasized the influence of recent tribes, especially the Cree. We therefore cannot safely assume that Assiniboine conceptions about Inktomi were coincident with those of the Lakota. My Assiniboine consultants did not share these visual images of Inktomi but said only that he was like a man but not really. The conception of Inktomi as a funny and foolish character is an indigenous one that displays an ironic humor in relation to things normally treated with reverence by Euro-Americans. It is not an ethnocentric restructuring by non-Indians.

6. See also the description in Dorsey 1897:224.

7. The Lakota myth told by George Sword to Walker (1983:57) suggests that Inktomi, represented as son of Íyą 'rock', is weary of being laughed at and devises a scheme that leads to shame and disharmony among the spirits. Inktomi is pun-

ished by no longer being associated with them. Although he is allowed to keep his power, humankind shall be warned of his tricks and cautioned against him.

8. The purpose here is not a detailed analysis of Genesis as origin myth, but a summary of the folk model that is based upon Genesis. See Leach 1969 for a structural analysis of Genesis.

9. Compare this with the Lakota narrative told to Neihardt by Black Elk in which competition and not cooperation decides the order of things. The competition takes the form of a great race around the circle of the earth between the four-leggeds (animals) and the two-leggeds (birds, but representing humans in the race). In this case, because the Magpie won on behalf of the two-leggeds, humans are able to eat the buffalo and not the reverse.

10. The presence of the camera when Rose Weasel told her stories had the unintended effect of silencing this anticipated audience response. Mrs. Weasel complained after telling her first story because no one had said "hą" in the right places. Her audience, however, had decided it would spoil the videotaping and ignored her request! (See Tedlock 1983 for discussion of the presence of technology in the "story of how a story was made" and as part of ethnography as interaction.)

11. "Kinesphere" is a technical term used by Rudolph Laban (the creator of Labanotation) for an imaginary sphere of three-dimensional space around a person that extends as far as the individual can reach in any direction.

12. This makes Kendon's (1989:2) suggested distinction between "primary" and "alternate" sign languages somewhat problematical. As Kendon himself suggests, however, the use of PST as a lingua franca necessarily freed it from close connection to any one spoken language grammar, despite the fact that the simultaneous use of speech and signing was widespread (West 1960:2, 76). The kinds of relationships between words and signs may differ markedly from those found by Kendon among users of Walbiri (Australian Aboriginal) sign language.

13. Field notes, Earthboy, Book 1. Earthboy often used the term "word" for what I have called a PST sign, indicating a lack of any important distinction between the two as far as he was concerned. Another example of this occurred during discussion of a polysemic PST sign that accompanied the spoken words "if it's gonna be that way" (žéc'en tušten). He said, "If you use that word [sign] again [in a different context] it means TRUE, the same sign."

14. "Degrees of Freedom" is a technical term used in the context of a semasiological approach to human movement. It designates exactly how many of the three intersecting planes of movement an isolated body part is capable of moving in, based upon the limitations set by its anatomical structure. That is, while your elbow can only bend and straighten (using one plane), your wrist can bend and straighten (one plane), tilt side to side (a second plane), and rotate around its axis (a third plane). So the elbow has only one degree of freedom while the wrist has three. The whole body has a total of ninety-five degrees of freedom, permutations of which create all theoretically possible movement. The

Laban script is also based upon this system of making finite all possible movements of the joints of the body. This making finite in order to analyze and tran-
scribe is no different from that engaged in by linguists who identify the limitations set by the structure of the mouth in creating all the sounds we find in
spoken languages of the world, a level that they call phonetic. Setting out theoretical models for these kinds of structural universals in relation to human movement has been an important breakthrough for the study of human movement
previously plagued by problems of how to "measure" and make finite the seemingly infinite complexity of the whole body moving (see Williams 1975 and 1991,
Chaps. 8 and 9 for further exegesis).

7. THE PRIMACY OF MOVEMENT IN ASSINIBOINE CULTURE

1. Specialists may wonder why I have chosen to use an illustration from
Tomkins 1926, given that his book is a popular one written especially for Boy
Scouts (a topic worthy of investigation in its own right) and so is perhaps viewed
as a doubtful source. My reasons are partly pragmatic in that Tomkins uses all
six pictographic representations to which I refer in the same illustration. But
also, in defense of Tomkins' work, it must be said that although an amateur
enthusiast, Tomkins was a man whom the Sioux had named *Waḅli Wíyuta* 'Sign-
talking Eagle'. He lived around Cheyenne Agency, Pierre, and Fort Pierre from
1885 to 1894 learning PST among Sioux and other sign talkers. For the most
part, I have found his picture dictionary of signs to correspond fairly accurately
to historical records and present-day knowledge of PST.

Some caution is indeed necessary when dealing with Tomkins' treatment
of pictographs. While inscriptions on rock, birch bark, and hides were widespread in indigenous North America and served many communicative and
mnemonic functions, Tomkins may well have invented these "pictographic stories" himself. I have not yet come across any other records of stories or messages written in the spiral form that Tomkins presents (1926:89), and he may
have taken this idea from Dakota winter counts (see Mallery 1886 for examples).
Most of the pictographic "building blocks" used by Tomkins can also be found
in the more scholarly collections of Schoolcraft and Mallery, however (e.g., SKY
as half circle in Schoolcraft 1851–1857, vol. 1, pp. 390, 407; RIVER in Schoolcraft
1851–1857, vol. 2, plate 57; TRADE in Mallery 1886:220). A good example of a
message written using pictographs of this kind and written by an Assiniboine
person can be found in Denig [1930] 1961:603.

Further examples of pictographs representing the movement paths of signs
are described in Mallery 1886:219–221 and 1893:639–641, e.g., PIPE, HUNGER,
LITTLE CHIEF, DAKOTA, NOON. The only two exceptions to this I have encountered to date are (a) a seated human figure signifying "pipe" in which the
Dakota artist drew a tiny human figure making the sign PIPE instead of draw-

ing a pipe (see Batiste Goode's winter count in Mallery 1886:219); and (b) "Afraid of Him" a name sign in Red Cloud's census that shows the handshape and arm position from the sign AFRAID (Mallery 1886:639). It is interesting to note in passing that Dakota pictographs of persons who were prisoners are depicted without hands to denote helplessness (Mallery 1886:242).

2. An investigation of some of the methods used to measure and record bodily movement by early nonverbal communication specialists, for example, reveals a particular conception of the nature of human movement that is common to many of them and that may be much more widespread than those particular investigators' problems with measurement. I suggest that for many people in Euro-American societies, "movement" is conceived of as a series of positions of the body or its parts, such that a series of photographs or positions of limbs plotted on a two-dimensional graph are deemed adequate records of movement. This would appear to be entirely consistent with the kind of mathematical view of the world inherited from the Platonic search for the absolute—that is, a search for some point in intellectual understanding that fixes the world as a constant. From this perspective, change (in this case movement) is illusion, mere appearance that is to be eliminated. What is real is what is fixed and constant. Zeno's famous paradox illustrates this view: there is no movement, just a series of positions. Movement is thereby reduced to point.

All this would seem to be continuous with a complex ontological dualism in Western culture between the material and the nonmaterial. This has an effect on the status of body movement because it coincides with the kind of body/mind dualism concretized by Descartes, wherein the body is reduced to sensating matter, in direct contrast to the nonmaterial nature of mind/soul. Contemporary philosophy of science suggests rather a dynamic view of substance as having causal powers, which provides a whole different basis for viewing human movement and connecting mind to body. See Introduction for further discussion.

3. Munn also notes that "the Walbiri graphic symbolism is closely bound up with linguistic communication in Walbiri thought and usage," thereby providing evidence of links between the visual and the vocal in this culture also. The graphic designs are used on the body in ceremonials, and in conversation and storytelling when they are drawn in the sand. Munn tells us that they enter Walbiri imagination as a kind of visual language for ordering meaning. As these are a people who also use a sign language extensively (see Kendon 1989), one wonders what kinds of links might exist between spoken, graphic, and signed systems.

4. Ray DeMallie (personal communication) and Buechel's Lakota grammar (1939:72).

5. The following brief exchange between a seven-year-old girl and myself illustrates the point:

Do you have a husband?
No.
Do you live with some other people?
No, I live all by myself.
(With disdain) Don't you have any *relatives*?

6. Buechel's Lakota dictionary includes a list of fifty-three words that use *wacį* Many of these have to do with thinking of various kinds, ranging from "to be quick to comprehend" and "to be intelligent, wise" to be "fickle-minded" and "bewildered." What is distinctive about this list is the inclusion of many words that involve what English speakers would distinguish as being involved with feeling rather than thinking, e.g., "to be kind," "to be discouraged," "to be contented," "to be sad on account of," "to trust in," "to be patient," "to comfort," "to trust in." These are all general attributes of persons and states of persons toward others that I have termed "disposition."

7. Harris (1980) and Goody (1977a, 1977b) have both "robustly denounced the sweeping reduction of alien cultural forms to the diagrammatic habits of a single literate canon" (Herzfeld 1987:39). See also Fabian 1983, Chap. 4, for a critique of "visualism" in anthropology, wherein what can be mapped, diagrammed, and charted has been privileged in ethnographic accounts.

8. The fool dance was an Assiniboine ceremony led by someone who had the rights to do so. It was a sacred ceremony that included a lot of fun and foolishness; see Lowie 1909:62–66. The last fool dance at Fort Belknap occurred in 1975 but was not passed on by its owner Al First-Sound. At the sun dance in Lodgepole, June 1989, however, a group of young men from Canada dressed as fools and danced counterclockwise around the sun dance lodge using the same antics described in the former fool dance. They also appeared at the *húteśa* powwow at Frazer on the Fort Peck Reservation and danced the "wrong" way around the dance arbor. The leader of this group explained that his grandfather in Canada had the rights to this dance long ago, and that he himself had attended the last fool dance at Fort Belknap in 1975. Having since dreamed about it, he felt the dream was an indication that he should "take it up for the people" again.

9. Further examples can be found in Mallery 1886, 1893; Mooney 1979; and Howard 1960, 1976, 1979. See also discussion of winter counts in DeMallie 1982.

10. For example, a young actor in the powerful black South African theater production "The Voices of Sarafina" (PBS, August 19, 1990) made reference to what people in the townships have come to call a "black smile." In the context of relentless oppression and violence, this has come to symbolize the internalization of tremendous pain and suffering and the shared awareness of injustices, covered in a simple empty smile that means "All that is too painful—we still have somehow to get on with life."

8. CONCLUSIONS

1. I am not sure that Vico's reversal of the import of this schema, but not its overall assumption, really assists the anti-Cartesian project he was engaged in. It still removes gesture from spoken expression but simply places a more positive value on it as a precursor to metaphorical speech. See Herzfeld 1987:191.

2. See, for example, how the Indian Offenses Act banned dances and other religious and marriage practices in Rodnick 1938:12–13.

3. On "emotion" see Lutz 1988 and the 1986b collection edited by Harré. On "knowledge" and "passion" see M. Rosaldo 1980. On "person" and "self" the collections of Carrithers, Collins, and Lukes (1985), White and Kirkpatrick (1985), and Marsella, DeVos, and Hsu (1985) are representative. On "history" see Sahlins 1985 and R. Rosaldo 1980. Also Herzfeld 1981, 1984.

4. Harré, following Wittgenstein on the problem of rules, correctly insists: "A rule is formulated by observation of behavior, the production of which may not involve the deployment of that rule or any other. . . . The internalizer's program makes the mistake of supposing that just because a rule can be formulated to capture a regularity of conduct, that rule must be operative in the production of that conduct—if not 'consciously,' then in the secret workings of the mental or physical system of which the individual is composed" (Warner 1990:143).

5. See Piaget 1954; Bates, Bretherton, Shore, and McNew 1983; Bowerman 1980.

6. Merleau-Ponty's notion of "bodily intentionality" seems to posit an original and primary bodily experience as a way of access to the world and the object without having to make use of any symbolic or social function. It is both individual and essentially preconceptual or nonconceptual. The body through habit develops its own form of understanding (1962:142–145) and has a unique form of intentionality that is not reducible to the intentionality of thought (1962:137, 243). He fails to explain how this might work and indeed seems to suggest that no explanation can be forthcoming; it is an "ultimate fact" (1962:194). Woodruff Smith (1988:51–52) has criticized this and suggested that we need to distinguish several forms of awareness that are interwoven. For example, first there is kinesthetic awareness of one's body and bodily movement in one's conscious *action* when picking up a shovel. Next, in that action there is one's out-of-focal-awareness *of* one's acting. Third, there is one's perception of things in the environment—say, in seeing and touching the shovel one is picking up in order to dig a hole. These three forms of intentionality are interdependent. One cannot perform the action of picking up a shovel without a kinesthetic awareness of one's movement, a perception of the object, and a (probably) out-of-focal-awareness of picking up the shovel, not to mention a background cultural understanding of the activity of digging. One also cannot see the shovel without turning one's eyes toward it, or feel it without reaching one's hand out to touch it.

These various forms cannot be reduced to the others, whether reducing action to cognition or cognition to action, and none is foundational for the others.

APPENDIX B: KINETIC KEY

1. Labanotation was invented by Rudolph Laban (1879–1958), a choreographer and dancer. Working in Austria and Germany (1926), he set out to devise a notation system that could record *any* human movement, although initially it was used only in choreographic contexts. Laban was intrigued by Greek concerns with mathematics, the movement of planetary spheres, and the Bauhaus movement in visual art and architecture. He had wide interests in movement in diverse situations, from the dynamic components of the physical working environment in industry to mime. Labanotation—or Kinetography Laban, as it is known in Europe—came to be used primarily for the recording and preservation of professional theater and dance works in the United States and in Europe and the traditional dances of Eastern Europe. This background has led to an erroneous conception that it is a *dance* notation rather than a movement notation system. Williams pioneered its use in anthropology when she completed a movement score of the Roman Catholic post-Tridentine mass in 1975, and it is used by several of her former students, the author included. Kaeppler also uses Labanotation in her work.

2. See, for example, seminal articles by Haugen [1957] 1969 and Hallowell 1955 and current work on deixis and spatial orientation in Hanks 1990, Havilland 1993, Levinson 1991, McNeill and Levy 1982, Talmy 1983, Williams 1988 and 1990. Lakoff and Johnson (1980) articulate such values as found in metaphors attached to spatial direction among English speakers. Johnson 1987 and Lakoff 1987 develop these ideas considerably in relation to embodiment.

3. Laban also created a detailed classification and transcription system for the dynamic aspects of movement that he called Eukinetics and later Effort. This work was further developed in the United States and is known as Effort-Shape. An earlier emphasis on "inner attitudes" has made this system of interest to psychology in therapeutic settings and in personality diagnosis. Assumptions of universality were highly problematic, however, as the classifications involved and the interpretation of meaning that accompanied them were made according to the values that Europeans and Euro-Americans tend to attach to different uses of energy, spatial directions, and parts of the body.

BIBLIOGRAPHY

ALFORD, R. D.
1987.   *Naming and Identity: A Cross-Cultural Study of Personal Naming
        Practices.* New Haven, Conn.: HRAF.
ALLEN, J. L.
1985.   The Garden-Desert Continuum: Competing Views of the Great Plains
        in the Nineteenth Century. *Great Plains Quarterly* 5:207–220.
ARDENER, E.
1973.   'Behaviour': A Social Anthropological Criticism. *Journal of the
        Anthropological Society of Oxford* 4(3):153–155. Reprinted in Ardener
        1989.
1978.   Some Outstanding Problems in the Analysis of Events. ASA Confer-
        ence paper, 1973. In *Yearbook of Symbolic Anthropology.* E. Schwimmer,
        ed. London: Hurst. Reprinted in Ardener 1989:86–104.
1989.   *Edwin Ardener: The Voice of Prophecy and Other Essays.* M. Chapman,
        ed. Oxford: Blackwell.
ARGYLE, M.
1975.   *Bodily Communication.* London: Methuen.
ARMSTRONG, D.
1983.   *Political Anatomy of the Body: Medical Knowledge in Britain in the
        Twentieth Century.* Cambridge: Cambridge University Press.
AUSTIN, J. L.
1962.   *How to Do Things with Words.* 2d ed. J. O. Urmson and M. Sbisa, eds.
        Cambridge: Harvard University Press.
BAKER, C., AND D. COKELY
1980.   *American Sign Language: A Teacher's Resource Text on Grammar and
        Culture.* Silver Spring, Md.: T.J. Publishers.
BASSO, K.
1969.   "To Give Up on Words": Silence in Western Apache Culture. *South-
        western Journal of Anthropology* 24(3):252–266.

1979.   *Portraits of the Whiteman: Linguistic Play and Cultural Symbols among the Western Apache.* Cambridge: Cambridge University Press.

1984.   "Stalking with Stories": Names, Places, and Moral Narratives among the Western Apache. In *Text, Play and Story: The Construction and Reconstruction of Self and Society.* E. Bruner, ed. Pp. 19–55. AES Proceedings. Washington, D.C.: American Ethnological Society.

1988.   "Speaking with Names": Language and Landscape among the Western Apache. *Cultural Anthropology* 3:99–130.

BASTIEN, J. W.
1985.   Qollahuaya-Andean Body Concepts: A Topographical-Hydrolic Model of Physiology. *American Anthropologist* 87:595–611.

BATES, E., I. BRETHERTON, C. SHORE, AND S. MCNEW
1983.   Names, Gestures and Objects: Symbolization in Infancy and Aphasia. In *Children's Language.* K. E. Nelson, ed. Vol. 4:59–123. New York: Gardner Press.

BAUMAN, R.
1977.   *Verbal Art as Performance.* Prospect Heights, Ill.: Waveland.

1986.   *Story, Performance and Event: Contextual Studies in Oral Narrative.* Cambridge: Cambridge University Press.

BAUMAN, R., AND J. SHERZER
1989.   Eds. *Explorations in the Ethnography of Speaking.* 2d ed. Cambridge: Cambridge University Press.

BELLUGI, U., AND E. S. KLIMA
1982.   From Gesture to Sign: Deixis in a Visual Gestural Language. In Jarvella and Klein 1982:297–313.

BENTHALL, J., AND T. POLHEMUS
1975.   Eds. *The Body as a Medium of Expression.* London: Institute of Contemporary Arts.

BENVENISTE, E.
1971.   *Problems in General Linguistics.* Coral Gables: University of Florida Press.

BERLIN, B., AND P. KAY
1969.   *Basic Color Terms: Their Universality and Evolution.* Berkeley: University of California Press.

BERNSTEIN, B.
1964.   Elaborated and Restricted Codes: Their Social Origins and Some Consequences. In *The Ethnography of Communication.* J. J. Gumperz and D. Hymes, eds. Pp. 55–69. Washington, D.C.: American Anthropological Association.

BEST, D.
1974.   *Expression in Movement and the Arts.* London: Lepus.

1978.   *Philosophy and Human Movement.* London: Allen and Unwin.

BHASHKAR, R.
1978.   *A Realist Theory of Science*. Atlantic Highlands, N.J.: Humanities Press.
BIRDWHISTELL, R. L.
1970.   *Kinesics in Context: Essays on Body Motion Communication*. Philadelphia: University of Pennsylvania Press.
BLACKING, J.
1977.   Ed. *The Anthropology of the Body*. ASA Monograph 15. London: Academic Press.
BOAS, F.
1911.   Ed. Introduction to *The Handbook of American Indian Languages*. Bulletin 40, pt 1. Pp. 1–83. Washington, D.C.: Bureau of American Ethnology, Smithsonian Institution.
BOAS, F., AND E. DELORIA
1941.   Dakota Grammar. *Memoirs of the National Academy of Sciences* 23(2).
BOURDIEU, P.
1977.   *Outline of a Theory of Practice*. R. Nice, trans. Cambridge: Cambridge University Press.
1984.   *Distinction: A Social Critique of the Judgement of Taste*. R. Nice, trans. Cambridge: Harvard University Press.
BOWERMAN, M.
1980.   Systematizing Semantic Knowledge: Changes Over Time in the Child's Organization of Word Meaning. *Child Development* 49:977–987.
BRAIN, R.
1979.   *The Decorated Body*. New York: Harper & Row.
BROWN, J. E.
1953.   Ed. *The Sacred Pipe: Black Elk's Account of the Seven Rites of the Oglala Sioux*. Norman: University of Oklahoma Press.
BUECHEL, E., S.J.
1939.   *A Grammar of Lakota*. St. Francis, S.Dak.: Rosebud Educational Society.
[1970] 1983.   *A Dictionary of the Teton Dakota Sioux Language: Lakota-English, English-Lakota*. P. Manhart, S.J., ed. Pine Ridge, S.Dak.: Red Cloud Indian School.
BÜHLER, K.
[1934] 1982.   The Deictic Field of Language and Deictic Words. In Jarvella and Klein 1982:9–30.
BURKS, A. W.
1949.   Icon, Index, and Symbol. *Journal of Philosophical and Phenomenological Research* 9(4):673–689.
BURTON, R. F.
1861.   *The City of Saints*. New York: Harper and Brothers.

CARRITHERS, M., S. COLLINS, AND S. LUKES
1985.   Eds. *The Category of the Person: Anthropology, Philosophy, History.* Cambridge: Cambridge University Press.

CATLIN, G.
[1844] 1973. *Letters and Notes on the Manners, Customs and Conditions of the North American Indians.* Vols. 1, 2. New York: Dover.

CAZDEN, C. B., AND V. P. JOHN
1986.   Learning in American Indian Children. In *Styles of Learning among American Indians: An Outline for Research.* Washington, D.C.: Center for Applied Linguistics.

CHAPMAN, M.
1982.   "Semantics" and the "Celt." In *Semantic Anthropology.* D. Parkin, ed. ASA Monograph 22. Pp. 123–144. London: Academic Press.

CHESAREK, R., AND S. CHESAREK
1988.   Paper presented at Eighth Annual Conference on Siouan and Caddoan Linguistics Conference, Billings, Mont. July 17–18.

CLARK, E.
1977.   *From Gesture to Word: On the Natural History of Deixis in Language Acquisition.* In *Human Growth and Development.* J. S. Bruner and A. Garton, eds. Oxford: Oxford University Press.

CLARK, W. P.
1885.   *The Indian Sign Language.* Philadelphia: L. R. Hammersley.

CLIFFORD, J.
1988.   *The Predicament of Culture.* Cambridge: Harvard University Press.

CODY, I. E.
1952.   *How: Sign Talk in Pictures.* Hollywood, Calif.: H. H. Boelter Lithography.

COLLINSON, W. E.
1937.   *Indication: A Study of Demonstratives, Articles and Other 'Indicators'.* Monograph 17, *Language.* Baltimore: Linguistic Society of America.

COUES, E.
[1897] 1965. *The Manuscript Journals of Alexander Henry and of David Thompson, 1799–1814.* New York.

COULTER, J.
1979.   *The Social Construction of Mind.* London: Macmillan.
1989.   *Mind in Action.* Oxford: Polity Press and Blackwell.

COWAN, J.
1990.   *Dance and the Body Politic in Northern Greece.* Princeton Modern Greek Studies. Princeton: Princeton University Press.

CROFT, W.
1990.   *Typology and Universals.* Cambridge: Cambridge University Press.

DANTO, A.

1990.   Review of *Gone Primitive: Savage Intellects, Modern Lives* by Marianna Torgovnick. *New York Times Book Review,* June 24.

DAVIES, B., AND R. HARRÉ.

1990.   Positioning: The Discursive Production of Selves. *Journal for the Theory of Social Behaviour* 20(1):43–63.

DELORIA, E.

1937–1938.   Ed. and trans. Dakota Commentary on Walker's Texts. MS 30(x8a.5), Boas Collection, American Philosophical Society Library, Philadelphia.

1938.   Dakota Texts from the Sword Manuscripts. MS 30(x8a.18), Boas Collection, American Philosophical Society Library, Philadelphia.

ca. 1940.   Lakota-English Lexicon. Manuscript, American Philosophical Society Library, Philadelphia.

DELORIA, V.

1973.   *God is Red.* New York: Dell.

DEMALLIE, R. J.

1982.   Ed. Introduction to Part 3, Time and History, in *Lakota Society* by J. R. Walker. Pp. 111–122. Lincoln: University of Nebraska Press.

1984.   Ed. *The Sixth Grandfather: Black Elk's Teachings Given to John Neihardt.* Lincoln: University of Nebraska Press.

In press.   Ed. *Handbook of North American Indians.* Vol. 13, *The Plains.* Washington, D.C.: Smithsonian Institution.

DEMALLIE, R. J., AND R. H. LAVENDA

1977.   Wakan: Plains Siouan Concepts of Power. In *The Anthropology of Power: Ethnographic Studies from Asia, Oceania and the New World.* R. D. Fogelson and R. N. Adams, eds. New York: Academic Press.

DENIG, E. T.

[1930] 1961.   *Five Indian Tribes of the Upper Missouri.* J. C. Ewers, ed. Norman: University of Oklahoma Press.

DERRIDA, J.

1976.   *Of Grammatology.* G. C. Spivak, trans. Baltimore: Johns Hopkins University Press.

DESCARTES, R.

[1641] 1986.   *Discourse on Method and Meditations on First Philosophy.* 2d ed. D. A. Cress, trans. Indianapolis: Hackett.

DE SMET, P.

1863.   *Western Missions and Missionaries: A Series of Letters.* New York: James B. Kirker.

DODGE, R. I.

1877.   *The Plains of the Great West.* New York: G. P. Putnam & Sons.

1882.   The Sign Language: Wonderful Expertness of Indian Sign Talkers. In
          Our Wild Indians: 33 yrs Personal Experience among the Red Men of the
          Great West. Reprinted in Sebeok and Umiker-Sebeok 1978 (2):3–18.
DORSEY, G., AND A. KROEBER
1903.   Traditions of the Arapaho. *Field Columbian Museum Anthropology*
          Series 5:1–475.
DORSEY, J. O.
1890.   Indian Personal Names. *American Anthropologist* 3:263–268.
1894.   A Study of Siouan Cults. *BAE Annual Report* 11:351–544. Washington,
          D.C.: Smithsonian Institution.
1897.   Siouan Sociology: A Posthumous Paper. *BAE Annual Report* 15:207–
          244. Washington, D.C.: Smithsonian Institution.
DOUGLAS, M.
1966.   *Purity and Danger: An Analysis of Concepts of Pollution and Taboo.*
          London: Routledge & Kegan Paul.
1970.   *Natural Symbols.* London: Barrie and Rockcliff. ·
DURR, D., AND B. FARNELL
1981.   Spatial Orientation and the Notion of Constant Oppositions. *Journal*
          for the Anthropological Study of Human Movement (JASHM) 1(4):
          226–245.
ECO, U.
1976.   *A Theory of Semiotics.* Bloomington: Indiana University Press.
EGGAN, F.
1975.   From History to Myth: A Hopi Example. In *Essays in Social Anthropol-*
          ogy and Ethnology. Studies in Anthropology, Series in Social, Cultural
          and Linguistic Anthropology 1. Chicago: Department of Anthropol-
          ogy, University of Chicago.
EPÉE, ABBÉ C.-M. DE L'
1776.   L'Institution des sourds et muets par la voie des signes methodiques.
          Paris: Nyon. Reprinted 1860 as The True Method of Educating the
          Deaf and Dumb, Confirmed by Long Experience. F. Green, trans.
          Annals of the Deaf 12:1–132.
EWERS, J.
1974.   Ethnological Report on the Blackfeet and Gros Ventre Tribes of
          Indians. In *Blackfeet Indians.* American Indian Ethnohistory Series.
          D. Agee Horr, ed. New York: Garland.
FABIAN, J.
1983.   *Time and the Other: How Anthropology Makes Its Object.* New York:
          Columbia University Press.
FARNELL, B.
1984.   Visual Communication and Literacy: An Anthropological Enquiry

into Plains Indian and American Sign Languages. Master's thesis, New York University.

1985.   The Hands of Time: An Exploration into Some Features of Deixis in American Sign Language. *JASHM* 3(3):100–116.

1988.   Where 'the Mind' Is a Verb: Sign-Talk of the Plains Indians Revisited. Paper presented at AAA Meeting. In Farnell 1994.

1989.   Sign-Talk of the Plains: The Visual Record. Paper presented to Visual Research Conference, Society for Visual Anthropology, Washington, D.C. November 14.

1995.   Ed. *Action Sign Systems in Cultural Context: The Visible and the Invisible in Movement and Dance.* Metuchen, N.J.: Scarecrow Press.

In press. Ethno-Graphics and the Moving Body. *MAN.*

FAST, J.

1970.   *Body Language.* New York: Evans.

FERNANDEZ, J.

1986.   *Persuasions and Performances: The Play of Tropes in Culture.* Bloomington: Indiana University Press.

FEY, H. E., AND D. MCNICKLE

[1959] 1970. *Indians and Other Americans: Two Ways of Life Meet.* New York: Harper and Row.

FILLMORE, C. J.

1966.   Deictic Categories in the Semantics of 'Come'. *Foundations of Language* 2: 219–227.

1970.   Subjects, Speakers and Roles. *Synthese* 21:251–274. Reprinted 1972 in *Semantics of Natural Language.* D. Davidson and G. Harman, eds. Pp. 1–24. Dortrecht, Holland: Reidel.

FISHER, S., AND S. E. CLEVELAND

1958.   *Body Image and Personality.* Princeton: Van Nostrand.

FLETCHER, A. C.

1884.   *Indian Ceremonies.* Peabody Museum of Ethnology and Archaeology Report 16.

1899.   A Pawnee Ritual Used When Changing a Man's Name. *American Anthropologist* 1:82–97.

FLETCHER, A. C., AND F. LA FLESCHE

[1911] 1972. *The Omaha Tribe.* Annual Report of the Bureau of Ethnology 27. Washington, D.C.: Government Printing Office. Reprinted 1972, University of Nebraska Press, Lincoln.

FOUCAULT, M.

1973.   *The Birth of the Clinic: An Archaeology of Medical Perception.* New York: Pantheon.

1978.   *The History of Sexuality.* Vol. 1, *An Introduction.* New York: Pantheon.

1979.   *Discipline and Punish: The Birth of the Prison*. New York: Random House.

FOWLER, L.
1982.   *Arapahoe Politics, 1851–1978: Symbols in Crises of Authority*. Lincoln: University of Nebraska Press.
1987.   *Shared Symbols, Contested Meanings. Gros Ventre Culture and History, 1778–1984*. Ithaca: Cornell University Press.

FREI, H.
1944.   Systeme de Deictiques. *Acta Linguistica* 4:111–129.

FREUND, P. E. S.
1982.   *The Civilized Body: Social Domination, Control and Health*. Philadelphia: Temple University Press.

FRIEDMAN, L.
1975.   Space, Time and Person Reference in American Sign Language. *Language* 51:940–961.

FRIEDRICH, P.
1979.   The Symbol and Its Relative Non-Arbitrariness. In *Language, Context and the Imagination*. Pp. 1–61. Stanford: Stanford University Press.
1986.   Linguistic Relativism and Poetic Indeterminacy: A Reformulation of Sapir's Position. In *The Language Parallax*. Pp. 16–53. Austin: University of Texas Press.

FRISHBURG, N.
1975.   Arbitrariness and Iconicity: Historical Change in American Sign Language. *Language* 51:696–719.

GIDDENS, A.
1984.   *The Constitution of Society*. Berkeley: University of California Press.
1987.   Interview. In *Sociologists on Sociology*. B. Mullen, ed. Pp. 92–144. London/Sydney: Croom Helm.

GOFFMAN, E.
1956.   *The Presentation of Self in Everyday Life*. Edinburgh: Edinburgh University Press.
1974.   *Frame Analysis*. New York: Harper.
1981.   *Forms of Talk*. Oxford: Blackwell.

GOODY, J.
1977a.   Literacy and Classification: On Turning the Tables. In *Text and Context: The Social Anthropology of Tradition*. J. K. Jain, ed. Pp. 205–222. ASA Essays in Social Anthropology 2. Philadelphia: Institute for the Study of Human Issues.
1977b.   *The Domestication of the Savage Mind*. Cambridge: Cambridge University Press.

GOULD, S. J.
1977.   *Ontogeny and Phylogeny*. Cambridge: Harvard University Press, Belknap Press.

GOULDNER, A. W.
1970.   *The Coming Crisis of Western Sociology*. New York: Free Press.
GRENE, M.
1985.   Perception, Interpretation and the Sciences: Toward a New Philoso-
         phy of Science. In *Evolution at the Crossroads: The New Biology and the
         New Philosophy of Science*. M. Grene, ed. Cambridge: MIT Press.
GUEMPLE, D. L.
1965.   Saunik: Name Sharing as a Factor Governing Eskimo Kinship Terms.
         Ethnology 4:323–335.
GUMPERTZ, J. J., AND D. HYMES
1964.   *The Ethnography of Communication*. Washington, D.C.: American
         Anthropological Association.
1972.   *Directions in Sociolinguistics: The Ethnography of Communication*. New
         York: Holt, Rinehart and Winston.
HADLEY, L. F.
1893.   *Indian Sign Talk*. Chicago: Baker and Co.
HALL, E. T.
1966.   *The Hidden Dimension*. New York: Anchor Books.
HALLOWELL, A. I.
1955.   Cultural Factors in Spatial Orientation. In *Culture and Experience*.
         Philadelphia: University of Pennsylvania Press.
HAMILTON, E., AND H. CAIRNS
1961.   Eds. *Plato: The Collected Dialogues*. Princeton: Princeton University
         Press.
HAMLYN, D.
1987.   *A History of Western Philosophy*. New York: Penguin, Viking Press.
HAMPSHIRE, S.
1965.   *Thought and Action*. London: Chatto & Windus.
HANKS, W.
1990.   *Referential Practice: Language and Lived Space among the Maya*. Chicago:
         University of Chicago Press.
HARPER, R. G., A. N. WIENS, AND J. D. MATARAZZO
1978.   *Nonverbal Communication: The State of the Art*. New York: John Wiley
         & Sons.
HARRÉ, R.
1970.   Powers. *British Journal of the Philosophy of Science* 21:81–101.
1971.   The Shift to an Anthropomorphic Model of Man. *Journal of the
         Anthropological Society of Oxford* 2(1).
1984.   *Personal Being*. Cambridge: Harvard University Press.
1986a.   Mind as a Social Formation. In Margolis, Krausz, and Burien 1986.
1986b.   Ed. *The Social Construction of Emotions*. Oxford: Blackwell.
1986c.   *Varieties of Realism*. Oxford: Blackwell.
1987.   The Social Construction of Selves. In *Self and Identity: Psychosocial*

Perspectives. K. Yardley and T. Honess, eds. Pp. 41–52. New York: John Wiley and Sons.

1992. *Physical Being.* Oxford: Blackwell.

HARRÉ, R., AND E. H. MADDON

1977. *Causal Powers.* Oxford: Blackwell.

HARRÉ, R., AND P. F. SECORD

1972. *The Explanation of Social Behaviour.* Oxford: Blackwell.

HARRINGTON, J. R.

n.d. New Materials on the Name of the Missouri. Unpublished manuscript. National Anthropological Archives, Smithsonian Institution, Washington, D.C.

HARRIS, R.

1980. *The Language Makers.* Ithaca: Cornell University Press.

1981. *The Language Myth.* New York: St. Martin's Press.

1987. *The Language Machine.* Ithaca: Cornell University Press.

HAUGEN, E.

[1957] 1969. The Semantics of Icelandic Orientation. In *Cognitive Anthropology.* S. A. Tyler, ed. Pp. 330–342. New York: Holt, Rinehart and Winston.

HAVILLAND, J.

1986. Complex Referential Gestures. Draft prepared at the Center for Advanced Study in the Behavioral Sciences, Stanford.

1993. Anchoring, Iconicity, and Orientation in Guugu Yimithirr Pointing Gestures. *Journal of Linguistic Anthropology* 3(1):3–45.

HEATH, S. B.

1983. *Ways with Words: Language, Life and Work in Communities and Classrooms.* Cambridge: Cambridge University Press.

HENSON, H.

1974. *British Social Anthropologists and Language.* Oxford: Clarendon Press.

HERTZ, R.

[1909] 1960. The Pre-eminence of the Right Hand. In *Death and the Right Hand.* R. Needham, ed. and trans. Aberdeen: Aberdeen University Press.

HERZFELD, M.

1981. An Indigenous Theory of Meaning and Its Elicitation in Performative Context. *Semiotica* 34:113–141.

1982. Disemia. In *Semiotics 1980.* M. Herzfeld and M. D. Lehnhart, eds. Pp. 205–215. New York and London: Plenum Press.

1984. *The Poetics of Manhood: Contest and Identity in a Cretan Mountain Village.* Princeton: Princeton University Press.

1987. *Anthropology through the Looking Glass: Critical Ethnography in the Margins of Europe.* Cambridge: Cambridge University Press.

HEWES, G.

1955. World Distribution of Certain Postural Habits. *American Anthropologist* 57(2):231–244.

HINDE, E.
1972.   Ed. *Non-Verbal Communication*. Cambridge: Cambridge University Press.
HJELMSLEV, L.
1937.   *La Nature du pronom*. Reprinted 1959 in L. Hjelmslev, *Essais linguistiques*. Travaux du Cercle Linguistique de Copenhague 12. Copenhagen: Akademisk Forlag.
HODGE, F. W.
1910.   *Handbook of American Indians*. BAE Bulletin 30. Washington, D.C.: Smithsonian Institution, Government Printing Office.
HODGEN, M. T.
[1964] 1971.   *Early Anthropology in the Sixteenth and Seventeenth Centuries*. Philadelphia: University of Pennsylvania Press.
HOFFMAN, W. J.
1893.   *The Menominee Indians*. BAE Annual Report 14:11–328.
HOFFMEISTER, R. J.
1978.   The Development of Demonstrative Pronouns, Locatives and Personal Pronouns in the Acquisition of American Sign Language. Ph.D. diss., University of Minnesota.
HOFSINDE, R.
1941.   Talk without Talk. *Natural History* 47:32–39.
HOLQUIST, M.
1990.   *Dialogism: Bakhtin and His World*. London and New York: Routledge.
HOWARD, J. H.
1960.   Two Dakota Winter Count Texts. *North Dakota History* 27:64–79.
1976.   Yanktonai Ethnohistory and the John K. Bear Winter Count. Memoir 11. *Plains Anthropologist* 21(73).
1979.   *The British Museum Winter Count*. British Museum Occasional Paper 4.
HUDSON, L.
1982.   *Bodies of Knowledge: The Psychological Significance of the Nude in Art*. New York: Weidenfeld & Nicholson.
HUMPHRIES, T., C. PADDEN, AND T. J. O'ROURKE
1980.   *A Basic Course in American Sign Language*. Silver Spring, Md.: T. J. Publishers.
HUNT, D. C.
1982.   *Legacy of the West*. Center for Western Studies, Jocelyn Art Museum. Lincoln: University of Nebraska Press.
HUTCHINSON, A.
1977.   *Labanotation*. 3d ed. New York: Routledge/Theatre Arts Books.
HYMES, D.
1974.   *Foundations in Sociolinguistics*. Philadelphia: University of Pennsylvania Press.
1971.   Competence and Performance in Linguistic Theory. In *Language*

Acquisition: Models and Methods. R. Huxley and E. Ingram, eds. New York: Academic Press.

1975.   Breakthrough into Performance. In *Folklore and Communication.* D. Ben-Amos and K. S. Goldstein, eds. Pp. 11–74. The Hague: Mouton.

1981.   *"In Vain I Tried to Tell You": Essays in Native American Ethnopoetics.* Philadelphia: University of Pennsylvania Press.

JACKSON, M.

1983.   Knowledge of the Body. *MAN* 18:327–345.

1989.   *Paths towards a Clearing.* Bloomington: Indiana University Press.

JAHNER, E.

1983.   Ed. Introduction to *Lakota Myth* by J. R. Walker. Pp. 1–40. Lincoln: University of Nebraska Press.

1980.   Language Change and Cultural Dynamics: A Study of Lakota Verbs of Movement. In *Languages in Conflict.* P. Schach, ed. Lincoln: University of Nebraska Press.

JAKOBSON, R.

[1957] 1971.   Shifters, Verbal Categories and the Russian Verb. In *Selected Writings of Roman Jakobson* 2:130–147. The Hague: Mouton.

1960.   Linguistics and Poetics. In *Style in Language.* T. Sebeok, ed. Pp. 350–377. Cambridge: MIT Press.

1965.   Quest for the Essence of Language. Address to the Academy of Arts and Sciences. *Diogenes* 51. Reprinted in Jakobson 1987:409–427.

1974.   A Glance at the Development of Semiotics. P. Baudoin, trans. Reprinted in Jakobson 1987:436–454.

1978.   *Six Lectures on Sound and Meaning.* Cambridge: MIT Press.

1987.   *Language in Literature.* K. Pomorska and S. Rudy, eds. Cambridge: Harvard University Press, Belknap Press.

JARVELLA, RJ., AND W. KLEIN

1982.   Eds. *Speech, Place, and Action.* Chichester: John Wiley.

JESPERSON, O.

[1922] 1964.   *Language: Its Nature, Development, and Origin.* New York: Norton.

JESUIT RELATIONS.

[1610–1791] 1896–1901.   *Travels and Explorations of the Jesuit Missionaries in New France.* R. G. Thwaites, ed. Cleveland: Burrows Brothers.

JOHNSON, M.

1987.   *The Body in the Mind: The Bodily Basis of Meaning, Imagination and Reason.* Chicago: University of Chicago Press.

JONES, W.

1907.   Fox Texts. *Publications of the American Ethnological Society* 1:1–383.

KAEPPLER, A.

1972.   Method and Theory in Analyzing Dance Structure with an Analysis of Tongan Dance. *Ethnomusicology* 16(2):173–217.

1985.   Structured Movement Systems in Tonga. In *Society and the Dance: The*

Social Anthropology of Performance and Process. P. Spencer, ed. Pp. 92–118. Cambridge: Cambridge University Press.

1986. Cultural Analysis, Linguistic Analogies and the Study of Dance in Anthropological Perspective. In *Explorations in Ethnomusicology: Essays in Honor of David P. McAllester.* C. J. Frisbie, ed. Detroit Monographs in Musicology 9. Detroit: Information Coordinators.

1988. The Visible and the Invisible in Hawaiian Dance. In Farnell 1995.

KEATING, W. H.

1824. *Narrative of an Expedition to the Source of St. Peter's River, Lake Winnipeg, Lake of the Woods, etc.* Philadelphia: H. C. Carey & I. Lea.

KEGL, J. A.

1977. Pronominalization in American Sign Language. Unpublished manuscript, MIT.

KENDALL, M. B.

1980. Exegesis and Translation: Northern Yuman Names as Texts. *Journal of Anthropological Research* 36(3):261–273.

KENDON, A.

1972. Some Relationships between Body Motion and Speech: An Analysis of an Example. In *Studies in Dyadic Communication.* A. Seigman and B. Pope, eds. Pp. 177–210. Elmsford, N.Y.: Pergamon Press.

1980a. Gesticulation and Speech: Two Aspects of the Process of Utterance. In *Nonverbal Communication and Language.* M. R. Key, ed. The Hague: Mouton.

1980b. Gesticulation, Speech, and the Gesture Theory of Language Origins. In *Sign and Culture.* W. C. Stokoe, ed. Pp. 334–362. Silver Spring, Md.: Linstock Press.

1982. The Study of Gesture: Some Observations on Its History. *Semiotic Inquiry* 2:45–62.

1983. Gesture and Speech: How They Interact. In *Nonverbal Interaction.* J. M. Wieman and R. P. Harrison, eds. Beverly Hills, Calif.: Sage Publications.

1986. Iconicity in Walpiri Sign Language. In *Iconicity: Essays on the Nature of Culture.* P. Bouissac, M. Herzfeld, and R. Posner, eds. Pp. 437–446. Tübingen: Stauffenburg Verlag.

1989. *Sign Languages of Aboriginal Australia.* Cambridge: Cambridge University Press.

KLIMA, E., AND U. BELLUGI

1979. *The Signs of Language.* Cambridge: Harvard University Press.

KROEBER, A. L.

1907–1908. Gros Ventre Myths and Tales. *Anthropological Papers of the American Museum of Natural History* 1:55–139.

1958. Sign Language Enquiry. *International Journal of American Linguistics (IJAL)* 24:1–19.

KROEBER, K.

1981.   Ed. *Traditional Literatures of the American Indian: Texts and Interpretations*. Lincoln: University of Nebraska Press.

KRUPAT, A.

1992.   *Ethno-Criticism: Ethnography, History, Literature*. Berkeley: University of California Press.

KUHN, T.

1962.   *The Structure of Scientific Revolutions*. Chicago: University of Chicago Press.

KURYLOWICZ, J.

1972.   The Role of Deictic Elements in Linguistic Evolution. *Semiotica* 5:174–183.

LA BARRE, W.

1947.   The Expression of Emotion in Man and Animals. *Journal of Personality* 16:49–68.

LABOV, W.

1968.   *A Study of the Nonstandard English of Negro and Puerto Rican Speakers in New York City*. New York: Columbia University Press.

LAKOFF, G.

1987.   *Women, Fire and Dangerous Things*. Chicago: University of Chicago Press.

LAKOFF, G., AND M. JOHNSON

1980.   *Metaphors We Live By*. Chicago: University of Chicago Press.

LANGER, S.

1942.   *Philosophy in a New Key: A Study in the Symbolism of Reason, Rite and Art*. Cambridge: Harvard University Press.

LAWLER, J. M.

1979.   Mimicry in Natural Language. In *The Elements: A Parasession on Linguistic Units and Levels*. Chicago: Chicago Linguistic Society, University of Chicago.

LEACH, E.

1969.   *Genesis as Myth and Other Essays*. London: Jonathan Cape.

LEVINSON, S.

1991.   Relativity in Spatial Conception and Description. Working Paper #1. Nijmegen, Netherlands: Cognitive Anthropology Research Group, Max Planck Institute for Psycholinguistics.

LINDE, E.

1987.   Explanatory Systems in Oral Life Stories. In *Cultural Models in Language and Thought*. D. Holland and N. Quinn, eds. Pp. 343–366. Cambridge and New York: Cambridge University Press.

LOMAX, A.

1971.   Choreometrics and Ethnographic Film-Making. *Film-Maker's Newsletter* 4(4).

LOWIE, R. H.
1909.   The Assiniboine. *Anthropological Papers of the American Museum of Natural History* 4(1).

LUNTLEY, M.
1989.   Understanding Anthropologists. *Inquiry* 25:199–216.

LUTZ, C.
1988.   *Unnatural Emotions: Everyday Sentiments on a Micronesian Atoll and Their Challenge to Western Theory.* Chicago: University of Chicago Press.

LYELL, C.
1830.   *Principles of Geology.* London: J. Murray.

LYONS, J.
1977.   *Semantics.* Vol. 2. Cambridge: Cambridge University Press.

MACINTYRE, A.
1981.   *After Virtue: A Study in Moral Theory.* Notre Dame, Ind.: University of Notre Dame Press.

1986.   The Intelligibility of Action. In Margolis, Krausz, and Burien 1986.

MALINOWSKI, B.
[1948] 1954.   *Magic, Science and Religion, and Other Essays.* New York: Doubleday Anchor Books.

MALLERY, G.
ca. 1879.   Sample illustration for use by collectors. Mallery Papers, BAE Collections, National Anthropological Archives, Washington, D.C.

1880a.   Introduction to *The Study of Sign Language among the North American Indians as Illustrating the Gesture Speech of Mankind.* Washington, D.C.: Bureau of Ethnology. Reprinted in Sebeok and Umiker-Sebeok 1978 (1):1–76.

1880b.   *A Collection of Gesture Signs and Signals of the North American Indians with Some Comparisons.* Washington, D.C.: Smithsonian Institution. Reprinted in Sebeok and Umiker-Sebeok 1978 (1):77–406.

1881.   Sign Language among the North American Indians. *BAE Annual Report* 1:269–552. Washington, D.C.: Smithsonian Institution. Reprinted 1972. The Hague: Mouton.

1886.   Pictographs of the North American Indians. *BAE Annual Report* 4:1–256. Washington, D.C.: Smithsonian Institution.

1893.   Picture Writing of the American Indians. *BAE Annual Report* 10. Washington, D.C.: Smithsonian Institution. Reprinted 1972. New York: Dover Publications.

MARGOLIS, J., M. KRAUSZ, AND R. M. BURIEN
1986.   Eds. *Rationality, Relativism and the Human Sciences.* Dortrecht: Martinus Nijhoff.

MARSELLA, J., G. DEVOS, AND F. L. K. HSU
1985.   Eds. *Culture and Self: Asian and Western Perspectives.* New York: Tavistock Publications.

MARTIN, E.
1987.   *The Woman in the Body: A Cultural Analysis of Reproduction*. Boston: Beacon Press.

MAUSS, M.
[1935] 1973.   Techniques of the Body. *Economy and Society* 2(1):70–88.
[1938] 1985.   A Category of the Human Mind: The Notion of the Person, the Notion of the Self. In *The Category of the Person: Anthropology, Philosophy, History*. M. Carrithers, S. Collins, and S. Lukes, eds. Pp. 1–25. Cambridge: Cambridge University Press.
[1950] 1979.   *Sociology and Psychology: Essays*. London: Routledge & Kegan Paul.

MCNEILL, D.
1985.   So You Think Gestures Are Nonverbal? *Psychological Review* 92(3):350–371.
1992.   *Hand and Mind: What Gestures Reveal about Thought*. Chicago: University of Chicago Press.

MCNEILL, D., AND E. LEVY
1982.   Conceptual Representations in Language Activity and Gesture. In Jarvella and Klein 1982:271–295.

MEAD, G. H.
1933.   *Mind, Self and Society*. Chicago: University of Chicago Press.

MELVILLE, H.
1963.   *Moby-Dick or, the Whale*. Vol. 7 of *The Works of Herman Melville*, standard edition. New York: Russell and Russell.

MERLEAU-PONTY, M.
1962.   *Phenomenology of Perception*. C. Smith, trans. New York: Humanities Press.
1963.   *The Structure of Behaviour*. A. L. Fisher, trans. Boston: Beacon Press.

MILLER, D. R.
1986.   Montana Assiniboine Identity. A Cultural Account of an American Indian Ethnicity. Ph. D. diss., Indiana University.

MOMADAY, N. S.
1976.   Native American Attitudes to the Environment. In *Seeing with a Native Eye*. W. H. Capps, ed. New York: Harper & Row.

MOONEY, J.
[1898] 1979.   *Calendar History of the Kiowa Indians*. Washington, D.C.: Smithsonian Institution Press. Reprinted from *BAE Annual Report* 17.

MÜHLHÄUSLER, P., AND R. HARRÉ.
1990.   *Pronouns and People: The Linguistic Construction of Social and Personal Identity*. Oxford: Blackwell.

MUNN, N.
1973.   *Walbiri Iconography*. Ithaca and London: Cornell University Press.

NEIHARDT, J. G.
[1932] 1972. *Black Elk Speaks: Being the Life Story of a Holy Man of the Oglala Sioux*. New York: William Morrow & Co.

NOYES, A. J.
1917.   *In the land of Chinook*. Helena, Mont.: State Publishing Co.

NUCKOLLS, J.
1990.   Sound Symbolism in Quechua. Paper presented to Anthropology Department, Indiana University, Bloomington.

ONG, W.
1982.   *Orality and Literacy: The Technologizing of the Word*. London: Methuen.

PADDON, W.
1979.   Verbs in American Sign Language. Working paper, University of California, San Diego.
1980.   Complement Structures in American Sign Language. Working paper, University of California, San Diego.

PAGE, J.
1990.   A Comparative Study of Two Movement Writing Systems: Laban and Benesh Notations. Master's thesis, University of Sydney, Australia.

PARKS, D., AND R. J. DEMALLIE
1989.   Sioux and Assiniboine Dialects. Paper presented at American Anthropological Association Meeting, Washington, D.C. November.

PARSONS, T.
1978.   Action Theory and the Human Condition. New York: Free Press.

PEIRCE, C. S.
1931–1958. *Collected Papers*. Vols. 1–6, C. Hartshorne and P. Weiss, eds. Vols. 7, 8, A. W. Burks, ed. Cambridge: Harvard University Press.
1956.   *The Philosophy of Peirce: Selected Writings*. J. Buchler, ed. London: Routledge Kegan and Paul.

PETITOT, E.
1886.   *Traditions indiennes du Canada Nord-Ouest*. Paris.

PHILIPS, S. U.
[1974] 1989. Warm Springs 'Indian Time': How the Regulation of Participation Affects the Progression of Events. In *Explorations in the Ethnography of Speaking*. R. Bauman and J. Sherzer, eds. Pp. 92–109.
1983.   *The Invisible Culture: Communication in Classroom and Community on the Warm Springs Indian Reservation*. New York: Longmans.

PHILIPSEN, G., AND D. CARBAUGH
1986.   A Bibliography of Fieldwork in the Ethnography of Speaking. *Language in Society* 15:387–397.

PIAGET, J.
1954.   *The Construction of Reality in the Child*. M. Cook, trans. New York: Basic Books.

PICK, H. L., AND L. P. ACREDOLO

1983.   Eds. *Spatial Orientation: Theory, Research and Application.* New York and London: Plenum Press.

POCOCK, D.

1973.   The Idea of a Personal Anthropology. Paper for the Decennial Conference of the Association of Social Anthropologists (ASA), Oxford, July.

POLANYI, M.

1958.   *Personal Knowledge.* Chicago: University of Chicago Press.

1967.   *The Tacit Dimension.* New York: Anchor Books, Doubleday.

POLHEMUS, T.

1978.   *The Body Reader. Social Aspects of the Human Body.* New York: Pantheon.

POUWER, J.

1973.   On Signification in Fieldwork. *Journal of Symbolic Anthropology* 1, July. The Hague: Mouton.

RABINOW, P.

1983.   Humanism as Nihilism: The Bracketing of Truth and Seriousness in American Cultural Anthropology. In *Social Science as Moral Inquiry.* N. Haan, R. Bellah, P. Rabinow, and W. Sullivan, eds. Pp. 52–75. New York: Columbia University Press.

RADIN, P.

1959.   *The Trickster: A Study in American Indian Mythology.* New York: Bell Publishing.

REDDY, M. J.

1979.   The Conduit Metaphor—A Case of Frame Conflict in Our Language about Language. In *Metaphor and Thought.* A. Ortner, ed. Pp. 284–325. Cambridge: Cambridge University Press.

REYNOLDS, V.

1982.   Behaviour, Action and Act in Relation to Strategies and Decision-making. In *The Analysis of Action.* M. von Cranach and R. Harré, eds. Pp. 329–342. Cambridge: Cambridge University Press.

RODNICK, D.

1938.   *The Fort Belknap Assiniboine of Montana: A Study in Culture Change.* New Haven, Conn. Reprinted 1978. New York: AMS Press.

ROSALDO, M.

1980.   *Knowledge and Passion: Ilongot Notions of Self and Social Life.* Cambridge: Cambridge University Press.

1982.   The Things We Do with Words: Ilongot Speech Acts and Speech Act Theory in Philosophy. *Language in Society* 11:203–237.

ROSALDO, R.

1980.   *Ilongot Headhunting, 1883–1974: A Study in History and Society.* Stanford: Stanford University Press.

1984.   Ilongot Naming: The Play of Associations. In Tooker and Conklin 1984:11–24.

RYLE, G.

1949.   *The Concept of Mind.* London: Hutchinson.

SAHLINS, M.

1976.   Colors and Cultures. *Semiotica* 16:1–22. Reprinted 1977 in *Symbolic Anthropology.* J. Dolgin, D. Kemnitzer, and D. Schneider, eds. New York: Columbia University Press.

1985.   *Islands of History.* Chicago: University of Chicago Press.

SAPIR, E.

1921.   *Language.* New York: Harcourt, Brace and World.

1933.   Language. In *Encyclopedia of the Social Sciences* 9: 155–169. Reprinted 1985 in *Selected Writings of Edward Sapir.* D. Mandelbaum, ed. Berkeley: University of California Press.

[1949] 1985. *Selected Writings in Language Culture and Personality.* D. Mandelbaum, ed. Berkeley: University of California.

SAUSSURE, F. DE

[1916] 1966. *Course in General Linguistics.* C. Bally, A. Sechehaye, and A. Riedlinger, eds. W. Baskin, trans. New York: McGraw-Hill.

1967.   *Cours de linguistique generale: Edition critique.* Vol. 1. R. Engler, ed. Wiesbaden: Otto Harrassowitz.

1974.   *Cours de linguistique generale: Edition critique.* Vol. 2. R. Engler, ed. Wiesbaden: Otto Harrassowitz.

SAYCE, A. H.

1880.   Sign Language among the American Indians. *Nature* 22(5):93–94.

SCHEPER-HUGHES, N., AND M. M. LOCK

1987.   The Mindful Body: A Prolegomenon to Future Work in Medical Anthropology. *Medical Anthropology Quarterly* 1:6–41.

SCHERER, K. R., AND P. EKMAN

1981.   *Handbook of Methods in Nonverbal Communication.* New York: Cambridge University Press.

SCHOOLCRAFT, H. R.

1851–1857. Ed. *Information Respecting the History, Condition and Prospects of the Indian Tribes of the United States.* 6 vols. Philadelphia: Lippincott, Grambo and Co.

1856.   *The Myth of Hiawatha.* Philadelphia: J. B. Lippincott.

SCOTT, H. L.

1898.   The Sign Language of the Plains Indians. *Archives of the International Folklore Association* 1:206–220. Reprinted in Sebeok and Umiker-Sebeok 1978 (2):53–67.

1912–1934. Manuscript collection. National Anthropological Archives, Smithsonian Institution, Washington, D.C.

1934.   The Indian Sign Language. Film Dictionary. Record Gp. 106.13,
         106.14, 106.15, National Archives Audiovisual Division, Washington,
         D.C.

SEARLE, J.
1969.   *Speech Acts: An Essay in the Philosophy of Language.* Cambridge:
         Cambridge University Press.

SEBEOK, T., AND J. UMIKER-SEBEOK
1978.   Eds. *Aboriginal Sign Languages of the Americas and Australia.* Vols. 1, 2.
         New York: Plenum.

SETON, E. T.
1918.   *Sign Talk.* New York: Doubleday, Page & Co.

SHEETS-JOHNSTONE, M.
1981.   Thinking in Movement. *Journal of Aesthetics and Arts Criticism*
         39(4):399–407.

SHERZER, J.
1973.   Verbal and Nonverbal Deixis: The Pointed Lip Gesture among the
         San Blas Kuna. *Language in Society* 2:117–131.

1983.   *Kuna Ways of Speaking: An Ethnographic Perspective.* Austin: University
         of Texas Press.

1987a.   Strategies in Text and Context: Kuna Kaa Kwento. In *Recovering the
         Word: Essays on Native American Literature.* B. Swann and A. Krupat,
         eds. Berkeley: University of California Press.

1987b.   A Discourse-centered Approach to Language and Culture. *American
         Anthropologist* 89:295–309.

SHERZER, J., AND A. C. WOODBURY
1987.   Eds. *Native American Discourse: Poetics and Rhetoric.* Cambridge:
         Cambridge University Press.

SICARD, ABBÉ R. A. C.
1808.   *Theorie des signes pour l'instruction des sourds muets.* 2 vols. Paris.

SIEGMAN, A. W., AND S. FELDSTEIN
[1978] 1987. Eds. *Nonverbal Behaviour and Communication.* 2d. ed. Hillsdale,
         N.J.: Lawrence Erlbaum.

SILVERSTEIN, M.
1976.   Shifters, Linguistic Categories and Cultural Description. In *Meaning
         in Anthropology.* K. H. Basso and H. A. Selby, eds. Albuquerque:
         University of New Mexico Press.

1977.   Cultural Prerequisites to Grammatical Analysis. In *Linguistics and
         Anthropology,* Georgetown University Round Table on Language and
         Linguistics 1977. M. Saville-Troike, ed. Pp. 139–151. Washington,
         D.C.: Georgetown University Press.

1987.   Monoglot "Standard" in America. *Working Papers and Proceedings* 13.
         Chicago: Center for Psychosocial Studies.

SIMMS, S. C.
1903.   Traditions of the Crow. *Field Columbian Museum Anthropology Series*
         2:281–324.
SINGER, M.
1984.   *Man's Glassy Essence: Exploration in Semiotic Anthropology.*
         Bloomington: Indiana University Press.
SPENCER, P.
1985.   Ed. *Society and the Dance.* Cambridge: Cambridge University Press.
SPERBER, D.
1975.   *Rethinking Symbolism.* A. L. Morton, trans. New York: Cambridge
         University Press.
STANDING BEAR, L.
1933.   *Land of the Spotted Eagle.* Boston: Houghton Mifflin.
STOCKING, G.
1983.   Ed. *Observer's Observed: Essays on Ethnographic Fieldwork.* History of
         Anthropology, vol. 1. Madison: University of Wisconsin Press.
STOKOE, W.
1960.   Sign Language Structure. In *Studies in Linguistics Occasional Paper 8.*
         Buffalo, N.Y.: University of Buffalo Press. Reprinted 1978. Silver
         Spring, Md.: Linstock Press.
TALMY, L.
1983.   How Language Structures Space. In *Spatial Orientation: Theory,*
         Research, and Application. H. Pick and L. Acredolo, eds. Pp. 225–282.
         New York: Plenum Press.
TAYLOR, A. R.
1975.   Non-Verbal Communication in Aboriginal North America: The
         Plains Sign Language. In Sebeok and Umiker-Sebeok 1978 (2).
TAYLOR, A. R., AND D. ROOD
1972.   *Lessons in Lakhota.* University of Colorado Lakhota Project. Prelimi-
         nary draft.
TAYLOR, C.
1985.   *Human Agency and Language.* Cambridge: Cambridge University
         Press.
TEDLOCK, D.
1983.   *The Spoken Word and the Work of Interpretation.* Philadelphia: Univer-
         sity of Philadelphia Press.
THWAITES, R. G.
1904–1907. Ed. *Early Western Travels, 1748–1846.* Vols. 1–32. Cleveland.
TODOROV, T.
1985.   *Mikhail Bakhtin: The Dialogical Principle.* W. Godzich, trans. Minneapo-
         lis: University of Minnesota Press.
TOMKINS, W.
1926.   *Universal Indian Sign Language of the Plains Indians of North America.*

San Diego: Published by author. Reprinted 1969. New York: Dover Publications.

TOOKER, E., ED., AND H. C. CONKLIN

1984.   *Naming Systems: 1980 Proceedings of the American Ethnological Society.* Washington, D.C.: American Ethnological Society.

TOULMIN, S.

1990.   *Cosmopolis: The Hidden Agenda of Modernity.* Chicago: University of Chicago Press.

TURNER, B.

1984.   *The Body in Society.* Oxford: Blackwell.

TYLOR, E. B.

[1865] 1964.   *Researches into the Early History of Mankind and the Development of Civilization.* Chicago: University of Chicago Press, Phoenix Books.

ULLMANN, S.

1962.   *Semantics.* Oxford: Blackwell and New York: Barnes and Noble.

URCIUOLI, B.

1984.   The Cultural Construction of Linguistic Variation. Ph.D. diss., University of Chicago.

1988.   Discussion Essay: The Indexical Structure of Visibility. In Farnell 1995.

1992.   Time, Talk and Class: New York Puerto Ricans as Temporal and Linguistic Others. In *The Politics of Time.* H. J. Rutz, ed. AES Monograph 4. Washington, D.C.: American Anthropological Association.

VAN WINKLE, B.

1983.   Where It's at: Giving Spatial Directions in Washoe English. Paper delivered at Central States Anthropology Society Annual Meeting, Cleveland, Ohio. April.

VARELA, C.

1983.   Cartesianism Revisited: The Ghost in the Moving Machine. *JASHM* 2(3):143–157.

1984.   Pocock, Williams, Gouldner: Initial Reactions of Three Social Scientists to the Problem of Objectivity. *JASHM* 3(2):53–73.

1992.   Cartesianism Revisited: The Ghost in the Moving Machine or in the Lived Body. *JASHM* 7(4):5–64.

In press.   *Freud to Mead: The Third Psychologist's Fallacy and the Social Nature of Unawareness.*

VERDENIUS, W. J.

[1949] 1972.   *Mimesis: Plato's Doctrine of Artistic Imitation and Its Meaning to Us.* Leiden, Holland: E. J. Brill.

VOEGELIN, C. F.

1958.   Sign Language Analysis: On One Level or Two? *IJAL* 24:71–77.

VYGOTSKY, L.

1962.   *Thought and Language.* Cambridge: MIT Press.

WALKER, J. R.

1917.   The Sun Dance and Other Ceremonies of the Oglala Division of the
         Teton Dakota. *American Museum of Natural History Anthropological
         Papers* 16(2):50–221.

1980.   *Lakota Belief and Ritual.* R. J. DeMallie and E. A. Jahner, eds. Lincoln:
         University of Nebraska Press.

1982.   *Lakota Society.* R. J. DeMallie, ed. Lincoln: University of Nebraska
         Press.

1983.   *Lakota Myth.* E. A. Jahner, ed. Lincoln: University of Nebraska Press.

WARNER, T.

1990.   Locating Agency. *Annals of Theoretical Psychology* 6:133–145.

WEBER, M.

1947.   *The Theory of Social and Economic Organization.* London: Free Press.

WELCH, J.

1976.   *Riding the Earthboy 40.* New York: Harper & Row.

WEST, L. M., JR.

1960.   The Sign Language: An Analysis. Ph.D. diss., Indiana University.

WHITE, G. M., AND J. KIRKPATRICK

1985.   Eds. *Person, Self, and Experience: Exploring Pacific Ethnopsychologies.*
         Berkeley: University of California Press.

WHORF, B. L.

1941.   Languages and Logic. *Technological Review* 43:250–272. Reprinted in
         Whorf 1956:233–245.

1956.   *Language, Thought and Reality.* J. B. Carroll, ed. Cambridge: MIT Press.

WIED, MAXIMILIAN, PRINZ VON

[1843] 1905. Travels in the Interior of North America 1832–1834. In *Early
         Western Travels, 1748–1846.* R. G. Thwaites, ed. Vols. 22–24. Cleve-
         land: Arthur H. Clark.

WIGET, A.

1987.   Telling the Tale: A Performance Analysis of a Hopi Coyote Story. In
         Recovering the Word: Essays on Native American Literature. B. Swann
         and A. Krupat, eds. Pp. 297–338. Berkeley: University of California
         Press.

WILBUR, R.

1979.   *American Sign Language and Sign Systems: Research and Applications.*
         Baltimore: University Park Press.

WILLIAMS, D.

1975.   The Role of Movement in Selected Symbolic Systems. D. Phil.,
         Oxford University.

1976.   An Exercise in Applied Personal Anthropology. *JASHM* 3(3):139–167.

1980a.   *Sacred Spaces: A Preliminary Enquiry into the Dominican High Mass.*
         Summer Institute of Linguistics Publications. Austin: University of
         Texas.

1980b.   Taxonomies of the Body. Pt. 1, *JASHM* 1(1):1–19. Pt. 2, *JASHM*
          1(2):98–122.
1981.   Introduction to special issue on semasiology. *JASHM* 1(4):207–225.
1982.   Semasiology. In *Semantic Anthropology*. ASA vol. 22. D. Parkin, ed. Pp.
          161–181. London: Academic Press.
1986.   Pre-figurements of Art: A Reply to Sebeok. *JASHM* 4(2):68–90.
1988.   Space, Intersubjectivity and the Conceptual Imperative: Three
          Ethnographic Cases. Paper presented at AAA Meeting. In Farnell
          1995.
1990.   *Ceci n'est pas un "Wallaby."* Paper presented at the Visual Research
          Conference, Society for Visual Anthropology, AAA Meeting, New
          Orleans. December.
1991.   *Ten Lectures on Theories of the Dance*. Metuchen, N.J.: Scarecrow Press.
WILLIAMS, D., AND B. FARNELL
1990.   *A Beginning Text on Movement Writing for Non-Dancers*. Canberra:
          Australian Institute for Aboriginal Studies.
WISSLER, C., AND D. C. DUVALL
1908.   The Mythology of the Blackfoot Indians. *Anthropological Papers of the
          American Museum of Natural History* 2:1–162.
WITTGENSTEIN, L.
[1953] 1958. *Philosophical Investigations*. English text of 3d ed. G. E. M.
          Anscombe, trans. New York: Macmillan.
1980.   *Remarks on the Philosophy of Psychology*. Vols. 1, 2. Oxford: Blackwell.
WOOD, W. R., AND T. D. THIESSEN
1985.   Eds. *Early Fur Trade on the Northern Plains*. Norman: University of
          Oklahoma Press.
WOODRUFF SMITH, D.
1988.   Bodily versus Cognitive Intentionality? *Nous* 22:51–52.

INDEX